ABOUT THIS PUBLICATION

FOR SERVICE ASSISTANCE

Customer Service
1.704.898.0770

North Carolina General Statues is published by The Muliti-Media Group of Greater Charlotte in Charlotte, North Carolina. Copyright 2015 by the Multi-Media Group of Greater Charlotte. This book or parts thereof may not be reproduced in any form, stored in a retrieval system, or transmitted in any form by any means—electronic, mechanical, photocopy, recording or otherwise—without prior written permission of the publisher, except as provided by United States of America copyright law.

The records required by U.S. Code 2257(a) through (c) and the pertinent regulations 28 C.F.R. Cli. 1, Part 75 with respect to this publication and all materials associated with such records are maintained by The Multi-Media Group of Greater Charlotte, Publisher and available for review by Attorney General.

www.visionbooks.org

Copyright © 2015 by MMGGC
All rights reserved!

TID: 5107785
ISBN (10) digit: 1503243516
ISBN (13) digit: 978-1503243514

123-4-56789-01239-Paperback
123-4-56789-01239-Hardback

First Edition

090520140547

Printed in the United States of America

2015 EDITION

North Carolina Criminal Law And Procedure-Pamphlet # 75

Printed In conjunction with the Administration of the Courts

North Carolina Criminal Law and Procedure
Pamphlet Reference Guide

Chapters	Pamphlet
Chapter 1 Civil Procedure	1
Chapter 1 Civil Procedure (Continue)	2
Chapter 1A Rules of Civil Procedure	2
Chapter 1B Contribution.	2
Chapter 1C Enforcement of Judgments.	2
Chapter 1D Punitive Damages.	2
Chapter 1E Eastern Band of Cherokee Indians.	2
Chapter 1F North Carolina Uniform Interstate Depositions and Discovery Act.	2
Chapter 2 - Clerk of Superior Court [Repealed and Transferred.]	3
Chapter 3 - Commissioners of Affidavits and Deeds [Repealed.]	3
Chapter 4 - Common Law	3
Chapter 5 - Contempt [Repealed.]	3
Chapter 5A - Contempt	3
Chapter 6 - Liability for Court Costs	3
Chapter 7 - Courts [Repealed and Transferred.]	3
Chapter 7A – Judicial Department	3
Chapter 7A – Continuation (Judicial Department)	4
Chapter 7A – Continuation (Judicial Department)	5
Chapter 7B - Juvenile Code	5
Chapter 8 - Evidence	6
Chapter 8A - Interpreters for Deaf Persons [Recodified.]	6
Chapter 8B - Interpreters for Deaf Persons	6
Chapter 8C - Evidence Code	6
Chapter 9 - Jurors	6
Chapter 10 - Notaries [Repealed.]	6
Chapter 10A - Notaries [Recodified.]	6
Chapter 10B - Notaries	6
Chapter 11 - Oaths	6
Chapter 12 - Statutory Construction	6
Chapter 13 - Citizenship Restored	6
Chapter 14 - Criminal Law	7
Chapter 14 –Criminal Law (Continuation)	8
Chapter 15 - Criminal Procedure	9
Chapter 15A - Criminal Procedure Act (Continuation)	10
Chapter 15A - Criminal Procedure Act (Continuation)	11
Chapter 15B - Victims Compensation	11
Chapter 15C - Address Confidentiality Program	11
Chapter 16 - Gaming Contracts and Futures	11
Chapter 17 - Habeas Corpus	11

Chapter 17A - Law-Enforcement Officers [Recodified.]	11
Chapter 17B - North Carolina Criminal Justice Education and Training System [Recodified.] Chapter 17C - North Carolina Criminal Justice Education and Training Standards Commission	11
Chapter 17D - North Carolina Justice Academy	11
Chapter 17E - North Carolina Sheriffs' Education and Training Standards Commission	11
Chapter 18 - Regulation of Intoxicating Liquors [Repealed.]	12
Chapter 18A - Regulation of Intoxicating Liquors [Repealed.]	12
Chapter 18B - Regulation of Alcoholic Beverages	12
Chapter 18C - North Carolina State Lottery	12
Chapter 19 - Offenses against Public Morals	12
Chapter 19A - Protection of Animals	12
Chapter 20 - Motor Vehicles	13
Chapter 20 - Motor Vehicles (Continuation)	14
Chapter 20 - Motor Vehicles (Continuation)	15
Chapter 20 - Motor Vehicles (Continuation)	16
Chapter 21 - Bills of Lading	17
Chapter 22 - Contracts Requiring Writing	17
Chapter 22A - Signatures	17
Chapter 22B - Contracts Against Public Policy	17
Chapter 22C - Payments to Subcontractors	17
Chapter 23 - Debtor and Creditor	17
Chapter 24 – Interest	17
Chapter 25 – Uniform Commercial Code	18
Chapter 25 – Uniform Commercial Code (Continuation)	19
Chapter 25A – Retail Installment Sales Act	20
Chapter 25B - Credit	20
Chapter 25C - Sales of Artwork	20
Chapter 26 - Suretyship	20
Chapter 27 - Warehouse Receipts [Repealed.]	20
Chapter 28 - Administration [Repealed.]	20
Chapter 28A - Administration of Decedents' Estates	20
Chapter 28B - Estates of Absentees in Military Service	20
Chapter 28C - Estates of Missing Persons	20
Chapter 29 - Intestate Succession	21
Chapter 30 - Surviving Spouses	21
Chapter 31 - Wills	21
Chapter 31A - Acts Barring Property Rights	21
Chapter 31B - Renunciation of Property and Renunciation of Fiduciary Powers Act	21
Chapter 31C - Uniform Disposition of Community Property Rights at Death Act	21
Chapter 32 - Fiduciaries	21
Chapter 32A - Powers of Attorney	21
Chapter 33 - Guardian and Ward [Repealed and Recodified.]	21

Chapter 33A - North Carolina Uniform Transfers to Minors Act	21
Chapter 33B - North Carolina Uniform Custodial Trust Act	21
Chapter 34 - Veterans' Guardianship Act	22
Chapter 35 - Sterilization Procedures	22
Chapter 35A - Incompetency and Guardianship	22
Chapter 36 - Trusts and Trustees [Repealed.]	22
Chapter 36A - Trusts and Trustees	22
Chapter 36B - Uniform Management of Institutional Funds Act [Repealed.]	22
Chapter 36C - North Carolina Uniform Trust Code	22
Chapter 36D - North Carolina Community Third Party Trusts, Pooled Trusts	23
Chapter 36E - Uniform Prudent Management of Institutional Funds Act	23
Chapter 37 - Allocation of Principal and Income [Repealed.]	23
Chapter 37A - Uniform Principal and Income Act	23
Chapter 38 - Boundaries	23
Chapter 38A - Landowner Liability	23
Chapter 39 - Conveyances	23
Chapter 39A - Transfer Fee Covenants Prohibited	23
Chapter 40 - Eminent Domain [Repealed.]	23
Chapter 40A - Eminent Domain	23
Chapter 41 - Estates	23
Chapter 41A - State Fair Housing Act	23
Chapter 42 - Landlord and Tenant	23
Chapter 42A - Vacation Rental Act	23
Chapter 43 - Land Registration	23
Chapter 44 - Liens	24
Chapter 44A - Statutory Liens and Charges	24
Chapter 45 - Mortgages and Deeds of Trust	24
Chapter 45A - Good Funds Settlement Act	24
Chapter 46 - Partition	24
Chapter 47 - Probate and Registration	25
Chapter 47A - Unit Ownership	25
Chapter 47B - Real Property Marketable Title Act	25
Chapter 47C - North Carolina Condominium Act	25
Chapter 47D - Notice of Settlement Act [Expired.]	25
Chapter 47E - Residential Property Disclosure Act	25
Chapter 47F - North Carolina Planned Community Act	25
Chapter 47G - Option to Purchase Contracts	25
Chapter 47H - Contracts for Deed	25
Chapter 48 - Adoptions	26
Chapter 48A - Minors	26
Chapter 49 - Bastardy	26
Chapter 49A - Rights of Children	26
Chapter 50 - Divorce and Alimony	26
Chapter 50A - Uniform Child-Custody Jurisdiction and	

Enforcement Act	26
Chapter 50B - Domestic Violence	26
Chapter 50C - Civil No-Contact Orders	26
Chapter 51 - Marriage	26
Chapter 52 - Powers and Liabilities of Married Persons	27
Chapter 52A - Uniform Reciprocal Enforcement of Support Act [Repealed.]	27
Chapter 52B - Uniform Premarital Agreement Act	27
Chapter 52C - Uniform Interstate Family Support Act	27
Chapter 53 - Banks	27
Chapter 53A - Business Development Corporations and North Carolina Capital Resource Corporations	28
Chapter 53B - Financial Privacy Act	28
Chapter 54 - Cooperative Organizations	28
Chapter 54A - Capital Stock Savings and Loan Associations [Repealed.]	28
Chapter 54B - Savings and Loan Associations	29
Chapter 54C - Savings Banks	29
Chapter 55 - North Carolina Business Corporation Act	30
Chapter 55A - North Carolina Nonprofit Corporation Act	31
Chapter 55B - Professional Corporation Act	31
Chapter 55C - Foreign Trade Zones	31
Chapter 55D - Filings, Names, and Registered Agents for Corporations, Nonprofit Corporations, and Partnerships	31
Chapter 56 - Electric, Telegraph and Power Companies [Repealed.]	31
Chapter 57 - Hospital, Medical and Dental Service Corporations [Recodified.]	31
Chapter 57A - Health Maintenance Organization Act [Recodified.]	31
Chapter 57B - Health Maintenance Organization Act [Recodified.]	31
Chapter 57C - North Carolina Limited Liability Company Act.	31
Chapter 58 - Insurance.	32
Chapter 58 - Insurance (Continuation)	33
Chapter 58 - Insurance (Continuation)	34
Chapter 58 - Insurance (Continuation)	35
Chapter 58 - Insurance (Continuation)	36
Chapter 58 - Insurance (Continuation)	37
Chapter 58 - Insurance (Continuation)	38
Chapter 58A - North Carolina Health Insurance Trust Commission [Recodified.]	38
Chapter 59 - Partnership.	39
Chapter 59B - Uniform Unincorporated Nonprofit Association Act.	39
Chapter 60 - Railroads and Other Carriers [Repealed and Transferred.]	39
Chapter 61 - Religious Societies	39
Chapter 62 - Public Utilities	39

Chapter 62 - Public Utilities (Continuation)	40
Chapter 62A - Public Safety Telephone Service And Wireless Telephone Service	40
Chapter 63 - Aeronautics	40
Chapter 63A - North Carolina Global TransPark Authority	40
Chapter 64 - Aliens	40
Chapter 65 – Cemeteries	40
Chapter 66 - Commerce and Business	41
Chapter 67 - Dogs	41
Chapter 68 - Fences and Stock Law	41
Chapter 69 - Fire Protection	41
Chapter 70 - Indian Antiquities, Archaeological Resources and Unmarked Human Skeletal Remains Protection	42
Chapter 71 - Indians [Repealed.]	42
Chapter 71A - Indians	42
Chapter 72 - Inns, Hotels and Restaurants	42
Chapter 73 - Mills	42
Chapter 74 - Mines and Quarries	42
Chapter 74A - Company Police [Repealed.]	42
Chapter 74B - Private Protective Services Act [Repealed.]	42
Chapter 74C - Private Protective Services	42
Chapter 74D - Alarm Systems	42
Chapter 74E - Company Police Act	42
Chapter 74F - Locksmith Licensing Act	42
Chapter 74G - Campus Police Act	42
Chapter 75 - Monopolies, Trusts and Consumer Protection	42
Chapter 75A - Boating and Water Safety	43
Chapter 75B - Discrimination in Business	43
Chapter 75C - Motion Picture Fair Competition Act	43
Chapter 75D - Racketeer Influenced and Corrupt Organizations	43
Chapter 75E - Unlawful Activities in Connection With Certain Corporate Transactions	43
Chapter 76 - Navigation	43
Chapter 76A - Navigation and Pilotage Commissions	43
Chapter 77 - Rivers, Creeks, and Coastal Waters	43
Chapter 78 - Securities Law [Repealed.]	43
Chapter 78A - North Carolina Securities Act	43
Chapter 78B - Tender Offer Disclosure Act [Repealed.]	43
Chapter 78C - Investment Advisers	43
Chapter 78D - Commodities Act	43
Chapter 79 - Strays [Repealed.]	43
Chapter 80 - Trademarks, Brands, etc.	44
Chapter 81 - Weights and Measures [Recodified.]	44
Chapter 81A - Weights and Measures Act of 1975.	44
Chapter 82 - Wrecks [Repealed.]	44
Chapter 83 - Architects [Recodified.]	44

Chapter 83A - Architects	44
Chapter 84 - Attorneys-at-Law	44
Chapter 84A - Foreign Legal Consultants	44
Chapter 85 - Auctions and Auctioneers [Repealed.]	44
Chapter 85A - Bail Bondsmen and Runners [Recodified.]	44
Chapter 85B - Auctions and Auctioneers	44
Chapter 85C - Bail Bondsmen and Runners [Recodified.]	44
Chapter 86 - Barbers [Recodified.]	44
Chapter 86A - Barbers	44
Chapter 87 - Contractors	44
Chapter 88 - Cosmetic Art [Repealed.]	44
Chapter 88A - Electrolysis Practice Act	44
Chapter 88B - Cosmetic Art	45
Chapter 89 - Engineering and Land Surveying [Recodified.]	45
Chapter 89A - Landscape Architects	45
Chapter 89B - Foresters	45
Chapter 89C - Engineering and Land Surveying	45
Chapter 89D - Landscape Contractors	45
Chapter 89E - Geologists Licensing Act	45
Chapter 89F - North Carolina Soil Scientist Licensing Act	45
Chapter 89G - Irrigation Contractors	45
Chapter 90 - Medicine and Allied Occupations	45
Chapter 90 - Medicine and Allied Occupations (Continuation)	46
Chapter 90 - Medicine and Allied Occupations (Continuation)	47
Chapter 90 - Medicine and Allied Occupations (Continuation)	48
Chapter 90A - Sanitarians and Water and Wastewater Treatment Facility Operators	48
Chapter 90B - Social Worker Certification and Licensure Act	48
Chapter 90C - North Carolina Recreational Therapy Licensure Act	48
Chapter 90D - Interpreters and Transliterators	48
Chapter 91 - Pawnbrokers [Repealed.]	48
Chapter 91A - Pawnbrokers Modernization Act of 1989	48
Chapter 92 - Photographers [Deleted.]	48
Chapter 93 - Certified Public Accountants	48
Chapter 93A - Real Estate License Law	49
Chapter 93B - Occupational Licensing Boards	49
Chapter 93C - Watchmakers [Repealed.]	49
Chapter 93D - North Carolina State Hearing Aid Dealers and Fitters Board.	49
Chapter 93E - North Carolina Appraisers Act	49
Chapter 94 - Apprenticeship	49
Chapter 95 - Department of Labor and Labor Regulations	49
Chapter 95 - Department of Labor and Labor Regulations (Continuation)	50
Chapter 96 - Employment Security	50
Chapter 97 - Workers' Compensation Act	50
Chapter 97 - Workers' Compensation Act (Continuation)	51

Chapter 98 - Burnt and Lost Records	51
Chapter 99 - Libel and Slander	51
Chapter 99A - Civil Remedies for Criminal Actions	51
Chapter 99B - Products Liability	51
Chapter 99C - Actions Relating to Winter Sports Safety and Accidents	51
Chapter 99D - Civil Rights	51
Chapter 99E - Special Liability Provisions	51
Chapter 100 - Monuments, Memorials and Parks	51
Chapter 101 - Names of Persons	51
Chapter 102 - Official Survey Base	51
Chapter 103 - Sundays, Holidays and Special Days	51
Chapter 104 - United States Lands	51
Chapter 104A - Degrees of Kinship	51
Chapter 104B - Hurricanes or Other Acts of Nature	51
Chapter 104C - Atomic Energy, Radioactivity and Ionizing Radiation [Repealed and Recodified.]	51
Chapter 104D - Southern States Energy Compact	51
Chapter 104E - North Carolina Radiation Protection Act	51
Chapter 104F - Southeast Interstate Low-Level Radioactive Waste Management Compact [Repealed]	51
Chapter 104G - North Carolina Low-Level Radioactive Waste Management Authority Act of 1987 [Repealed]	51
Chapter 105 - Taxation	51
Chapter 105 - Taxation (Continuation)	52
Chapter 105 - Taxation (Continuation)	53
Chapter 105 - Taxation (Continuation)	54
Chapter 105A - Setoff Debt Collection Act	55
Chapter 105B - Defaulted Student Loan Recovery Act	55
Chapter 106 - Agriculture	55
Chapter 106 - Agriculture (Continue)	56
Chapter 106 - Agriculture (Continue)	57
Chapter 107 - Agricultural Development Districts [Repealed.]	57
Chapter 108 - Social Services [Repealed and Recodified.]	57
Chapter 108A - Social Services	57
Chapter 108B - Community Action Programs	58
Chapter 108C Medicaid and Health Choice Provider Requirements.	58
Chapter 108D Medicaid Managed Care for Behavioral Health Services.	58
Chapter 109 - Bonds [Recodified.]	58
Chapter 110 - Child Welfare	58
Chapter 111 - Aid to the Blind	58
Chapter 112 - Confederate Homes and Pensions [Repealed.]	58
Chapter 113 - Conservation and Development	58
Chapter 113 - Conservation and Development (Continuation)	59

Chapter 113A - Pollution Control and Environment	59
Chapter 113A - Pollution Control and Environment (Continuation)	60
Chapter 113B - North Carolina Energy Policy Act of 1975	60
Chapter 114 - Department of Justice	60
Chapter 115 - Elementary and Secondary Education [Repealed.]	60
Chapter 115A - Community Colleges, Technical Institutes, and Industrial Education Centers [Repealed.]	60
Chapter 115B - Tuition and Fee Waivers	60
Chapter 115C - Elementary and Secondary Education	60
Chapter 115C - Elementary and Secondary Education (Continuation)	61
Chapter 115C - Elementary and Secondary Education (Continuation)	62
Chapter 115C - Elementary and Secondary Education (Continuation)	63
Chapter 115D - Community Colleges	63
Chapter 115E - Private Educational Facilities Finance Act [Recodified]	63
Chapter 116 - Higher Education	63
Chapter 116 - Higher Education (Continuation)	63
Chapter 116A - Escheats and Abandoned Property [Repealed.]	64
Chapter 116B - Escheats and Abandoned Property	64
Chapter 116C - Continuum of Education Programs	64
Chapter 116D - Higher Education Bonds	64
Chapter 116E -Education Longitudinal Data System	64
Chapter 117 - Electrification	64
Chapter 118 - Firemen's and Rescue Squad Workers' Relief and Pension Funds [Recodified.]	64
Chapter 118A - Firemen's Death Benefit Act [Repealed.]	64
Chapter 118B - Members of a Rescue Squad Death Benefit Act [Repealed.]	64
Chapter 119 - Gasoline and Oil Inspection and Regulation	64
Chapter 120 - General Assembly	65
Chapter 120 - General Assembly (Continuation)	66
Chapter 120 - General Assembly (Continuation)	67
Chapter 120C - Lobbying	67
Chapter 121 - Archives and History	67
Chapter 122 - Hospitals for the Mentally Disordered [Repealed.]	67
Chapter 122A - North Carolina Housing Finance Agency	67
Chapter 122B - North Carolina Agricultural Facilities Finance Act [Repealed.]	67
Chapter 122C - Mental Health, Developmental Disabilities, and Substance Abuse Act of 1985	67
Chapter 122C - Mental Health, Developmental Disabilities, and Substance Abuse Act of 1985 (Continuation)	68

Chapter 122D - North Carolina Agricultural Finance Act	68
Chapter 122E - North Carolina Housing Trust and Oil Overcharge Act	68
Chapter 123 - Impeachment	69
Chapter 123A - Industrial Development [Repealed.]	69
Chapter 124 - Internal Improvements	69
Chapter 125 - Libraries	69
Chapter 126 - State Personnel System	69
Chapter 127 - Militia [Repealed.]	69
Chapter 127A - Militia	69
Chapter 127B - Military Affairs	69
Chapter 127C - Advisory Commission on Military Affairs	69
Chapter 128 - Offices and Public Officers	69
Chapter 128 - Offices and Public Officers (Continuation)	70
Chapter 129 - Public Buildings and Grounds	70
Chapter 130 - Public Health [Repealed.]	70
Chapter 130A - Public Health	70
Chapter 130A - Public Health (Continuation)	71
Chapter 130A - Public Health (Continuation)	72
Chapter 130B - Hazardous Waste Management Commission [Repealed.]	72
Chapter 131 - Public Hospitals [Repealed.]	72
Chapter 131A - Health Care Facilities Finance Act	72
Chapter 131B - Licensing of Ambulatory Surgical Facilities [Repealed.]	72
Chapter 131C - Charitable Solicitation Licensure Act [Repealed.]	72
Chapter 131D - Inspection and Licensing of Facilities	72
Chapter 131E - Health Care Facilities and Services	72
Chapter 131E - Health Care Facilities and Services (Continuation)	73
Chapter 131F - Solicitation of Contributions	73
Chapter 132 - Public Records	73
Chapter 133 - Public Works	74
Chapter 134 - Youth Development [Recodified.]	74
Chapter 134A - Youth Services [Repealed.]	74
Chapter 135 - Retirement System for Teachers and State Employees; Social Security; Health Insurance Program for Children	74
Chapter 135 - Retirement System for Teachers and State Employees; Social Security; Health Insurance Program for Children (Continuation)	75
Chapter 136 - Transportation	75
Chapter 136 - Transportation (Continuation)	76
Chapter 137 - Rural Rehabilitation [Repealed.]	76
Chapter 138 - Salaries, Fees and Allowances	76
Chapter 138A - State Government Ethics Act	76

Chapter 139 - Soil and Water Conservation Districts	76
Chapter 140 - State Art Museum; Symphony and Art Societies	76
Chapter 140A - State Awards System	76
Chapter 141 - State Boundaries	76
Chapter 142 - State Debt	76
Chapter 143 - State Departments, Institutions, and Commissions	77
Chapter 143 - State Departments, Institutions, and Commissions (Continuation)	78
Chapter 143 - State Departments, Institutions, and Commissions (Continuation)	79
Chapter 143 - State Departments, Institutions, and Commissions (Continuation)	80
Chapter 143A - State Government Reorganization	80
Chapter 143B - Executive Organization Act of 1973	80
Chapter 143B - Executive Organization Act of 1973 (Continuation)	81
Chapter 143B - Executive Organization Act of 1973 (Continuation)	82
Chapter 143C - State Budget Act	83
Chapter 143D - The State Governmental Accountability and Internal Control Act	83
Chapter 144 - State Flag, Official Governmental Flags, Motto, and Colors	83
Chapter 145 - State Symbols and Other Official Adoptions.	83
Chapter 146 - State Lands	83
Chapter 147 - State Officers	83
Chapter 148 - State Prison System	84
Chapter 149 - State Song and Toast	84
Chapter 150 - Uniform Revocation of Licenses [Repealed.]	84
Chapter 150A - Administrative Procedure Act [Recodified.]	84
Chapter 150B - Administrative Procedure Act	84
Chapter 151 - Constables [Repealed.]	84
Chapter 152 - Coroners	84
Chapter 152A - County Medical Examiner [Repealed.]	84
Chapter 152A - County Medical Examiner [Repealed.] (Continuation)	84
Chapter 153 - Counties and County Commissioners [Repealed.]	84
Chapter 153A - Counties	84
Chapter 153A - Counties (Continue)	85
Chapter 153B - Mountain Resources Planning Act	85
Chapter 153C - Uwharrie Regional Resources Act	85
Chapter 154 - County Surveyor [Repealed.]	85
Chapter 155 - County Treasurer [Repealed.]	85

Chapter 156 - Drainage	85
Chapter 156 – Drainage (Continuation)	86
Chapter 157 - Housing Authorities and Projects	86
Chapter 157A - Historic Properties Commissions [Transferred.]	86
Chapter 158 - Local Development	86
Chapter 159 - Local Government Finance	86
Chapter 159 - Local Government Finance (Continuation)	87
Chapter 159A - Pollution Abatement and Industrial Facilities Financing Act [Unconstitutional.]	87
Chapter 159B - Joint Municipal Electric Power and Energy Act	87
Chapter 159C - Industrial and Pollution Control Facilities Financing Act	87
Chapter 159D - The North Carolina Capital Facilities Financing Act	87
Chapter 159E - Registered Public Obligations Act	87
Chapter 159F - North Carolina Energy Development Authority [Repealed.]	87
Chapter 159G - Water Infrastructure	87
Chapter 159H - [Reserved.]	87
Chapter 159I - Solid Waste Management Loan Program and Local Government Special Obligation Bonds	87
Chapter 160 - Municipal Corporations [Repealed And Transferred.]	87
Chapter 160A - Cities and Towns	88
Chapter 160A - Cities and Towns (Continuation)	89
Chapter 160B - Consolidated City-County Act	89
Chapter 160C - Baseball Park Districts [Repealed.]	90
Chapter 161 - Register of Deeds	90
Chapter 162 - Sheriff	90
Chapter 162A - Water and Sewer Systems	90
Chapter 162B Continuity of Local Government in Emergency.	90
Chapter 163 Elections and Election Laws.	90
Chapter 163 Elections and Election Laws. (Continuation)	91
Chapter 164 Concerning the General Statutes of North Carolina.	92
Chapter 165 Veterans.	92
Chapter 166 Civil Preparedness Agencies [Repealed.]	92
Chapter 166A North Carolina Emergency Management Act.	92
Chapter 167 State Civil Air Patrol [Repealed.]	92
Chapter 168 Persons with Disabilities.	92
Chapter 168A Persons With Disabilities Protection Act.	92

§ 135-70. Transfer of members to another system.

(a) Any member whose membership service is terminated other than by retirement or death and, who, while still a member of this Retirement System becomes a member of either the Teachers' and State Employees' Retirement System or the North Carolina Local Governmental Employees' Retirement System, may elect to retain his membership in this Retirement System by not withdrawing his accumulated contributions hereunder. Any such member shall retain all the rights, credits and benefits obtaining to him under this Retirement System at the time of such termination of service while he is a member of such other system and does not withdraw his contributions hereunder.

(a1) The accumulated contributions and creditable service of any member whose service as a member of this Retirement System has been or is terminated other than by retirement or death and who, while still a member of this Retirement System, became or becomes a member, as defined in G.S. 135-1(13), of the Teachers' and State Employees' Retirement System for a period of five or more years may, upon application of the member, be transferred from this Retirement System to the Teachers' and State Employees' Retirement System. In order to effect the transfer of a member's creditable service from this Retirement System to the Teachers' and State Employees' Retirement System, there shall be transferred from this Retirement System to the Teachers' and State Employees' Retirement System the sum of (i) the accumulated contributions of the member credited in the annuity savings fund and (ii) the amount of reserve held in this Retirement System as a result of previous contributions by the employer on behalf of the transferring member.

(b) Any member who becomes eligible for benefits under more than one system may file application therefor with each retirement system to the end that each retirement system shall pay appropriate benefits without transfer of funds between the systems.

(c) The Board of Trustees shall effect such rules as it may deem necessary to administer the provisions of the preceding subsections of this section and to prevent any duplication of service credits or benefits that might otherwise occur. (1973, c. 640, s. 1; 1983 (Reg. Sess., 1984), c. 1031, s. 21; 2003-284, s. 30.18(d).)

§ 135-70.1. Transfer of members from the Local Governmental Employees' Retirement System, the Teachers' and State Employees' Retirement System, or the Legislative Retirement System.

(a) The accumulated contributions, creditable service, and reserves, if any, of a former teacher or employee, as defined in G.S. 135-1(25), 135-1(10), and 128-21(10), respectively, or a former member of the General Assembly who is a member of the Consolidated Judicial Retirement System for a period of five or more years may, upon application of the member, be transferred from the Local Governmental Employees' Retirement System, the Teachers' and State Employees' Retirement System, or the Legislative Retirement System to the Consolidated Judicial Retirement System. The accumulated contributions, creditable service, and reserves of any member whose service as a teacher or employee or member of the General Assembly is terminated other than by retirement or death and who becomes a member of the Consolidated Judicial Retirement System may, upon application of the member, be transferred from the Local Governmental Employees' Retirement System, the Teachers' and State Employees' Retirement System, or the Legislative Retirement System to the Consolidated Judicial Retirement System. In order to effect the transfer of a member's creditable service from the Local Governmental Retirement System, the Teachers' and State Employees' Retirement System, or the Legislative Retirement System, to the Consolidated Judicial Retirement System, the accumulated contributions of each member credited in the annuity savings fund in the Local Governmental Employees' Retirement System, the Teachers' and State Employees' Retirement System, or the Legislative Retirement System shall be transferred and credited to the annuity savings fund in the Consolidated Judicial Retirement System.

(b) The Board of Trustees shall effect such rules as it may deem necessary to administer the preceding subsection and to prevent any duplication of service credits or benefits that might otherwise occur. (1999-237, s. 28.24(h); 2003-284, s. 30.18(e); 2005-276, s. 29.30A(h); 2005-345, s. 42.)

§ 135-71. Return to membership of retired former member.

(a) In the event that a retired former member should at any time return to membership service, his retirement allowance shall thereupon cease and he shall be restored as a member of the Retirement System.

(b) Upon his subsequent retirement, he shall be paid a retirement allowance determined as follows:

(1) For a member who earns at least three years' membership service after restoration to service, the retirement allowance shall be computed on the basis of his compensation and service before and after the period of prior retirement without restrictions; provided, that if the prior allowance was based on a social security leveling payment option, the allowance shall be adjusted actuarially for the difference between the amount received under the optional payment and what would have been paid if the retirement allowance had been paid without optional modification.

(2) For a member who does not earn three years' membership service after restoration to service, the retirement allowance shall be equal to the sum of the retirement allowance to which he would have been entitled had he not been restored to service, without modification of the election of an optional allowance previously made, and the retirement allowance that results from service earned since being restored to service; provided, that if the prior retirement allowance was based on a social security leveling payment option, the prior allowance shall be adjusted actuarially for the difference between the amount that would have been paid for each month had the payment not been suspended and what would have been paid if the retirement allowance had been paid without optional modification.

(3) Subdivision (2) of this section shall apply only to restored members whose initial retirement lasted for more than four calendar months. For restored members whose initial retirement lasted for four or fewer calendar months, subdivision (1) shall apply.

(c) Notwithstanding any other provision in this Chapter, the retirement allowance of a justice or judge shall not be affected by the compensation received as an emergency justice or judge.

(d) Notwithstanding the provisions of G.S. 135-70.1 to the contrary, a retired former member and/or beneficiary of the Teachers' and State Employees' Retirement System as defined in G.S. 135-1(6), whose retirement allowance from this System and/or from the Teachers' and State Employees' Retirement System ceases upon a return to membership service under this System, shall be permitted to transfer the accumulated contributions, creditable service, and reserves, if any, from the Teachers' and State Employees' Retirement System to this System on the same basis as provided for members of other retirement systems under G.S. 135-70.1, if the member attains five or more years of total membership service in this System, and completes at least three years of membership service subsequent to the member's return to membership service. (1973, c. 640, s. 1; 1983 (Reg. Sess., 1984), c. 1031, s. 22; c. 1106, s. 3; 1987, c. 738, s. 39(b); 2005-276, s. 29.30A(i).)

§ 135-72: Repealed by Session Laws 1999-237, s. 28.25.

§ 135-73. Termination or partial termination; discontinuance of contributions.

In the event of the termination or partial termination of the Retirement System or in the event of complete discontinuance of contributions under the Retirement System, the rights of all affected members to benefits accrued to the date of such termination, partial termination, or discontinuance, to the extent funded as of such date, or the amounts credited to the members' accounts, shall be nonforfeitable and fully vested. (1987, c. 177, s. 1(a), (b).)

§ 135-74. Internal Revenue Code compliance.

(a) Notwithstanding any other provisions of law to the contrary, compensation for any calendar year after 1988 in which employee or employer contributions are made and for which annual compensation is used for computing any benefit under this Article shall not exceed the higher of two hundred thousand dollars ($200,000) or the amount determined by the Commissioner of Internal Revenue as the limitation for calendar years after 1989; provided the imposition of the limitation shall not reduce a member's benefit below the amount determined as of December 31, 1988.

All the provisions in this subsection have been enacted to make clear that the Plan shall not base contributions or Plan benefits on annual compensation in excess of the limits prescribed by Section 401(a)(17) of the Internal Revenue Code, as adjusted from time to time, subject to certain federal grandfathering rules.

Effective January 1, 1996, the annual compensation of a member taken into account for determining all benefits provided under this Article shall not exceed one hundred fifty thousand dollars ($150,000), as adjusted pursuant to section 401(a)(17)(B) of the Internal Revenue Code and any regulations issued under the Code. However, with respect to a person who became a member of the Retirement System prior to January 1, 1996, the imposition of this limitation on compensation shall not reduce the amount of compensation which may be taken into account for determining the benefits of that member under this Article below the amount of compensation which would have been recognized under the provisions of this Article in effect on July 1, 1993.

Effective January 1, 2002, the annual compensation of a person, who became a member of the Retirement System on or after January 1, 1996, taken into account for determining all benefits accruing under this Article for any plan year after December 31, 2001, shall not exceed two hundred thousand dollars ($200,000) or the amount otherwise set by the Internal Revenue Code or determined by the Commissioner of Internal Revenue as the limitation for calendar years after 2002.

(b) Notwithstanding any other provisions of law to the contrary, the annual benefit payable on behalf of a member shall, if necessary, be reduced to the extent required by Section 415(b) and with respect to calendar years commencing prior to January 1, 2000, Section 415(e) of the Internal Revenue Code, as adjusted by the Secretary of the Treasury or his delegate pursuant to Section 415(d) of the Code. If a member is a participant under any qualified defined contributions plan that is required to be taken into account for the purposes of the limitation contained in Section 415 of the Internal Revenue Code, the annual benefit payable under this Article shall be reduced to the extent required by Section 415(e) prior to making any reduction under the defined contribution plan provided by the employer. However, with respect to a member who has benefits accrued under this Article but whose benefit had not commenced as of December 31, 1999, the combined plan limitation contained in Section 415(e) of the Internal Revenue Code shall not be applied to such member for calendar years commencing on or after January 1, 2000.

(c) On and after September 8, 2009, and for all Plan years to which the minimum distribution rules of the Internal Revenue Code are applicable, with respect to any member who has terminated employment, the Plan shall comply with federal income tax minimum distribution rules by applying a reasonable and good faith interpretation to Section 401(a)(9) of the Internal Revenue Code.

(d) This subsection applies to distributions and rollovers from the Plan. The Plan does not have mandatory distributions within the meaning of Section 401(a)(31) of the Internal Revenue Code. With respect to distributions from the Plan and notwithstanding any other provision of the Plan to the contrary that would otherwise limit a distributee's election under this Article, a distributee (including, after December 31, 2006, a non-spouse beneficiary if that non-spouse beneficiary elects a direct rollover only to an inherited traditional or Roth IRA as permitted under applicable federal law) may elect, at the time and in the manner prescribed by the Plan administrator, to have any portion of an eligible rollover distribution paid directly to an eligible retirement plan specified by the distributee in a direct rollover. As used in this subsection, an "eligible retirement plan" means an individual retirement account described in Section 408(a) of the Code, an individual retirement annuity described in Section 408(b) of the Code, an annuity plan described in Section 403(a) of the Code, on and after January 1, 2009, a Roth IRA, or a qualified trust described in Section 401(a) of the Code, that accepts the distributee's eligible rollover distribution. Effective on and after January 1, 2002, an eligible retirement plan also means an annuity contract described in Section 403(b) of the Code and an eligible plan under Section 457(b) of the Code that is maintained by a state, political subdivision of a state, or any agency or instrumentality of a state or political subdivision of a state and which agrees to separately account for amounts transferred into that plan from this Plan. As used in this subsection, a "direct rollover" is a payment by the Plan to the eligible retirement plan specified by the distributee. Provided, an eligible rollover distribution is any distribution of all or any portion of the balance to the credit of the distributee, except that an eligible rollover distribution shall not include: any distribution that is one of a series of substantially equal periodic payments (not less frequently than annually) made for the life (or life expectancy) of the distributee or the joint lives (or joint life expectancies) of the distributee and the distributee's designated beneficiary, or for a specified period of 10 years or more; any distribution to the extent such distribution is required under section 401(a)(9) of the Code; and the portion of any distribution that is not includible in gross income (determined without regard to the exclusion for net realized appreciation with respect to employer securities). Effective as of January 1, 2002, and notwithstanding the exclusion of any after-tax portion from such a rollover distribution in the preceding sentence, a portion of a distribution shall not fail to be an eligible rollover distribution merely because the portion consists of after-tax employee contributions which are not includible in gross income. That portion may be transferred, pursuant to applicable federal law, to an individual retirement account or annuity described in Section 408(a) or (b) of the Code, to a qualified defined benefit plan, or to a qualified defined contribution plan described in Section 401(a), 403(a), or 403(b) of the Code that agrees to separately account for amounts so transferred, including separately accounting for the portion of such distribution which is includible in gross income and the portion of such distribution which is not so includible. The definition of eligible retirement plan shall also apply in the case of a distribution to surviving spouse, or to a spouse or former spouse who is the alternate payee under a qualified domestic relations order, as defined in Section 414(p) of the Internal Revenue Code, or a court-ordered equitable distribution of marital property, as provided under G.S. 50-20.1. Effective on and after January 1, 2007, notwithstanding any other provision of this subsection, a nonspouse beneficiary of a deceased member may elect, at the time and in the manner prescribed by the administrator of the Board of Trustees of this Retirement System, to directly roll over any portion of the beneficiary's distribution from the Retirement System; however, such rollover shall conform with the provisions of section 402(c)(11) of the Code. (1989, c. 276, s. 4; 1993, c. 531, s. 8; 1995, c. 361, s. 2; 2002-71, s. 8; 2009-66, s. 1(b); 2012-130, s. 4(d).)

§ 135-75. Deduction for payments allowed.

(a) Any beneficiary who is a member of a domiciled employees' or retirees' association that has at least 2,000 members, the majority of whom are active or retired employees of the State or public school employees, may authorize, in writing, the periodic deduction from the beneficiary's retirement benefits a designated lump sum to be paid to the employees' or retirees' association. The authorization shall remain in effect until revoked by the beneficiary. A plan of deductions pursuant to this section shall become void if the employees' or retirees' association engages in collective bargaining with the State, any political subdivision of the State, or any local school administrative unit.

(b) Any beneficiary eligible for coverage under the State Health Plan may also authorize, in writing, the monthly deduction from the beneficiary's retirement benefits of a designated lump sum to be paid to the State Health Plan for any dependent whom the beneficiary wishes to cover under the State Health Plan. In the event that the beneficiary's own State Health Plan coverage is contributory, in whole or in part, the beneficiary may also authorize a designated lump sum to be paid to the State Health Plan on behalf of the beneficiary. In addition, a beneficiary may similarly authorize the deduction for supplemental voluntary insurance benefits, provided that the deduction is authorized by the Department of State Treasurer and is payable to a company with which the Department of State Treasurer has or had an exclusive contractual relationship.

Any such authorization shall remain in effect until revoked by the beneficiary. (2002-126, s. 6.4(e); 2012-178, s. 4(d).)

§ 135-75.1. Forfeiture of retirement benefits for certain felonies committed while serving as elected government official.

(a) Except as provided in G.S. 135-56(g), the Board of Trustees shall not pay any retirement benefits or allowances, except for a return of member contributions plus interest, to any member who is convicted of any felony under the federal laws listed in subsection (b) of this section or the laws of this State listed in subsection (c) of this section if all of the following apply:

(1) The federal or State offense is committed while serving as a justice, judge, district attorney, or clerk of superior court.

(2) The conduct on which the federal or State offense is based is directly related to the member's service as a justice, judge, district attorney, or clerk of superior court.

(b) The federal offenses covered by this section are as follows:

(1) A felony violation of 18 U.S.C. § 201 (Bribery of public officials and witnesses), 18 U.S.C. § 286 (Conspiracy to defraud the Government with respect to claims), 18 U.S.C. § 287 (False, fictitious or fraudulent claims), 18 U.S.C. § 371 (Conspiracy to commit offense or to defraud United States), 18 U.S.C. § 597 (Expenditures to influence voting), 18 U.S.C. § 599 (Promise of appointment by candidate), 18 U.S.C. § 606 (Intimidation to secure political contributions), 18 U.S.C. § 641 (Public money, property, or records), 18 U.S.C. § 666 (Embezzlement and theft), 18 U.S.C. § 1001 (Statements or entries generally), 18 U.S.C. § 1341 (Frauds and swindles), 18 U.S.C. § 1343 (Fraud by wire, radio, or television), 18 U.S.C. § 1503 (Influencing or injuring officer or juror generally), 18 U.S.C. § 1951 (Interference with commerce by threats or violence), 18 U.S.C. § 1952 (Interstate and foreign travel or transportation in aid of racketeering enterprises), 18 U.S.C. § 1956 (Laundering of monetary instruments), 18 U.S.C. § 1962 (Prohibited activities), or section 7201 of the Internal Revenue Code (Attempt to evade or defeat tax).

(2) Reserved for future codification purposes.

(c) The offenses under the laws of this State covered by this section are as follows:

(1) A felony violation of Article 29, 30, or 30A of Chapter 14 of the General Statutes (Relating to bribery, obstructing justice, and secret listening) or G.S. 14-228 (Buying and selling offices), or Part 1 of Article 14 of Chapter 120 of the General Statutes (Code of Legislative Ethics), Article 20 or 22 of Chapter 163 of the General Statutes (Relating to absentee ballots, corrupt practices and other offenses against the elective franchise, and regulating of contributions and expenditures in political campaigns).

(2) Perjury or false information as follows:

a. Perjury committed under G.S. 14-209 in falsely denying the commission of an act that constitutes an offense within the purview of an offense listed in subdivision (1) of subsection (c) of this section.

b. Subornation of perjury committed under G.S. 14-210 in connection with the false denial of another as specified by subdivision (2) of this subsection.

c. Perjury under Article 22A of Chapter 163 of the General Statutes.

(d) All monies forfeited under this section shall be remitted to the Civil Penalty and Forfeiture Fund. (2007-179, s. 4(a).)

§ 135-75.1A. Forfeiture of retirement benefits for certain felonies related to employment or holding office.

(a) Except as provided in G.S. 135-56(j), the Board of Trustees shall not pay any retirement benefits or allowances, except for a return of member contributions plus interest, to any member who is convicted of any felony under federal law or the laws of this State if all of the following apply:

(1) The offense is committed while the member is in service.

(2) The conduct resulting in the member's conviction is directly related to the member's office or employment.

(b) Subdivision (2) of subsection (a) of this section shall apply to felony convictions where the court finds under G.S. 15A-1340.16(d)(9) or other applicable State or federal procedure that the member's conduct is directly related to the member's office or employment.

(c) If a member or former member whose benefits under the System were forfeited under this section, except for the return of member contributions plus interest, subsequently receives an unconditional pardon of innocence, or the conviction is vacated or set aside for any reason, then the member or former member may seek a reversal of the benefit forfeiture by presenting sufficient evidence to the State Treasurer. If the State Treasurer determines a reversal of the benefit forfeiture is appropriate, then all benefits will be restored upon repayment of all accumulated contributions plus interest. Repayment of all accumulated contributions that have been received by the individual under the forfeiture provisions of this section must be made in a total lump-sum payment with interest compounded annually at a rate of six and one-half percent (6.5%) for each calendar year from the year of forfeiture to the year of repayment. An individual receiving a reversal of benefit forfeiture must receive reinstatement of the service credit forfeited. (2012-193, s. 5.)

§ 135-75.2. Improper receipt of decedent's retirement allowance.

A person is guilty of a Class 1 misdemeanor if the person, with the intent to defraud, receives money as a result of cashing, depositing, or receiving a direct deposit of a decedent's retirement allowance and the person (i) knows that he or she is not entitled to the decedent's retirement allowance, (ii) receives the benefit at least two months after the date of the retiree's or beneficiary's death, and (iii) does not attempt to inform this Retirement System of the retiree's or beneficiary's death. (2011-232, s. 10(c); 2013-288, s. 9(d).)

§ 135-76: Reserved for future codification purposes.

Article 4A.

Uniform Solicitorial Retirement Act of 1974.

§§ 135-77 through 135-83: Repealed by Session Laws 1983 (Regular Session 1984), c. 1031, s. 24.

Article 4B.

Uniform Clerks of Superior Court Retirement Act of 1975.

§§ 135-84 through 135-86: Repealed by Session Laws 1983 (Regular Session, 1984), c. 1031, s. 24.

§ 135-87. Reserved for future codification purposes.

§ 135-88. Reserved for future codification purposes.

§ 135-89. Reserved for future codification purposes.

Article 5.

Supplemental Retirement Income Act of 1984.

§ 135-90. Short title and purpose.

(a) This Article shall be known and may be cited as the "Supplemental Retirement Income Act of 1984".

(b) The purpose of the Article is to attract and hold qualified employees and officials of the State of North Carolina and its political subdivisions by permitting them to participate in a profit sharing or salary reduction form of deferred compensation which will provide supplemental retirement income payments upon retirement, disability, termination, hardship, and death as allowed under section 401(k), or any other relevant section, of the Internal Revenue Code of 1954 as amended. As used in this Article, the term "profit" means the excess revenue over expenditures prior to the expenditure of the amount which may be optionally made available for employees to be placed in trust by the State and its political subdivisions on behalf of the employees and officials covered by this Article. (1983 (Reg. Sess., 1984), c. 975.)

§ 135-91. Administration.

(a)   The provisions of this Article shall be administered by the Department of State Treasurer and the Supplemental Retirement Board of Trustees established in G.S. 135-96. The Department of State Treasurer and the Board of Trustees shall create a Supplemental Retirement Income Plan as of January 1, 1985, to be administered under the provisions of this Article.

(b)   The Supplemental Retirement Income Plan shall have the power and privileges of a corporation and shall be known as the "Supplemental Retirement Income Plan of North Carolina" and by this name all of its business shall be transacted.

(c)   The Department of State Treasurer and the Board of Trustees shall have full power and authority to adopt rules and regulations for the administration of the Plan, provided they are not inconsistent with the provisions of this Article. The Department of State Treasurer and Board of Trustees may appoint those agents, contractors, employees and committees as they deem advisable to carry out the terms and conditions of the Plan.

(d)   The Department of State Treasurer and the Board of Trustees shall be charged with a fiduciary responsibility for managing all aspects of the Plan, including the receipt, maintenance, investment, and disposition of all Plan assets.

(e)   The administrative costs of the Plan may be charged to members or deducted from members' accounts in accordance with nondiscriminatory procedures established by the Department of State Treasurer and Board of Trustees.

(f)   Each institution of The University of North Carolina shall report the data and other information to the Supplemental Retirement Income Plan pertaining to participants in the Optional Retirement Program as shall be required by the Department of State Treasurer and the Board of Trustees.

(g)   Each political subdivision of the State that sponsors a retirement or pension plan with members who are members of the Supplemental Retirement Income Plan shall report the data and other information to the Plan pertaining to members of the retirement or pension plan as shall be required by the Department of State Treasurer and the Board of Trustees. (1983 (Reg. Sess.,

1984), c. 975; 1985, c. 403, s. 1; 1989 (Reg. Sess., 1990), c. 948, s. 2; 2008-132, s. 1.)

§ 135-92. Membership.

(a)   The membership eligibility of the Supplemental Retirement Income Plan shall consist of any of the following who voluntarily elect to enroll:

(1)   Members of the Teachers' and State Employees' Retirement System; and

(2)   Members of the Consolidated Judicial Retirement System; and

(3)   Members of the Legislative Retirement System; and

(4)   Members of the Local Governmental Employees' Retirement System; and

(5)   Law enforcement officers as defined under G.S. 143-166.30 and G.S. 143-166.50; and

(6)   Participants in the Optional Retirement Program provided for under G.S. 135-5.1; and

(7)   Members of retirement and pension plans sponsored by political subdivisions of the State so long as such plans are qualified under Section 401(a) of the Internal Revenue Code of 1986 as amended from time to time.

(b)   The membership of any person in the Supplemental Retirement Income Plan shall cease upon:

(1)   The withdrawal of a member's accumulated account; or

(2)   Retirement under the provisions of the Supplemental Income Retirement Plan; or

(3)   Death. (1983 (Reg. Sess., 1984), c. 975; 1985, c. 403, s. 2; 1989 (Reg. Sess., 1990), c. 948, s. 1.)

§ 135-93. Contributions.

(a) Each member may elect to reduce his compensation by the amount of his contribution to the Supplemental Retirement Income Plan and that amount shall be held in the member's account. Members electing such a reduction in compensation may authorize payroll deductions for making contributions to the Plan.

(b) The State and any of its political subdivisions may make contributions to the Supplemental Retirement Income Plan on behalf of any of its members, provided these contributions are nondiscriminatory in accordance with the Internal Revenue Code of 1954 as amended, and are duly appropriated by their governing bodies, and the contributions are held in the member's account. Employer contributions to the Plan are declared expenditures for a public purpose.

(c) The Department of State Treasurer and Board of Trustees shall establish maximum annual additions that may be made to a member's account and provide for multiple plan reductions in accordance with the Internal Revenue Code of 1954 as amended. (1983 (Reg. Sess., 1984), c. 975.)

§ 135-94. Benefits.

(a) The Department of State Treasurer and the Board of Trustees shall establish a schedule of supplemental retirement income benefits for all members of the Supplemental Retirement Income Plan, subject to the following limitations:

(1) Except as provided in G.S. 143-166.30(g1) and G.S. 143-166.50(e2), the balance in each member's account shall be fully vested at all times and shall not be subject to forfeiture for any reason.

(2) All amounts maintained in a member's account shall be invested according to the member's election, as approved by the Department of State Treasurer and Board of Trustees, including but not limited to, a time deposit account, a fixed investment account, or a variable investment account. Transfers of accumulated funds shall be permitted among the various approved forms of investment.

(3) The Department of State Treasurer and Board of Trustees shall provide members with alternative payment options, including survivors' options, for the distribution of benefits from the Plan upon retirement, disability, termination, hardship, and death.

(4) With the consent of the Department of State Treasurer and the Board of Trustees, amounts may be transferred from other qualified plans to the Supplemental Retirement Income Plan, provided that the trust from which such funds are transferred permits the transfer to be made and, the transfer will not jeopardize the tax status of the Supplemental Retirement Income Plan.

(5) At the discretion of the Department of State Treasurer and Board of Trustees, a loan program may be implemented for members which complies with applicable State and federal laws and regulations.

(b) All provisions of the Plan shall be interpreted and applied by the Department of State Treasurer and Board of Trustees in a uniform and nondiscriminatory manner.

(c) All benefits under the Plan shall become payable on and after January 1, 1985.

(d) Contributions under the Plan may be made on and after January 1, 1985. (1983 (Reg. Sess., 1984), c. 975; 1993, c. 531, s. 9; 2012-193, s. 15.)

§ 135-95. Exemption from garnishment, attachment.

Except for the applications of the provisions of G.S. 143-166.30(g1), G.S. 143-166.50(e2), G.S. 110-136, and G.S. 110-136.3 et seq., and in connection with a court-ordered equitable distribution under G.S. 50-20, the right of a member in the Supplemental Retirement Income Plan to the benefits provided under this Article is nonforfeitable and exempt from levy, sale, and garnishment. (1983 (Reg. Sess., 1984), c. 975; 1985, c. 402; 1989, c. 665, s. 2; c. 792, s. 2.6; 2012-193, s. 16.)

§ 135-96. Supplemental Retirement Board of Trustees.

(a) The Supplemental Retirement Board of Trustees is established to administer the Supplemental Retirement Income Plan established under the provisions of this Article and the North Carolina Public Employee Deferred Compensation Plan established under G.S. 143B-426.24, and the North Carolina Public School Teachers' and Professional Educators' Investment Plan established under G.S. 115C-341.2.

(b) The Board consists of nine voting members, as follows:

(1) Six persons appointed by the Governor who have experience in finance and investments, one of whom shall be a State employee, and one of whom shall be a retired State or local governmental employee;

(2) One person appointed by the General Assembly upon the recommendation of the Speaker of the House of Representatives;

(3) One person appointed by the General Assembly upon the recommendation of the President Pro Tempore of the Senate; and

(4) The State Treasurer, ex officio, who shall be the Chair.

(c) The initial appointments by the General Assembly and two of the Governor's initial appointments shall be for one-year terms. The remainder of the initial appointments shall be for two-year terms. At the expiration of these initial terms, appointments shall be for two years and shall be made by the appointing authorities designated in subsection (b) of this section. A member shall continue to serve until the member's successor is duly appointed, but a holdover under this provision does not affect the expiration date of the succeeding term. No member of the Board may serve more than three consecutive two-year terms.

(d) Other than ex officio members, members appointed by the Governor shall serve at the Governor's pleasure. An ex officio member may designate in writing, filed with the Board, any employee of the member's department to act at any meeting of the Board from which the member is absent, to the same extent that the member could act if present in person at such meeting.

(e) The Board may retain the services of independent appraisers, auditors, actuaries, attorneys, investment counseling firms, statisticians, custodians, or other persons or firms possessing specialized skills or knowledge necessary for the proper administration of investment programs that the Board administers pursuant to this section. (2008-132, s. 2; 2009-378, s. 1; 2013-287, s. 1.)

§ 135-97. Immunity.

A person serving on the Supplemental Retirement Board of Trustees shall be immune individually from civil liability for monetary damages, except to the extent covered by insurance, for any act or failure to act arising out of that service, except where any of the following apply:

(1)   The person was not acting within the scope of that person's official duties.

(2)   The person was not acting in good faith.

(3)   The person committed gross negligence or willful or wanton misconduct that resulted in the damages or injury.

(4)   The person derived an improper personal financial benefit, either directly or indirectly, from the transaction.

(5)   The person incurred the liability from the operation of a motor vehicle. (2013-287, s. 5.)

§ 135-98 Reserved for future codification purposes.

§ 135-99 Reserved for future codification purposes.

Article 6.

Disability Income Plan of North Carolina.

§ 135-100. Short title and purpose.

(a)   This Article shall be known and may be cited as the "Disability Income Plan of North Carolina".

(b)   The purpose of this Article is to provide equitable replacement income for eligible teachers and employees who become temporarily or permanently disabled for the performance of their duty prior to retirement, and to encourage disabled teachers and employees who are able to work to seek gainful employment after a reasonable period of rehabilitation, and to provide for the accrual of retirement and ancillary benefits to the date the eligible teacher or employee meets the requirements for retirement under the provisions of this Chapter. (1987, c. 738, s. 29(q).)

§ 135-101. Definitions.

The following words and phrases as used in this Article, unless a different meaning is plainly required by the context, shall have the following meanings:

(1)   "Base rate of compensation" shall mean the regular monthly rate of compensation not including pay for shift premiums, overtime, or other types of extraordinary pay; in all cases of doubt, the Board of Trustees shall determine what is "base rate of compensation".

(2)   "Beneficiary" shall mean any person in receipt of a disability allowance or other benefit as provided in this Article.

(3)   "Benefits" shall mean the monthly disability income payments made pursuant to the provisions of this Article. In the event of death on or after the first day of a month, or in the event the short-term disability benefit ends on or after the first day of a month where the beneficiary is eligible and applies for an early service or a service retirement allowance the first of the following month, the monthly benefit shall not be prorated and shall equal the benefits paid in the previous month.

(4)   "Board of Trustees" shall mean the Board of Trustees of the Teachers' and State Employees' Retirement System as provided in G.S. 135-6.

(5)   "Compensation" shall mean any compensation as the term is defined in G.S. 135-1(7a).

(6)   "Disability" or "Disabled" shall mean the mental or physical incapacity for the further performance of duty of a participant or beneficiary; provided that such incapacity was not the result of terrorist activity, active participation in a

riot, committing or attempting to commit a felony, or intentionally self-inflicted injury.

(7)   "Earnings" shall mean all income for personal services rendered or otherwise receivable, including, but not limited to, salaries and wages, fees, commissions, royalties, awards and other similar items and self-employment; in all cases of doubt, the Board of Trustees shall determine what are "earnings".

(8)   "Employee" shall mean any employee as the term is defined in G.S. 135-1(10).

(9)   "Employer" shall mean any employer as the term is defined in G.S. 135-1(11).

(10)   "Medical Board" shall mean the board of physicians as provided in G.S. 135-102(d).

(11)   "Member" shall mean any member as the term is defined in G.S. 135-1(13).

(12)   "Membership service" shall mean any service as defined in G.S. 135-1(14).

(13)   "Participant" shall mean any teacher or employee eligible to participate in the Plan as provided in G.S. 135-103.

(14)   "Plan" shall mean the Disability Income Plan of North Carolina as provided in this Article.

(15)   "Retirement" shall mean the withdrawal from active service with a retirement allowance granted under the provisions of Article 1 of this Chapter.

(16)   "Retirement System" shall mean the Teachers' and State Employees' Retirement System of North Carolina as defined in G.S. 135-2.

(17)   "Service" shall mean service as a teacher or employee as defined in G.S. 135-1(10) or G.S. 135-1(25).

(18)   "State" shall mean the State of North Carolina.

(19) "Teacher" shall mean any teacher as the term is defined in G.S. 135-1(25).

(20) "Trial Rehabilitation" shall mean a return to service in any capacity, if the return occurs within the waiting period as provided in G.S. 135-104; shall mean a return to service in the same capacity that existed prior to the disability if the return occurs within the short-term disability period as provided in G.S. 135-105; and shall mean a return to service in any capacity and in any position provided the salary earned is equal to or greater than the salary upon which the long-term disability benefit is based immediately preceding the return to service, if the return occurs within the long-term disability period as provided in G.S. 135-106.

(21) "Workers' Compensation" shall mean any disability income benefits provided under the North Carolina Workers' Compensation Act, excluding any payments for a permanent partial disability rating. (1987, c. 738, s. 29(q); 1989, c. 717, ss. 7, 8; 1991 (Reg. Sess., 1992), c. 779, s. 1; 1993 (Reg. Sess., 1994), c. 769, s. 7.30(s); 2003-284, s. 30.20(j); 2004-78, s. 1; 2006-74, ss. 1, 2.)

§ 135-102. Administration.

(a) The provisions of this Article shall be administered by the Department of State Treasurer and the Board of Trustees of the Teachers' and State Employees' Retirement System and all expenses in connection with the administration of the Plan, except for expenses incurred by and properly charged to the employer, shall be charged against and paid from the trust fund as created and provided in this Article.

(b) The Plan shall have the power and privileges of a corporation and under the name of Disability Income Plan of North Carolina shall all of its business be transacted, all of its funds invested and all of its cash, securities and other property be held.

(c) The Department of State Treasurer and the Board of Trustees shall have the full power and authority to adopt rules for the administration of the Plan not inconsistent with the provisions of this Article. The Department of State Treasurer and the Board of Trustees may appoint those agents, contractors, and employees as they deem advisable to carry out the terms and conditions of the Plan.

(d) The Department of State Treasurer and the Board of Trustees shall designate a Medical Board to be composed of not fewer than three nor more than five physicians not eligible for benefits under the Plan. Other physicians, medical clinics, institutions or agencies may be employed to conduct such medical examinations and tests necessary to provide the Medical Board with clinical evidence as may be needed to determine eligibility for benefits under the Plan. The Medical Board shall investigate the results of medical examinations, clinical evidence, all essential statements and certifications by and on behalf of applicants for benefits and shall report in writing to the Board of Trustees the conclusions and recommendations upon all matters referred to it.

(e) The Department of State Treasurer and the Board of Trustees may provide the benefits according to the terms and conditions of the Plan as provided in this Article either by purchasing a contract or contracts with any insurance company licensed to do business in this State or by establishing a separate trust fund qualified under Section 501(c)(9) of the Internal Revenue Code of 1986. (1987, c. 738, s. 29(q).)

§ 135-103. Eligible participants.

(a) The eligible participants of the Disability Income Plan shall consist of:

(1) All teachers and employees in service and members of the Teachers' and State Employees' Retirement System or participants of the Optional Retirement Program on January 1, 1988.

(2) All persons who become teachers and employees or re-enter service as teachers or employees and are in service and members of the Teachers' and State Employees' Retirement System or participants of the Optional Retirement Program after January 1, 1988.

(b) The participation of any person in the Disability Income Plan shall cease upon:

(1) The termination of the participant's employment as a teacher or State employee, or

(2) The participant's retirement under the provisions of the Teachers' and Employees' Retirement System or the Optional Retirement Program, or

(3) The participant's becoming a beneficiary under the Plan, or

(4) The participant's death. (1987, c. 738, s. 29(q).)

§ 135-104. Salary continuation.

(a) A participant shall receive no benefits from the Plan for a period of 60 continuous calendar days from the onset of disability determined as the last actual day of service, the day of the disabling event if the disabling event occurred on a day other than a normal workday, or the day succeeding at least 365 calendar days after service as a teacher or employee, whichever is later. These 60 continuous calendar days may be considered the waiting period before benefits are payable from the Plan. During this waiting period, a participant may be paid such continuation of salary as provided by an employer through the use of sick leave, vacation leave or any other salary continuation. Any such continuation of salary as provided by an employer shall not include any period a participant or beneficiary is in receipt of Workers' Compensation benefits.

(b) During the waiting period a participant may return to service for trial rehabilitation for periods of not greater than five continuous days of service. Such return to service will not cause a new waiting period to begin but shall extend the waiting period by the number of days of service. (1987, c. 738, s. 29(q); 1989, c. 717, s. 9; 1991 (Reg. Sess., 1992), c. 779, s. 2.)

§ 135-105. Short-term disability benefits.

(a) Any participant who becomes disabled and is no longer able to perform his usual occupation may, after at least 365 calendar days succeeding his date of initial employment as a teacher or employee and at least one year of contributing membership service, receive a benefit commencing on the first day succeeding the waiting period; provided that the participant's employer and attending physician shall certify that such participant is mentally or physically incapacitated for the further performance of duty, that such incapacity was incurred at the time of active employment and has been continuous thereafter; provided further that the requirement for one year of contributing membership service must have been earned within 36 calendar months immediately preceding the date of disability and further, salary continuation used during the period as provided in G.S. 135-104 shall count toward the aforementioned one year requirement. As to the requirement that a participant applying for short term disability benefits have at least one year of contributing membership service within the 36 calendar months immediately preceding the date of disability, a participant who would have qualified for a benefit under this section but for service in the uniformed services shall not be denied a benefit under this section because of that interruption for military service provided all other requirements of this section are met.

Notwithstanding the requirement that the incapacity was incurred at the time of active employment, any participant who becomes disabled while on an employer approved leave of absence and who is eligible for and in receipt of temporary total benefits under The North Carolina Workers' Compensation Act, Article 1 of Chapter 97 of the General Statutes, will be eligible for all benefits provided under this Article.

(b)   The benefits as provided for in subsection (a) of this section shall commence on the first day following the waiting period and shall be payable for a period of 365 days as long as the participant continues to meet the definition of disability. However, a disabled participant may elect to receive any salary continuation as provided in G.S. 135-104 in lieu of short-term disability benefits; provided further, such election shall not extend the 365 days duration of short-term payments. An election to receive any salary continuation for any part of a given day shall be in lieu of any short-term benefit otherwise payable for that day, provided further, any lump-sum payout for vacation leave shall be treated as if the beneficiary or participant had exhausted the leave and shall be in lieu of any short-term benefit otherwise payable.

(c)   The monthly benefit as provided in subsection (a) of this section shall be equal to fifty percent (50%) of 1/12th of the annual base rate of compensation last payable to the participant prior to the beginning of the short-term benefit period as may be adjusted for percentage increases as provided under G.S. 135-108 plus fifty percent (50%) of 1/12th of the annual longevity payment to which the participant would be eligible, to a maximum of three thousand dollars ($3,000) per month reduced by monthly payments for Workers' Compensation to which the participant may be entitled. The monthly benefit shall be further reduced by the amount of any payments from the federal Veterans Administration, any other federal agency, or any payments made under the provisions of G.S. 127A-108, to which the participant or beneficiary may be entitled on account of the same disability. Provided, that should a participant have earnings in an amount greater than the short-term benefit, the amount of the short-term benefit shall be reduced on a dollar-for-dollar basis by the amount that exceeds the short-term benefit.

(d)   The provisions of this section shall be administered by the employer and further, the benefits during the first six months of the short-term disability period shall be the full responsibility of and paid by the employer; Provided, further, that upon the completion of the initial six months of the short-term disability period, the employer will continue to be responsible for the short-term benefits to the participant, however, such employer shall notify the Plan, at the conclusion of the short-term disability period or upon termination of short-term disability benefits, if earlier, of the amount of short-term benefits and State Health Insurance premiums paid by the employer and the Plan shall reimburse the employer the amounts so paid.

(e)   During the short-term disability period, a beneficiary may return to service for trial rehabilitation for periods of not greater than 40 continuous days of service. Such return will not cause the beneficiary to become a participant and will not require a new waiting period or short-term disability period to commence unless a different incapacity occurs. The period of rehabilitative employment shall not extend the period of the short-term disability benefits.

(f)   A participant or beneficiary of short-term disability benefits or his legal representative or any person deemed by the Board of Trustees to represent the participant or beneficiary, or the employer of the participant or beneficiary, may request the Board of Trustees to have the Medical Board make a determination of eligibility for the short-term disability benefits as provided in this section or to make a preliminary determination of eligibility for the long-term disability benefits as provided in G.S. 135-106. A preliminary determination of eligibility for long-term disability benefits shall not preclude the requirement that the Medical Board make a determination of eligibility for long-term disability benefits.

(g)   The Board of Trustees may extend the short-term disability benefits of a beneficiary beyond the benefit period of 365 days for an additional period of not more than 365 days; provided the Medical Board determines that the beneficiary's disability is temporary and likely to end within the extended period of short-term disability benefits. During the extended period of short-term disability benefits, payment of benefits shall be made by the Plan directly to the beneficiary. (1987, c. 738, s. 29(q); 1989, c. 717, s. 10; 1989 (Reg. Sess., 1990), c. 1032, s. 1; 1991 (Reg. Sess., 1992), c. 779, s. 3; 1993 (Reg. Sess.,

1994), c. 769, s. 7.30(t); 2003-284, s. 30.20(k); 2004-78, s. 2; 2007-325, s. 1; 2013-288, s. 6.)

§ 135-106. Long-term disability benefits.

(a)   Upon the application of a beneficiary or participant or of his legal representative or any person deemed by the Board of Trustees to represent the participant or beneficiary, any beneficiary or participant who has had five or more years of membership service may receive long-term disability benefits from the Plan upon approval by the Board of Trustees, commencing on the first day succeeding the conclusion of the short-term disability period provided for in G.S. 135-105, provided the beneficiary or participant makes application for such benefit within 180 days after the short-term disability period ceases, after salary continuation payments cease, or after monthly payments for Workers' Compensation cease, whichever is later; Provided, that the beneficiary or participant withdraws from active service by terminating employment as a teacher or State employee; Provided, that the Medical Board shall certify that such beneficiary or participant is mentally or physically incapacitated for the further performance of duty, that such incapacity was incurred at the time of active employment and has been continuous thereafter, and that such incapacity is likely to be permanent; Provided further that the Medical Board shall not certify any beneficiary or participant as disabled who is in receipt of any payments on account of the same incapacity which existed when the beneficiary first established membership in the Retirement System. The Board of Trustees may extend this 180-day filing requirement upon receipt of clear and convincing evidence that application was delayed through no fault of the disabled beneficiary or participant and was delayed due to the employers' miscalculation of the end of the 180-day filing period. However, in no instance shall the filing period be extended beyond an additional 180 days.

The Board of Trustees may require each beneficiary who becomes eligible to receive a long-term disability benefit to have an annual medical review or examination for the first five years and thereafter once every three years after the commencement of benefits under this section. However, the Board of Trustees may require more frequent examinations and upon the advice of the Medical Board shall determine which cases require such examination. Should any beneficiary refuse to submit to any examination required by this subsection or by the Medical Board, his long-term disability benefit shall be suspended until he submits to an examination, and should his refusal last for one year, his benefit may be terminated by the Board of Trustees. If the Medical Board finds that a beneficiary is no longer mentally or physically incapacitated for the further performance of duty, the Medical Board shall so certify this finding to the Board of Trustees, and the Board of Trustees may terminate the beneficiary's long-term disability benefits effective on the last day of the month in which the Medical Board certifies that the beneficiary is no longer disabled.

As to the requirement of five years of membership service, any participant or beneficiary who does not have five years of membership service within the 96 calendar months prior to conclusion of the short-term disability period or cessation of salary continuation payments, whichever is later, shall not be eligible for long-term disability benefits.

Notwithstanding the requirement that the incapacity was incurred at the time of active employment, any participant who becomes disabled while on an employer approved leave of absence and who is eligible for and in receipt of temporary total benefits under The North Carolina Workers' Compensation Act, Article 1 of Chapter 97 of the General Statutes, will be eligible for all benefits provided under this Article.

(b) After the commencement of benefits under this section, the benefits payable under the terms of this section during the first 36 months of the long-term disability period shall be equal to sixty-five percent (65%) of 1/12th of the annual base rate of compensation last payable to the participant or beneficiary prior to the beginning of the short-term disability period as may be adjusted for percentage increases as provided under G.S. 135-108, plus sixty-five percent (65%) of 1/12th of the annual longevity payment to which the participant or beneficiary would be eligible, to a maximum of three thousand nine hundred dollars ($3,900) per month reduced by any primary Social Security disability benefits to which the beneficiary may be entitled, effective as of the first of the month following the month of initial entitlement, and by monthly payments for Workers' Compensation to which the participant or beneficiary may be entitled. When primary Social Security disability benefits are increased by cost-of-living adjustments, the increased reduction shall be applied in the first month following the month in which the member becomes entitled to the increased Social Security benefit. The monthly benefit shall be further reduced by the amount of any monthly payments from the federal Department of Veterans Affairs, any other federal agency or any payments made under the provisions of G.S. 127A-108, to which the participant or beneficiary may be entitled on account of the same disability. Provided, in any event, the benefit payable shall be no less than ten dollars ($10.00) a month. However, a disabled participant may elect to receive any salary continuation as provided in G.S. 135-104 in lieu of long-term disability benefits; provided such election shall not extend the first 36 consecutive calendar months of the long-term disability period. An election to receive any salary continuation for any part of any given day shall be in lieu of any long-term benefit payable for that day, provided further, any lump-sum payout for vacation leave shall be treated as if the beneficiary or participant had exhausted the leave and shall be in lieu of any long-term benefit otherwise payable. Provided that, in any event, a beneficiary's benefit shall be reduced during the first 36 months of the long-term disability period by an amount, as determined by the Board of Trustees, equal to a primary Social Security retirement benefit to which the beneficiary might be entitled.

After 36 months of long-term disability, no further benefits are payable under the terms of this section unless the member has been approved and is in receipt of primary Social Security disability benefits. In that case the benefits payable shall be equal to sixty-five percent (65%) of 1/12th of the annual base rate of compensation last payable to the participant or beneficiary prior to the beginning of the short-term disability period as may be adjusted for percentage increases as provided under G.S. 135-108, plus sixty-five percent (65%) of 1/12th of the annual longevity payment to which the participant or beneficiary would be eligible, to a maximum of three thousand nine hundred dollars ($3,900) per month reduced by the primary Social Security disability benefits to which the beneficiary may be entitled, effective as of the first of the month following the month of initial entitlement, and by monthly payments for Workers' Compensation to which the participant or beneficiary may be entitled. When primary Social Security disability benefits are increased by cost-of-living adjustments, the increased reduction shall be applied in the first month following the month in which the member becomes entitled to the increased Social Security benefit. The monthly benefit shall be further reduced by the amount of any monthly payments from the federal Department of Veterans Affairs, for payments from any other federal agency, or for any payments made under the provisions of G.S. 127A-108, to which the participant or beneficiary may be entitled on account of the same disability. Provided, in any event, the benefit payable shall be no less than ten dollars ($10.00) a month.

Notwithstanding the foregoing, but subject to an additional integration with the five-year and 10-year retirement vesting provisions as set forth in this paragraph, the long-term disability benefit is payable so long as the beneficiary is disabled and is in receipt of a primary Social Security disability benefit until the earliest date at which the beneficiary who became a member prior to August 1, 2011, is eligible for an unreduced service retirement allowance from the

Retirement System, at which time the beneficiary would receive a retirement allowance calculated on the basis of the beneficiary's average final compensation at the time of disability as adjusted to reflect compensation increases subsequent to the time of disability and the creditable service accumulated by the beneficiary, including creditable service while in receipt of benefits under the Plan. In the case of any long-term disability beneficiary who became a member on and after August 1, 2011, and ordinarily would not be eligible for a retirement benefit without 10 years of membership service, for purposes of this conversion from long-term disability to service retirement, and for that purpose only, noncontributory creditable service granted while in receipt of disability benefits under this Article shall be deemed to be membership service, through the completion of 10 years of combined membership and noncontributory service on short-term and long-term disability benefits in total. In the event the beneficiary has not been approved and is not in receipt of a primary Social Security disability benefit, the long-term disability benefit shall cease after the first 36 months of the long-term disability period. When such a long-term disability recipient begins receiving this unreduced service retirement allowance from the System, that recipient shall not be subject to the six-month waiting period set forth in G.S. 135-1(20). However, a beneficiary shall be entitled to a restoration of the long-term disability benefit in the event the Social Security Administration grants a retroactive approval for primary Social Security disability benefits with a benefit effective date within the first 36 months of the long-term disability period. In such event, the long-term disability benefit shall be restored retroactively to the date of cessation.

(c) Notwithstanding the foregoing, a beneficiary in receipt of long-term disability benefits who has earnings during the long-term disability period shall have his long-term disability benefit reduced when the sum of the net long-term disability benefit and the earnings equals one hundred percent (100%) of monthly compensation adjusted as provided under G.S. 135-108. The net long-term benefit shall mean the long-term benefit amount payable as calculated under (b) above, after the reduction for Social Security benefits and Workers' Compensation benefits to which the beneficiary might be entitled, and after the reduction for any monthly payments from the federal Department of Veterans Affairs, for payments from any other federal agency, or for any payments made under the provisions of G.S. 127A-108, to which the participant or beneficiary may be entitled on account of the same disability. The net long-term disability benefit shall be reduced dollar-for-dollar for the amount of earnings in excess of the one hundred percent (100%) monthly limit. Any beneficiary exceeding the earnings limitations shall notify the Plan by the fifth of the month succeeding the month in which the earnings were received of the amount of earnings in excess of the limitations herein provided. Failure to report excess earnings may result in a suspension or termination of benefits as determined by the Board of Trustees.

(c1)   During the long-term disability period, a beneficiary may return to service for trial rehabilitation for periods of not greater than 36 months of continuous service. Such return will not cause the beneficiary to become a participant and will not require a new waiting period or short-term disability period to commence regardless of whether the beneficiary is unable to continue in service due to the same incapacity or a different incapacity.

A beneficiary who, during a period of trial rehabilitation, is unable to continue in service may be entitled to a restoration of the long-term disability benefit provided that the Medical Board certifies that the beneficiary is disabled in accordance with the laws in effect at the time of the Board's original approval for long-term disability benefits, either due to the same or a different incapacity, notwithstanding the requirement the incapacity has been continuous. In the event that the Medical Board determines that the long-term disability benefit should be restored, the restored benefit should be calculated in accordance with G.S. 135-106(b); should include any post-disability benefit adjustments as provided by G.S. 135-108; and shall continue as long as the beneficiary remains disabled until the beneficiary has received a total of 36 long-term disability payments. Continuation of long-term disability benefit payments beyond 36 total payments shall be dependent upon approval for primary Social Security disability benefits as required by G.S. 135-106(b).

A beneficiary who returns to service for a period of trial rehabilitation and who has continued in service for greater than 36 continuous months shall again become a participant, and any subsequent incapacity shall be treated as a new incapacity causing a new waiting period to begin. Such a beneficiary may be entitled to additional long-term disability benefits on account of the new incapacity provided the beneficiary meets all other requirements notwithstanding the requirement of five years of membership service within the 96 calendar months prior to becoming disabled or the cessation of continuous salary continuation payments.

(d)   Notwithstanding the foregoing, a participant or beneficiary who has applied for and been approved by the Medical Board for long-term disability benefits may make an irrevocable election, within 90 days from the date of notification of such approval, and prior to receipt of any long-term disability benefit payments, to forfeit all pending and accrued rights to the long-term disability benefit including any ancillary benefits and retire on an early service retirement allowance, effective with the first day of the month following the end of the short-term period, or receive a return of accumulated contributions from the Retirement System. (1987, c. 738, s. 29(q); 1989, c. 717, s. 11; 1989 (Reg. Sess., 1990), c. 1032, s. 2; 1991 (Reg. Sess., 1992), c. 779, s. 4; 1993 (Reg. Sess., 1994), c. 769, s. 7.30(u); 2003-284, s. 30.20(l); 2004-78, ss. 3, 4; 2005-91, s. 6.1; 2005-276, s. 29.30B(a), (b); 2006-74, ss. 3, 4(a), (b); 2007-325, s. 2; 2010-72, s. 7; 2011-294, s. 6; 2012-178, s. 5; 2013-288, s. 7; 2013-405, s. 2.)

§ 135-107. Optional Retirement Program.

Any participant of the Optional Retirement Program who becomes a beneficiary under the Plan shall be eligible to receive long-term disability benefits so long as the beneficiary is disabled and is in receipt of a primary Social Security disability benefit until the time the beneficiary would first qualify for an unreduced service retirement benefit had the beneficiary elected to be a member of the Teachers' and State Employees' Retirement System, and shall receive no service accruals as otherwise provided members of the Retirement System under the provisions of G.S. 135-4(y). In the event a beneficiary who was a participant in the Optional Retirement Program has not been approved and is not in receipt of a primary Social Security disability benefit, the long-term disability benefit shall cease after the first 36 months of the long-term disability period. However, a beneficiary shall be entitled to a restoration of the long-term disability benefit in the event the Social Security Administration grants a retroactive approval for primary Social Security disability benefits with a benefit effective date within the first 36 months of the long-term disability period. In such event, the long-term disability benefit shall be restored retroactively to the date of cessation. (1987, c. 738, s. 29(q); 2007-325, s. 3.)

§ 135-108. Post disability benefit adjustments.

The compensation upon which the short-term or long-term disability benefit is calculated under the provisions of G.S. 135-105(c) or G.S. 135-106(b) may be increased by any permanent across-the-board salary increase granted to employees of the State by the General Assembly and the benefits payable to beneficiaries shall be recalculated based upon the increased compensation, reduced by any percentage increase in Social Security benefits granted by the Social Security Administration times the amount used in the reduction of benefits for primary Social Security disability or retirement benefit as provided in G.S. 135-106(b). The provisions of this section shall be subject to future acts of the General Assembly. (1987, c. 738, s. 29(q); 2001-424, s. 32.32A.)

§ 135-109. Reports of earnings.

The Department of State Treasurer and Board of Trustees shall require each beneficiary to annually provide a statement of the beneficiary's income received as compensation for services, including fees, commissions, or similar items, income received from business, and benefits received from the Social Security Administration, the federal Veterans Administration, any other federal agency, under the North Carolina Workers' Compensation Act, or under the provisions of G.S. 127A-108. The benefit payable to a beneficiary who does not or refuses to provide the information requested within 60 days after such request shall not be paid a benefit until the information so requested is provided, and should such refusal or failure to provide such information continue for 240 days after such request the right of a beneficiary to a benefit under the Article may be terminated. (1987, c. 738, s. 29(q); 2003-359, s. 23.)

§ 135-110. Funding and management of funds.

(a) A trust fund is hereby created to which all receipts, transfers, appropriations, contributions, investment earnings and other income belonging to the Plan shall be deposited, and from which all benefits, expenses, and other charges against the Plan shall be disbursed. The Board of Trustees shall be the trustee of the funds created by this Article.

(b) The Board of Trustees shall on the basis of such economic and demographic assumptions duly adopted, determine and adopt a uniform percentage of compensation as is defined in Article 1 of this Chapter which would be sufficient to fund the benefits payable under this Article on a term cost method basis as recommended by an actuary engaged by the Board of Trustees. Such uniform percentage of compensation shall not be inconsistent with acts of the General Assembly as may be thereafter adopted.

(c) Each employer shall contribute monthly to the Plan an amount determined by applying the uniform percentage of compensation adopted by the

Board of Trustees multiplied by the compensation of teachers and employees reportable to the Retirement System or the Optional Retirement Program. Such monthly contribution shall be paid by the employer from the same source of funds from which the compensation of teachers and employees are paid.

(d) The State Treasurer shall be the custodian of the funds and shall invest the assets of the fund in accordance with the provisions of G.S. 147-69.2 and G.S. 147-69.3. (1987, c. 738, s. 29(q).)

§ 135-111. Applicability of other pension laws.

Subject to the provisions of this Article, the provisions of G.S. 135-9, entitled "Exemption from taxes, garnishment, attachment, etc."; G.S. 135-10, entitled "Protection against fraud"; G.S. 135-10.1, entitled "Failure to Respond"; and G.S. 135-17, entitled "Facility of payment" shall be applicable to this Article and to benefits paid pursuant to the provisions of this Article. (1987, c. 738, s. 29(q); 2005-91, s. 7; 2012-185, s. 3(b); 2013-288, s. 8.)

§ 135-111.1. Improper receipt of decedent's Disability Income Plan allowance.

A person is guilty of a Class 1 misdemeanor if the person, with the intent to defraud, receives money as a result of cashing, depositing, or receiving a direct deposit of a decedent's Disability Income Plan allowance and the person (i) knows that he or she is not entitled to the decedent's Disability Income Plan allowance, (ii) receives the benefit at least two months after the date of the beneficiary's death, and (iii) does not attempt to inform this Retirement System of the beneficiary's death. (2013-288, s. 9(a).)

§ 135-112. Transition provisions.

(a) Any participant in service as of the date of ratification of this Article and who becomes disabled after one year of membership service will be eligible for all benefits provided under this Article notwithstanding the requirement of five years' membership service to receive the long-term benefit; provided, however, any beneficiary who receives benefits as a result of this transition provision before completing five years of membership service shall receive lifetime benefits in lieu of service accruals under the Retirement System as otherwise provided in G.S. 135-4(y).

(b)   All benefit recipients under the former Disability Salary Continuation Plan provided for in G.S. 135-34 and the rules adopted thereto shall become beneficiaries under this Plan under the same provisions and conditions including the benefit amounts payable as were provided under the former Disability Salary Continuation Plan. Any benefit recipient under the former Disability Salary Continuation Plan who returns to service on or after January 1, 1988, who subsequently becomes disabled due to the same disabling condition within 90 days after restoration to service shall not become a participant of the Disability Income Plan but shall be entitled to a restoration of the disability benefit under the same provisions and conditions, including the benefit amounts payable, as were provided under the former Disability Salary Continuation Plan, and shall be entitled to make application for disability retirement benefits under the Retirement System under the same provisions and conditions as were provided members whose service terminated prior to January 1, 1988.

(c)   Any person who retired on a disability retirement allowance from the Teachers' and State Employees' Retirement System prior to the effective date of this Article shall be entitled to apply for and receive any benefits that would have otherwise been provided under the Disability Salary Continuation Plan provided for in G.S. 135-34 and shall become beneficiaries under this Plan, under the same provisions and conditions, including the benefit amounts payable, as were provided under the former Disability Salary Continuation Plan. (1987, c. 738, s. 29(q); 1989, c. 717, s. 12.)

§ 135-113. Reservation of power to change.

The benefits provided in this Article as applicable to a participant who is not a beneficiary under the provisions of this Article shall not be considered as a part of an employment contract, either written or implied, and the General Assembly reserves the right at any time and from time to time to modify, amend in whole or in part or repeal the provisions of this Article. (1987, c. 738, s. 29(q).)

§ 135-114. Reciprocity of membership service with the Legislative Retirement System and the Consolidated Judicial Retirement System.

Only for the purpose of determining eligibility for benefits accruing under this Article, membership service standing to the credit of a member of the Legislative Retirement System or the Consolidated Judicial Retirement System shall be added to the membership service standing to the credit of a member of the Teachers' and State Employees' Retirement System. However, in the event that a participant or beneficiary is a retired member of the Legislative Retirement System or the Consolidated Judicial Retirement System whose retirement benefit was suspended upon entrance into membership in the Teachers' and State Employees' Retirement System, such membership service standing to the credit of the retired member prior to retirement shall be likewise counted. Membership service under this section shall not be counted twice for the same period of time. (1993 (Reg. Sess., 1994), c. 769, s. 7.30(q).)

§ 135-115: Reserved for future codification purposes.

§ 135-116: Reserved for future codification purposes.

§ 135-117: Reserved for future codification purposes.

§ 135-118: Reserved for future codification purposes.

§ 135-119: Reserved for future codification purposes.

§ 135-120: Reserved for future codification purposes.

§ 135-121: Reserved for future codification purposes.

§ 135-122: Reserved for future codification purposes.

§ 135-123: Reserved for future codification purposes.

§ 135-124: Reserved for future codification purposes.

§ 135-125: Reserved for future codification purposes.

§ 135-126: Reserved for future codification purposes.

§ 135-127: Reserved for future codification purposes.

§ 135-128: Reserved for future codification purposes.

§ 135-129: Reserved for future codification purposes.

§ 135-130: Reserved for future codification purposes.

§ 135-131: Reserved for future codification purposes.

§ 135-132: Reserved for future codification purposes.

§ 135-133: Reserved for future codification purposes.

§ 135-134: Reserved for future codification purposes.

§ 135-135: Reserved for future codification purposes.

§ 135-136: Reserved for future codification purposes.

§ 135-137: Reserved for future codification purposes.

§ 135-138: Reserved for future codification purposes.

§ 135-139: Reserved for future codification purposes.

§ 135-140: Reserved for future codification purposes.

§ 135-141: Reserved for future codification purposes.

§ 135-142: Reserved for future codification purposes.

§ 135-143: Reserved for future codification purposes.

§ 135-144: Reserved for future codification purposes.

§ 135-145: Reserved for future codification purposes.

§ 135-146: Reserved for future codification purposes.

§ 135-147: Reserved for future codification purposes.

§ 135-148: Reserved for future codification purposes.

§ 135-149: Reserved for future codification purposes.

Article 7.

Qualified Excess Benefit Arrangement.

§ 135-150. Definitions.

The following words and phrases as used in this Article, unless a different meaning is plainly required by the context, have the following meanings:

(1) "Board of Trustees" means the Board of Trustees established by G.S. 135-6.

(2) "Internal Revenue Code" means the Internal Revenue Code of 1986, as amended from time to time.

(3) "Payee" means a retired member, or the survivor beneficiary of a member or retired member.

(4) "Qualified Excess Benefit Arrangement" means the qualified excess benefit arrangement under section 415(m) of the Internal Revenue Code established under this Article.

(5) "Retirement System" means the Teachers' and State Employees' Retirement System. (2013-405, s. 3(a).)

§ 135-151. Qualified Excess Benefit Arrangement.

(a) The Qualified Excess Benefit Arrangement (QEBA) is established effective January 1, 2014, and placed under the management of the Board of Trustees. The purpose of the QEBA is solely to provide the part of a retirement allowance or benefit that would otherwise have been payable by a Retirement System except for the limitations under section 415(b) of the Internal Revenue Code. The QEBA, as set forth in this Article, is intended to constitute a qualified governmental excess benefit arrangement under section 415(m) of the Internal Revenue Code.

(b)   Eligibility to Participate in the QEBA. - Effective as of January 1, 2014, a payee shall participate in the QEBA for any calendar year, or portion of the calendar year, during which he or she receives a retirement allowance or benefit payment on and after January 1, 2014, from the Teachers' and State Employees' Retirement System that is reduced due to the application of the maximum benefit provisions of section 415(b) of the Internal Revenue Code. For purposes of the QEBA, a payee is a retired member or survivor beneficiary of a member or retired member who is receiving monthly retirement benefit payments from a Retirement System.

(c)   Supplemental Benefit Payable Under the QEBA. - Effective January 1, 2014, a payee shall receive each month, commencing on and after January 1, 2014, a monthly supplemental benefit equal to the difference between the amount of that payee's monthly retirement benefit paid under the Teachers' and State Employees' Retirement System on and after January 1, 2014, and the amount that would have been payable to that payee from the Teachers' and State Employees' Retirement System in that month if not for the reduction due to the application of section 415(b) of the Internal Revenue Code. That supplemental benefit shall be computed and payable under the same terms, at the same time, and to the same person as the related benefit payable under the Retirement System. A payee cannot elect to defer the receipt of all or any part of the supplemental payments due under the QEBA. The supplemental benefit paid under this section shall be taxable under North Carolina law in the same manner as the benefit paid under the Teachers' and State Employees' Retirement System.

(d)   Funding of the QEBA. - The QEBA shall be unfunded within the meaning of federal tax laws. No payee contributions or deferrals, direct or indirect, by election or otherwise shall be made or allowed. The Board of Trustees, upon the recommendation of the actuary engaged by the Board of Trustees, shall determine the employer contributions required to pay the benefits due under the QEBA for each fiscal year. The required contributions shall be paid by all participating employers. The required contributions shall be deposited in a separate fund from the fund into which regular employer contributions are deposited for the Retirement System. The benefit liability for the QEBA shall be determined each fiscal year, and assets shall not be accumulated to pay benefits in future fiscal years.

(e) Treatment of Unused Assets. - Any assets of the QEBA plan not used to pay benefits in the current fiscal year shall be used for payment of the administrative expenses of the QEBA for the current or future fiscal years or shall be paid to the Retirement System as an additional employer contribution.

(f) Assets Subject to Claims of Creditors. - A payee, or a payee's beneficiary or heirs, shall have no right to, and shall have no property interest in, any assets held to support the liabilities created under this Article. To the extent that any person acquires the right to receive benefits under the QEBA, that right shall be no greater than the right of any unsecured general creditor of the State of North Carolina or such other applicable employer under this Article.

(g) Administration. - The QEBA shall be administered by the Board of Trustees, which shall compile and maintain all records necessary or appropriate for administration. The Board of Trustees shall have full discretionary authority to interpret, construe, and implement the QEBA and to adopt such rules and regulations as may be necessary or desirable to implement the provisions of the QEBA in accordance with section 415(m) of the Internal Revenue Code.

(h) No Assignment. - Except for the application of the provisions of G.S. 110-136 and G.S. 110-136.3, et seq., or in connection with a court-ordered equitable distribution under G.S. 50-20, any supplemental benefit under this Article shall be exempt from levy and sale, garnishment, attachment, or any other process, and shall be unassignable except as specifically otherwise provided in this Chapter.

(i) Reservation of Power to Change. - The General Assembly reserves the right at any time and, from time to time, to modify or amend, in whole or in part, any or all of the provisions of the QEBA. No member of the Retirement System and no beneficiary of such a member shall be deemed to have acquired any vested right to a supplemental payment under this Article.

(j) Sunset of Eligibility to Participate in the QEBA. - No member of the Teachers' and State Employees' Retirement System retiring on or after January 1, 2015, shall be eligible to participate in the QEBA, and the Retirement System shall not pay any new retiree more retirement benefits than allowed under the limitations of section 415(b) of the Internal Revenue Code. (2013-405, s. 3(a).)

Chapter 136.

Transportation.

Article 1.

Organization of Department of Transportation.

§§ 136-1 through 136-3: Repealed by Session Laws 1973, c. 507, s. 23.

§ 136-4. Chief Engineer.

There shall be a Chief Engineer, who shall be a career official and who shall be the administrative officer of the Department of Transportation for highway matters. The Chief Engineer shall be appointed by the Secretary of Transportation and he may be removed at any time by the Secretary of Transportation. He shall be paid a salary to be set in accordance with Chapter 126 of the General Statutes, the North Carolina Human Resources Act. The Chief Engineer shall have such powers and perform such duties as the Secretary of Transportation shall prescribe. (1921, c. 2, ss. 5, 6; C.S., s. 3846(g); 1933, c. 172, s. 17; 1957, c. 65, s. 2; 1961, c. 232, s. 2; 1965, c. 55, s. 3; 1973, c. 507, s. 22; 1975, c. 716, s. 7; 1977, c. 464, s. 11; 1983, c. 717, s. 45; 1983 (Reg. Sess., 1984), c. 1034, s. 164; 1985, c. 757, s. 191; 2012-85, s. 4; 2013-382, s. 9.1(c).)

§§ 136-4.1 through 136-5. Repealed by Session Laws 1973, c. 507, s. 23.

§ 136-5.1. Transportation system.

For the purpose of this Chapter, transportation system is defined as all modes of transportation infrastructure owned and maintained by the North Carolina Department of Transportation, including roads, highways, rail, ferry, aviation, public transportation, and bicycle and pedestrian facilities. (2009-266, s. 5.)

§§ 136-6 through 136-9. Repealed by Session Laws 1957, c. 65, s. 12.

§ 136-10. Audit and rules.

The operations of the Department of Transportation shall be subject to the oversight of the State Auditor pursuant to Article 5A of Chapter 147 of the General Statutes. Rules adopted by the Department of Transportation are subject to Chapter 150B of the General Statutes. (1921, c. 2, s. 24; C.S., s. 3846(m); 1933, c. 172, s. 7; 1957, c. 65, s. 4; 1973, c. 507, s. 5; 1977, c. 464, s. 7.1; 1983, c. 913, s. 25; 1991, c. 477, s. 5.)

§ 136-11: Repealed by Session Laws 2010-165, s. 1, effective August 2, 2010.

§ 136-11.1. Local consultation on transportation projects.

Prior to any action of the Board on a transportation project, the Department shall inform all municipalities and counties affected by a planned transportation project and request each affected municipality or county to submit within 45 days a written resolution expressing their views on the project. A municipality or county may designate a Transportation Advisory Committee to submit its response to the Department's request for a resolution. Upon receipt of a written resolution from all affected municipalities and counties or their designees, or the expiration of the 45-day period, whichever occurs first, the Board may take action. The Department and the Board shall consider, but shall not be bound by, the views of the affected municipalities and counties on each transportation project. The failure of a county or municipality to express its views within the time provided shall not prevent the Department or the Board from taking action. The Department shall not be required to send notice under this section if it has already received a written resolution from the affected county or municipality on the planned transportation project. "Action of the Board", as used in this section, means approval by the Board of: the Transportation Improvement Program and amendments to the Transportation Improvement Program; the Secondary Roads Paving Program and amendments to the Secondary Roads Paving Program; and individual applications for access and public service road projects, contingency projects, small urban projects, and spot safety projects that exceed one hundred fifty thousand dollars ($150,000). The 45-day notification provision may be waived upon a finding by the Secretary of Transportation that emergency action is required. Such findings must be reported to the Joint Legislative Transportation Oversight Committee. (1998-169, s. 3.)

§ 136-12. Reports to General Assembly; Transportation Improvement Program submitted to members and staff of General Assembly.

(a)   The Department of Transportation shall, on or before the tenth day after the convening of each regular session of the General Assembly of North Carolina, make a full printed, detailed report to the General Assembly, showing the construction and maintenance work and the cost of the same, receipts of license fees, and disbursements of the Department of Transportation, and such other data as may be of interest in connection with the work of the Department of Transportation. A full account of each road project shall be kept by and under the direction of the Department of Transportation or its representatives, to ascertain at any time the expenditures and the liabilities against all projects; also records of contracts and force account work. The account records, together with all supporting documents, shall be open at all times to the inspection of the Governor or road authorities of any county, or their authorized representatives, and copies thereof shall be furnished such officials upon request.

(a1)   Repealed by Session Laws 2011-145, s. 28.35(a), effective July 1, 2011.

(b)   At least 30 days before it approves a Transportation Improvement Program in accordance with G.S. 143B-350(f)(4) or approves interim changes to a Transportation Improvement Program, the Department shall submit the proposed Transportation Improvement Program or proposed interim changes to a Transportation Improvement Program to the following members and staff of the General Assembly:

(1)   The Speaker and the Speaker Pro Tempore of the House of Representatives;

(2)   The Lieutenant Governor and the President Pro Tempore of the Senate;

(3)   The Chairs of the House and Senate Appropriations Committees;

(4) Each member of the Joint Legislative Transportation Oversight Committee; and

(5) The Fiscal Research Division of the Legislative Services Commission. (1921, c. 2, s. 23; C.S., s. 3846(l); 1933, c. 172, s. 17; 1957, c. 65, s. 11; 1973, c. 507, s. 5; 1977, c. 464, s. 7.1; 1989, c. 692, s. 1.3; c. 770, s. 74.16; 1993, c. 321, s. 169.2(d); 1996, 2nd Ex. Sess., c. 18, s. 19.4(c); 2006-203, s. 74; 2011-145, s. 28.35(a).)

§ 136-12.1. Biennial report on off-premise sign regulatory program.

The Department of Transportation shall make a biennial report to the General Assembly beginning on January 1, 1993, on its Off-Premise Sign Regulatory Program.

The report shall include:

(1) The number of off-premise signs (billboards) that conform with State and local regulations and the number of off-premise signs that do not conform with State and local regulations in each county along federal-aid primary highways.

(2) The number of conforming and nonconforming off-premise signs on State-owned railroad right-of-way.

(3) The number of nonconforming off-premise signs removed during the fiscal year.

(4) The number of permitted tree cuttings and the number of illegal tree cuttings in front of off-premise signs.

(5) Expenses incurred in regulating off-premise signs and receipts from application and renewal permit fees. (1991, c. 689, s. 208.)

§ 136-12.2: Repealed by Session Laws 2011-145, s. 28.35(a), effective July 1, 2011.

§ 136-13. Malfeasance of officers and employees of Department of Transportation, members of Board of Transportation, contractors, and others.

(a) It is unlawful for any person, firm, or corporation to directly or indirectly corruptly give, offer, or promise anything of value to any officer or employee of the Department of Transportation or member of the Board of Transportation, or to promise any officer or employee of the Department of Transportation or any member of the Board of Transportation to give anything of value to any other person with intent:

(1) To influence any official act of any officer or employee of the Department of Transportation or member of the Board of Transportation;

(2) To influence such member of the Board of Transportation, or any officer or employee of the Department of Transportation to commit or aid in committing, or collude in, or allow, any fraud, or to make opportunity for the commission of any fraud on the State of North Carolina; and

(3) To induce a member of the Board of Transportation, or any officer or employee of the Department of Transportation to do or omit to do any act in violation of his lawful duty.

(b) It shall be unlawful for any member of the Board of Transportation, or any officer or employee of the Department of Transportation, directly or indirectly, to corruptly ask, demand, exact, solicit, accept, receive, or agree to receive anything of value for himself or any other person or entity in return for:

(1) Being influenced in his performance of any official act;

(2) Being influenced to commit or aid in committing, or to collude in, or allow, any fraud, or to make opportunity for the commission of any fraud on the State of North Carolina; and

(3) Being induced to do or omit to do any act in violation of his official duty.

(c) The violation of any of the provisions of this section shall be cause for forfeiture of public office and shall be a Class H felony which may include a fine of not more than twenty thousand dollars ($20,000) or three times the monetary equivalent of the thing of value whichever is greater. (1921, c. 2, s. 49; C.S., s. 3846(cc); 1933, c. 172, s. 17; 1957, c. 65, s. 11; 1965, c. 55, s. 7; 1973, c. 507,

s. 6; 1975, c. 716, s. 7; 1977, c. 464, ss. 7.1, 10, 10.1; 1979, c. 298, ss. 3, 4; 1993, c. 539, s. 1308; 1994, Ex. Sess., c. 24, s. 14(c).)

§ 136-13.1. Use of position to influence elections or political action.

No member of the Board of Transportation nor any officer or employee of the Department of Transportation shall be permitted to use his position to influence elections or the political action of any person. (1965, c. 55, s. 8; 1973, c. 507, s. 7; 1975, c. 716, s. 7; 1977, c. 464, ss. 7.1, 10.1; 1979, c. 298, s. 3.)

§ 136-13.2. Falsifying highway inspection reports.

(a) Any person who knowingly falsifies any inspection report or test report required by the Department of Transportation in connection with the construction of highways, shall be guilty of a Class H felony.

(b) Any person who directs a subordinate under his direct or indirect supervision to falsify an inspection report or test report required by the Department of Transportation in connection with the construction of highways, shall be guilty of a Class H felony.

(c) Repealed by Session Laws 1979, c. 786, s. 2, effective May 8, 1979. (1979, c. 523; c. 786, s. 2; 1981, c. 793, s. 1; 2005-96, s. 1.)

§ 136-14. Members not eligible for other employment with Department; no sales to Department by employees; members not to sell or trade property with Department; profiting from official position; misuse of confidential information by Board members.

(a) No Board member shall be eligible to any other employment in connection with the Department.

(b) No Board member or any salaried employee of the Department shall furnish or sell any supplies or materials, directly or indirectly, to the Department.

(c) No Board member shall, directly or indirectly, engage in any transaction involving the sale of or trading of real or personal property with the Department.

(d) No Board member shall profit in any manner by reason of the Board member's official action or official position, except to receive salary, fees and allowances as by law provided.

(e) No Board member shall take any official action or use the Board member's official position to profit in any manner the Board member's immediate family, a business with which the Board member or the Board member's immediate family has a business association, or a client of the Board member or the Board member's immediate family with whom the Board member, or the Board member's immediate family, has an existing business relationship for matters before the Board.

(f) No Board member shall attempt to profit from a proposed project of the Department if the profit is greater than that which would be realized by other persons living in the area where the project is located. If the profit under this subsection would be greater for the Board member than other persons living in the area where the project is located not only shall the member abstain from voting on that issue, but once the conflict of interest is apparent, the member shall not discuss the project with any other Board member or other officer or employee of the Department except to state that a conflict of interest exists. Under this subsection a Board member is presumed to profit if the profit would be realized by a Board member's immediate family, a business with which the Board member or the Board member's immediate family has a business association, or a client of the Board member or the Board member's immediate family with whom the Board member, or the Board member's immediate family, has an existing business relationship for matters before the Board. Violation of this subsection shall be a Class I felony.

(g) No Board member, in contemplation of official action by the Board member, by the Board, or in reliance on information that was made known to the Board member in the Board member's official capacity and that has not been made public, shall commit any of the following acts:

(1) Acquire a pecuniary interest in any property, transaction, or enterprise or gain any pecuniary benefit that may be affected by such information or official action; or

(2) Intentionally aid another to do any of the above acts.

(h) As used in this section, the following terms mean:

(1) "Board". - The Board of Transportation.

(2) "Board member". - A member of the Board of Transportation.

(3) "Business association". - A director, employee, officer, or partner of a business entity, or owner of more than ten percent (10%) interest in any business entity.

(4) "Department". - The Department of Transportation.

(5) "Immediate family". - Spouse, children, parents, brothers, and sisters.

(6) "Official action". - Actions taken while a Board member related to or in connection with the person's duties as a Board member including, but not limited to, voting on matters before the Board, proposing or objecting to proposals for transportation actions by the Department or the Board, discussing transportation matters with other Board members or Department staff or employees in an effort to further the matter after the conflict of interest has been discovered, or taking actions in the course and scope of the position as a Board member and actions leading to or resulting in profit.

(7) "Profit". - Receive monetary or economic gain or benefit, including an increase in value whether or not recognized by sale or trade.

(i) Except as otherwise provided in this section, a violation of this section shall be a Class H felony which may include a fine of not more than twenty thousand dollars ($20,000), or three times the value of the transaction, whichever amount is greater. (1933, c. 172, s. 10; 1957, c. 65, s. 11; 1965, c. 55, s. 9; 1973, c. 507, s. 8; 1975, c. 716, s. 7; 1977, c. 464, ss. 7.1, 10.2; 1979, ch. 298, s. 3; 1985, c. 689, s. 28; 1993, c. 539, s. 1309; 1994, Ex. Sess., c. 24, s. 14(c); 1998-169, s. 4.)

§ 136-14.1. Transportation engineering divisions.

For purposes of administering transportation activities, the Department of Transportation shall have authority to designate boundaries of transportation engineering divisions for the proper administration of its duties. (1957, c. 65, s. 5; 1965, c. 55, s. 10; 1973, c. 507, s. 9; 1975, c. 716, s. 7; 1993, c. 483, s. 2.)

§ 136-14.2. Division engineer to manage personnel.

Except for general departmental policy applicable to all of the State the division engineer shall have authority over all divisional personnel matters and over Department employees in his division making personnel decisions. (1975, 2nd Sess., c. 983, s. 92.)

§ 136-15. Establishment of administrative districts.

The Department of Transportation may establish such administrative districts as in its opinion shall be necessary for the proper and efficient performance of highway duties. The Department may from time to time change the number of such districts, or it may change the territory embraced within the several districts, when in its opinion it is in the interest of efficiency and economy to make such change. (1931, c. 145, s. 5; 1933, c. 172, s. 17; 1957, c. 65, s. 11; 1973, c. 507, s. 10; 1975, c. 716, s. 7.)

§ 136-16. Funds and property converted to State Highway Fund.

Except as otherwise provided, all funds and property collected by the Department of Transportation, including the proceeds from the sale of real property originally purchased with funds from the State Highway Fund, shall be paid or converted into the State Highway Fund. (1919, c. 189, s. 8; C.S., s. 3595; 1933, c. 172, s. 17; 1957, c. 65, s. 11; 1973, c. 507, s. 5; 1977, c. 464, s. 7.1; 2007-323, s. 27.15.)

§§ 136-16.1 through 136-16.3. Reserved for future codification purposes.

§§ 136-16.4, 136-16.5: Repealed by Session Laws 2013-360, s. 34.9, effective July 1, 2013.

§ 136-16.6: Repealed by Session Laws 2013-360, s. 34.14(i), effective January 1, 2014.

§§ 136-16.7 through 136-16.9: Repealed by Session Laws 2013-360, s. 34.9, effective July 1, 2013.

§ 136-16.10. Allocations by Department Chief Financial Officer to eliminate overdrafts.

The Chief Financial Officer of the Department of Transportation shall allocate at the beginning of each fiscal year from the various appropriations made to the Department of Transportation for State Construction, State Funds to Match Federal Highway Aid, State Maintenance, and Ferry Operations, sufficient funds to eliminate all overdrafts on State maintenance and construction projects, and these allocations shall not be diverted to other purposes. (1997-443, s. 32.3; 2010-165, s. 2.)

Article 2.

Powers and Duties of Department and Board of Transportation.

§ 136-17: Repealed by Session Laws 1973, c. 507, s. 3.

§ 136-17.1. Repealed by Session Laws 1977, c. 464, s. 13.

§ 136-17.2. Members of the Board of Transportation represent entire State.

The chairman and members of the Board of Transportation shall represent the entire State in transportation matters and not represent any particular person, persons, or area. The Board shall, from time to time, provide that one or more of its members or representatives shall publicly hear any person or persons concerning transportation matters in each of said geographic areas of the State. (1973, c. 507, s. 3; 1977, c. 464, s. 7.1; 1987, c. 783, s. 3; 1993, c. 483, s. 3.)

§ 136-17.2A: Repealed by Session Laws 2013-183, s. 4.3, effective July 1, 2013.

§ 136-18. Powers of Department of Transportation.

The said Department of Transportation is vested with the following powers:

(1)   The authority and general supervision over all matters relating to the construction, maintenance, and design of State transportation projects, letting of contracts therefor, and the selection of materials to be used in the construction of State transportation projects under the authority of this Chapter.

(2)   To take over and assume exclusive control for the benefit of the State of any existing county or township roads, and to locate and acquire rights-of-way for any new roads that may be necessary for a State highway system, and subject to the provisions of G.S. 136-19.5(a) and (b) also locate and acquire such additional rights-of-way as may be necessary for the present or future relocation or initial location, above or below ground, of telephone, telegraph, distributed antenna systems (DAS), broadband communications, electric and other lines, as well as gas, water, sewerage, oil and other pipelines, to be operated by public utilities as defined in G.S. 62-3(23) and which are regulated under Chapter 62 of the General Statutes, or by municipalities, counties, any entity created by one or more political subdivisions for the purpose of supplying any such utility services, electric membership corporations, telephone membership corporations, or any combination thereof, with full power to widen, relocate, change or alter the grade or location thereof, or alter the location or configuration of such lines or systems above or below ground, and to change or relocate any existing roads that the Department of Transportation may now own or may acquire; to acquire by gift, purchase, or otherwise, any road or highway, or tract of land or other property whatsoever that may be necessary for a State transportation system and adjacent utility rights-of-way: Provided, all changes or alterations authorized by this subdivision shall be subject to the provisions of G.S. 136-54 to 136-63, to the extent that said sections are applicable: Provided, that nothing in this Chapter shall be construed to authorize or permit the Department of Transportation to allow or pay anything to any county, township, city or town, or to any board of commissioners or governing body thereof, for any existing road or part of any road heretofore constructed by any such county, township, city or town, unless a contract has already been entered into with the Department of Transportation.

(3) To provide for such road materials as may be necessary to carry on the work of the Department of Transportation, either by gift, purchase, or condemnation: Provided, that when any person, firm or corporation owning a deposit of sand, gravel or other material, necessary, for the construction of the system of State highways provided herein, has entered into a contract to furnish the Department of Transportation any of such material, at a price to be fixed by said Department of Transportation, thereafter the Department of Transportation shall have the right to condemn the necessary right-of-way under the provisions of Article 9 of Chapter 136, to connect said deposit with any part of the system of State highways or public carrier, provided that easements to material deposits, condemned under this Article shall not become a public road and the condemned easement shall be returned to the owner as soon as the deposits are exhausted or abandoned by the Department of Transportation.

(4) To enforce by mandamus or other proper legal remedies all legal rights or causes of action of the Department of Transportation with other public bodies, corporations, or persons.

(5) To make rules, regulations and ordinances for the use of, and to police traffic on, the State highways, and to prevent their abuse by individuals, corporations and public corporations, by trucks, tractors, trailers or other heavy or destructive vehicles or machinery, or by any other means whatsoever, and to provide ample means for the enforcement of same; and the violation of any of the rules, regulations or ordinances so prescribed by the Department of Transportation shall constitute a Class 1 misdemeanor: Provided, no rules, regulations or ordinances shall be made that will conflict with any statute now in force or any ordinance of incorporated cities or towns, except the Department of Transportation may regulate parking upon any street which forms a link in the State highway system, if said street be maintained with State highway funds.

(6) To establish a traffic census to secure information about the relative use, cost, value, importance, and necessity of roads forming a part of the State highway system, which information shall be a part of the public records of the State, and upon which information the Department of Transportation shall, after due deliberation and in accordance with these established facts, proceed to order the construction of the particular highway or highways.

(7) To assume full and exclusive responsibility for the maintenance of all roads other than streets in towns and cities, forming a part of the State highway system from date of acquiring said roads. The Department of Transportation shall have authority to maintain all streets constructed by the Department of

Transportation in towns of less than 3,000 population by the last census, and such other streets as may be constructed in towns and cities at the expense of the Department of Transportation, whenever in the opinion of the Department of Transportation it is necessary and proper so to do.

(8)   To give suitable names to State highways and change the names as determined by the Board of Transportation of any highways that shall become a part of the State system of highways.

(9)   To employ appropriate means for properly selecting, planting and protecting trees, shrubs, vines, grasses or legumes in the highway right-of-way in the promotion of erosion control, landscaping and general protection of said highways; to acquire by gift or otherwise land for and to construct, operate and maintain roadside parks, picnic areas, picnic tables, scenic overlooks and other appropriate turnouts for the safety and convenience of highway users; and to cooperate with municipal or county authorities, federal agencies, civic bodies and individuals in the furtherance of those objectives. None of the roadside parks, picnic areas, picnic tables, scenic overlooks or other turnouts, or any part of the highway right-of-way shall be used for commercial purposes except for any of the following:

a.   Materials displayed in welcome centers in accordance with G.S. 136-89.56.

b.   Vending machines permitted by the Department of Transportation and placed by the Division of Services for the Blind, Department of Health and Human Services, as the State licensing agency designated pursuant to Section 2(a)(5) of the Randolph-Sheppard Act (20 USC 107a(a)(5)). The Department of Transportation shall regulate the placing of the vending machines in highway rest areas and shall regulate the articles to be dispensed.

c.   Activities permitted by a local government pursuant to an ordinance meeting the requirements of G.S. 136-27.4.

Every other use or attempted use of any of these areas for commercial purposes shall constitute a Class 1 misdemeanor, and each day's use shall constitute a separate offense.

(10)   To make proper and reasonable rules, regulations and ordinances for the placing or erection of telephone, telegraph, electric and other lines, above or below ground, signboards, fences, gas, water, sewerage, oil, or other pipelines,

and other similar obstructions that may, in the opinion of the Department of Transportation, contribute to the hazard upon any of the said highways or in any way interfere with the same, and to make reasonable rules and regulations for the proper control thereof. And whenever the order of the said Department of Transportation shall require the removal of, or changes in, the location of telephone, telegraph, electric or other lines, signboards, fences, gas, water, sewerage, oil, or other pipelines, or other similar obstructions, the owners thereof shall at their own expense, except as provided in G.S. 136-19.5(c), move or change the same to conform to the order of said Department of Transportation. Any violation of such rules and regulations or noncompliance with such orders shall constitute a Class 1 misdemeanor.

(11) To regulate, abandon and close to use, grade crossings on any road designated as part of the State highway system, and whenever a public highway has been designated as part of the State highway system and the Department of Transportation, in order to avoid a grade crossing or crossings with a railroad or railroads, continues or constructs the said road on one side of the railroad or railroads, the Department of Transportation shall have power to abandon and close to use such grade crossings; and whenever an underpass or overhead bridge is substituted for a grade crossing, the Department of Transportation shall have power to close to use and abandon such grade crossing and any other crossing adjacent thereto.

(12) The Department of Transportation shall have such powers as are necessary to comply fully with the provisions of the Intermodal Surface Transportation Efficiency Act of 1991, Pub. L. No. 102-240, 105 Stat. 1914 (1991), as amended, and all other federal aid acts and programs the Department is authorized to administer. The said Department of Transportation is hereby authorized to enter into all contracts and agreements with the United States government relating to survey, construction, improvement and maintenance of roads, urban area traffic operations studies and improvement projects on the streets on the State highway system and on the municipal system in urban areas, under the provisions of the present or future congressional enactments, to submit such scheme or program of construction or improvement and maintenance as may be required by the Secretary of Transportation or otherwise provided by federal acts, and to do all other things necessary to carry out fully the cooperation contemplated and provided for by present or future aid acts of Congress for the construction or improvement and maintenance of federal aid of State highways. The good faith and credit of the State are further hereby pledged to make available funds necessary to meet the requirements of the acts of Congress, present or future, appropriating money to

construct and improve rural post roads and apportioned to this State during each of the years for which federal funds are now or may hereafter be apportioned by the said act or acts, to maintain the roads constructed or improved with the aid of funds so appropriated and to make adequate provisions for carrying out such construction and maintenance. The good faith and credit of the State are further pledged to maintain such roads now built with federal aid and hereafter to be built and to make adequate provisions for carrying out such maintenance. Upon request of the Department of Transportation and in order to enable it to meet the requirements of acts of Congress with respect to federal aid funds apportioned to the State of North Carolina, the State Treasurer is hereby authorized, with the approval of the Governor and Council of State, to issue short term notes from time to time, and in anticipation of State highway revenue, and to be payable out of State highway revenue for such sums as may be necessary to enable the Department of Transportation to meet the requirements of said federal aid appropriations, but in no event shall the outstanding notes under the provisions of this section amount to more than two million dollars ($2,000,000).

(12a)   The Department of Transportation shall have such powers as are necessary to establish, administer, and receive federal funds for a transportation infrastructure banking program as authorized by the Intermodal Surface Transportation Efficiency Act of 1991, Pub. L. 102-240, as amended, and the National Highway System Designation Act of 1995, Pub. L. 104-59, as amended. The Department of Transportation is authorized to apply for, receive, administer, and comply with all conditions and requirements related to federal financial assistance necessary to fund the infrastructure banking program. The infrastructure banking program established by the Department of Transportation may utilize federal and available State funds for the purpose of providing loans or other financial assistance to governmental units, including toll authorities, to finance the costs of transportation projects authorized by the above federal aid acts. Such loans or other financial assistance shall be subject to repayment and conditioned upon the establishment of such security and the payment of such fees and interest rates as the Department of Transportation may deem necessary. The Department of Transportation is authorized to apply a municipality's share of funds allocated under G.S. 136-41.1 or G.S. 136-44.20 as necessary to ensure repayment of funds advanced under the infrastructure banking program. The Department of Transportation shall establish jointly, with the State Treasurer, a separate infrastructure banking account with necessary fiscal controls and accounting procedures. Funds credited to this account shall not revert, and interest and other investment income shall accrue to the account and may be used to provide loans and other financial assistance as provided under this subdivision. The Department of Transportation may establish such rules and policies as are necessary to establish and administer the infrastructure banking program. The infrastructure banking program authorized under this subdivision shall not modify the formula for the distribution of funds established by G.S. 136-189.11. Governmental units may apply for loans and execute debt instruments payable to the State in order to obtain loans or other financial assistance provided for in this subdivision. The Department of Transportation shall require that applicants shall pledge as security for such obligations revenues derived from operation of the benefited facilities or systems, other sources of revenue, or their faith and credit, or any combination thereof. The faith and credit of such governmental units shall not be pledged or be deemed to have been pledged unless the requirements of Article 4, Chapter 159 of the General Statutes have been met. The State Treasurer, with the assistance of the Local Government Commission, shall develop and adopt appropriate debt instruments for use under this subdivision. The Local Government Commission shall develop and adopt appropriate procedures for the delivery of debt instruments to the State without any public bidding therefor. The Local Government Commission shall review and approve proposed loans to applicants pursuant to this subdivision under the provisions of Articles 4 and 5, Chapter 159 of the General Statutes, as if the issuance of bonds was proposed, so far as those provisions are applicable. Loans authorized by this subdivision shall be outstanding debt for the purpose of Article 10, Chapter 159 of the General Statutes.

(12b) To issue "GARVEE" bonds (Grant Anticipation Revenue Vehicles) or other eligible debt-financing instruments to finance federal-aid highway projects using federal funds to pay a portion of principal, interest, and related bond issuance costs, as authorized by 23 U.S.C. § 122, as amended (the National Highway System Designation Act of 1995, Pub. L. 104-59). These bonds shall be issued by the State Treasurer on behalf of the Department and shall be issued pursuant to an order adopted by the Council of State under G.S. 159-88. The State Treasurer shall develop and adopt appropriate debt instruments, consistent with the terms of the State and Local Government Revenue Bond Act, Article 5 of Chapter 159 of the General Statutes, for use under this subdivision. Prior to issuance of any "GARVEE" or other eligible debt instrument using federal funds to pay a portion of principal, interest, and related bond issuance costs, the State Treasurer shall determine (i) that the total outstanding principal of such debt does not exceed the total amount of federal transportation funds authorized to the State in the prior federal fiscal year; or (ii) that the maximum annual principal and interest of such debt does not exceed fifteen percent (15%) of the expected average annual federal revenue shown for the period in the most recently adopted Transportation Improvement Program. Notes issued under the provisions of this subdivision may not be deemed to constitute a debt or liability of the State or of any political subdivision thereof, or a pledge of the full faith and credit of the State or of any political subdivision thereof, but shall be payable solely from the funds and revenues pledged therefor. All the notes shall contain on their face a statement to the effect that the State of North Carolina shall not be obligated to pay the principal or the interest on the notes, except from the federal transportation fund revenues as shall be provided by the documents governing the revenue note issuance, and that neither the faith and credit nor the taxing power of the State of North Carolina or of any of its political subdivisions is pledged to the payment of the principal or interest on the notes. The issuance of notes under this Part shall not directly or indirectly or contingently obligate the State or any of its political subdivisions to levy or to pledge any form of taxation whatever or to make any appropriation for their payment.

(13) The Department of Transportation may construct and maintain all walkways and driveways within the Mansion Square in the City of Raleigh and the Western Residence of the Governor in the City of Asheville including the approaches connecting with the city streets, and any funds expended therefor shall be a charge against general maintenance.

(14) The Department of Transportation shall have authority to provide roads for the connection of airports in the State with the public highway system, and to mark the highways and erect signals along the same for the guidance and protection of aircraft.

(15) The Department of Transportation shall have authority to provide facilities for the use of waterborne traffic and recreational uses by establishing connections between the highway system and the navigable and nonnavigable waters of the State by means of connecting roads and piers. Such facilities for recreational purposes shall be funded from funds available for safety or enhancement purposes.

(16) The Department of Transportation, pursuant to a resolution of the Board of Transportation, shall have authority, under the power of eminent domain and under the same procedure as provided for the acquirement of rights-of-way, to acquire title in fee simple to parcels of land for the purpose of exchanging the same for other real property to be used for the establishment of rights-of-way or for the widening of existing rights-of-way or the clearing of obstructions that, in the opinion of the Department of Transportation, constitute dangerous hazards

at intersections. Real property may be acquired for such purposes only when the owner of the property needed by the Department of Transportation has agreed in writing to accept the property so acquired in exchange for that to be used by the Department of Transportation, and when, in the opinion of the Department of Transportation, an economy in the expenditure of public funds and the improvement and convenience and safety of the highway can be effected thereby.

(17) The Department of Transportation is hereby authorized and required to maintain and keep in repair, sufficient to accommodate the public school buses, roads leading from the state-maintained public roads to all public schools and public school buildings to which children are transported on public school buses to and from their homes. Said Department of Transportation is further authorized to construct, pave, and maintain school bus driveways and sufficient parking facilities for the school buses at those schools. The Department of Transportation is further authorized to construct, pave, and maintain all other driveways and entrances to the public schools leading from public roads not required in the preceding portion of this subdivision.

(18) To cooperate with appropriate agencies of the United States in acquiring rights-of-way for and in the construction and maintenance of flight strips or emergency landing fields for aircraft adjacent to State highways.

(19) To prohibit the erection of any informational, regulatory, or warning signs within the right-of-way of any highway project built within the corporate limits of any municipality in the State where the funds for such construction are derived in whole or in part from federal appropriations expended by the Department of Transportation, unless such signs have first been approved by the Department of Transportation.

(20) The Department of Transportation is hereby authorized to maintain and keep in repair a suitable way of ingress and egress to all public or church cemeteries or burial grounds in the State notwithstanding the fact that said road is not a part of the state-maintained system of roads. For the purpose of this subdivision a public or church cemetery or burial ground shall be defined as a cemetery or burial ground in which there are buried or permitted to be buried deceased persons of the community in which said cemetery or burial ground is located, but shall not mean a privately owned cemetery operated for profit or family burial plots.

(21) The Department of Transportation is hereby authorized and directed to remove all dead animals from the traveled portion and rights-of-way of all primary and secondary roads and to dispose of such animals by burial or otherwise. In cases where there is evidence of ownership upon the body of any dead dog, the Department of Transportation shall take reasonable steps to notify the owner thereof by mail or other means.

(22) No airport or aircraft landing area shall be constructed or altered where such construction or alteration when undertaken or completed may reasonably affect motor vehicle operation and safety on adjoining public roads except in accordance with a written permit from the Department of Transportation or its duly authorized officers. The Department of Transportation is authorized and empowered to regulate airport and aircraft landing area construction and alteration in order to preserve safe clearances between highways and airways and the Department of Transportation is authorized and empowered to make rules, regulations, and ordinances for the preservation of safe clearances between highways and airways. The Department of Transportation shall be responsible for determining safe clearances and shall fix standards for said determination which shall not exceed the standards adopted for similar purposes by the United States Bureau of Public Roads under the Federal Aid Highway Act of 1958. Any person, firm, corporation or airport authority constructing or altering an airport or aircraft landing area without obtaining a written permit as herein provided, or not in compliance with the terms of such permit, or violating the provisions of the rules, regulations or ordinances promulgated under the authority of this section shall be guilty of a Class 1 misdemeanor; provided, that this subdivision shall not apply to publicly owned and operated airports and aircraft landing areas receiving federal funds and subject to regulation by the Federal Aviation Authority.

(23) When in the opinion of the Department of Transportation an economy in the expenditure of public funds can be effected thereby, the Department of Transportation shall have authority to enter into agreements with adjoining states regarding the planning, location, engineering, right-of-way acquisition and construction of roads and bridges connecting the North Carolina State highway system with public roads in adjoining states, and the Department of Transportation shall have authority to do planning, surveying, locating, engineering, right-of-way acquisition and construction on short segments of roads and bridges in adjoining states with the cost of said work to be reimbursed by the adjoining state, and may also enter into agreements with adjoining states providing for the performance of and reimbursement to the adjoining state of the cost of such work done within the State of North Carolina by the adjoining state:

Provided, that the Department of Transportation shall retain the right to approve any contract for work to be done in this State by an adjoining state for which the adjoining state is to be reimbursed.

(24)   The Department of Transportation is further authorized to pave driveways leading from state-maintained roads to rural fire district firehouses which are approved by the North Carolina Fire Insurance Rating Bureau and to facilities of rescue squads furnishing ambulance services which are approved by the North Carolina State Association of Rescue Squads, Inc.

(25)   The Department of Transportation is hereby authorized and directed to design, construct, repair, and maintain paved streets and roads upon the campus of each of the State's institutions of higher education, at state-owned hospitals for the treatment of tuberculosis, state-owned orthopedic hospitals, juvenile correction centers, mental health hospitals and retarded centers, schools for the deaf, and schools for the blind, when such construction, maintenance, or repairs have been authorized by the General Assembly in the appropriations bills enacted by the General Assembly. Cost for such construction, maintenance, and repairs shall be borne by the Highway Fund. Upon the General Assembly authorizing the construction, repair, or maintenance of a paved road or drive upon any of the above-mentioned institutions, the Department of Transportation shall give such project priority to insure that it shall be accomplished as soon as feasible, at the minimum cost to the State, and in any event during the biennium for which the authorization shall have been given by the General Assembly.

(26)   The Department of Transportation, at the request of a representative from a board of county commissioners, is hereby authorized to acquire by condemnation new or additional right-of-way to construct, pave or otherwise improve a designated State-maintained secondary road upon presentation by said board to the Department of Transportation of a duly verified copy of the minutes of its meeting showing approval of such request by a majority of its members and by the further presentation of a petition requesting such improvement executed by the abutting owners whose frontage on said secondary road shall equal or exceed seventy-five percent (75%) of the linear front footage along the secondary road sought to be improved. This subdivision shall not be construed to limit the authority of the Department of Transportation to exercise the power of eminent domain.

(27)   The Department of Transportation is authorized to establish policies and promulgate rules providing for voluntary local government, property owner or

highway user participation in the costs of maintenance or improvement of roads which would not otherwise be necessary or would not otherwise be performed by the Department of Transportation and which will result in a benefit to the property owner or highway user. By way of illustration and not as a limitation, such costs include those incurred in connection with drainage improvements or maintenance, driveway connections, dust control on unpaved roads, surfacing or paving of roads and the acquisition of rights-of-way. Local government, property owner and highway user participation can be in the form of materials, money, or land (for right-of-way) as deemed appropriate by the Department of Transportation. The authority of this section shall not be used to authorize, construct or maintain toll roads or bridges.

(28) The Department of Transportation may obtain land, either by gift, lease or purchase which shall be used for the construction and maintenance of ridesharing parking lots. The Department may design, construct, repair, and maintain ridesharing parking facilities.

(29) The Department of Transportation may establish policies and adopt rules about the size, location, direction of traffic flow, and the construction of driveway connections into any street or highway which is a part of the State Highway System. The Department of Transportation may require the construction and public dedication of acceleration and deceleration lanes, and traffic storage lanes and medians by others for the driveway connections into any United States route, or North Carolina route, and on any secondary road route with an average daily traffic volume of 4,000 vehicles per day or more.

(29a) To coordinate with all public and private entities planning schools to provide written recommendations and evaluations of driveway access and traffic operational and safety impacts on the State highway system resulting from the development of the proposed sites. All public and private entities shall, upon acquiring land for a new school or prior to beginning construction of a new school, relocating a school, or expanding an existing school, request from the Department a written evaluation and written recommendations to ensure that all proposed access points comply with the criteria in the current North Carolina Department of Transportation "Policy on Street and Driveway Access". The Department shall provide the written evaluation and recommendations within a reasonable time, which shall not exceed 60 days. This subdivision shall not be construed to require the public or private entities planning schools to meet the recommendations made by the Department, except those highway improvements that are required for safe ingress and egress to the State highway system.

(29b) The Department of Transportation shall consider exceptions to the sight distance requirement for driveway locations in instances where the curves of the road are close and frequent. Exceptions shall be granted in instances where sufficient sight distance can be provided or established through other means such as advisory speed signs, convex mirrors, and advanced warning signs. When appropriate, the Department shall consider lowering the speed limit on the relevant portion of the road. The Department may require a driveway permit applicant to cover the cost of installing the appropriate signage around the driveway, including speed limit reduction and driveway warning signs, and may also require the applicant to install and maintain convex or other mirrors to increase the safety around the driveway location.

This subdivision applies only to sections of roadway where the minimum sight distance as defined in the published "Policy on Street and Driveway Access to North Carolina Highways" is not available for a proposed driveway.

(30) Consistent with G.S. 130A-309.14(a1), the Department of Transportation shall review and revise its bid procedures and specifications set forth in Chapter 136 of the General Statutes to encourage the purchase or use of reusable, refillable, repairable, more durable, and less toxic supplies and products. The Department of Transportation shall require the purchase or use of such supplies and products in the construction and maintenance of highways and bridges to the extent that the use is practicable and cost-effective. The Department shall prepare an annual report on October 1 of each year to the Environmental Review Commission as required under G.S. 130A-309.14(a1).

(31) The Department of Transportation is authorized to designate portions of highways as scenic highways, and combinations of portions of highways as scenic byways, for portions of those highways that possess unusual, exceptional, or distinctive scenic, recreational, historical, educational, scientific, geological, natural, wildlife, cultural or ethnic features. The Department shall remove, upon application, from any existing or future scenic highway or scenic byway designation, highway sections that:

a. Have no scenic value,

b. Have been designated or would be so designated solely to preserve system continuity, and

c. Are adjacent to property on which is located one or more permanent structures devoted to a commercial or industrial activity and on which a commercial or industrial activity is actually conducted, in an unzoned area or an area zoned commercial or industrial pursuant to a State or local zoning ordinance or regulation, except for commercial activity related to tourism or recreation.

The Department shall adopt rules and regulations setting forth the criteria and procedures for the designation of scenic highways and scenic byways under this subsection.

Those portions of highways designated as scenic by the Department prior to July 1, 1993, are considered to be designated as scenic highways and scenic byways under this subsection but the Department shall remove from this designation portions of those highway sections that meet the criteria set forth in this subsection, if requested.

(32) The Department of Transportation may perform dredging services, on a cost reimbursement basis, for a unit of local government if the unit cannot obtain the services from a private company at a reasonable cost. A unit of local government is considered to be unable to obtain dredging services at a reasonable cost if it solicits bids for the dredging services in accordance with Article 8 of Chapter 143 of the General Statutes and does not receive a bid, considered by the Department of Transportation Engineering Staff, to be reasonable.

(33) The Department of Transportation is empowered and directed, from time to time, to carefully examine into and inspect the condition of each railroad, its equipment and facilities, in regard to the safety and convenience of the public and the railroad employees. If the Department finds any equipment or facilities to be unsafe, it shall at once notify the railroad company and require the company to repair the equipment or facilities.

(34) The Department of Transportation may conduct, in a manner consistent with federal law, a program of accident prevention and public safety covering all railroads and may investigate the cause of any railroad accident. In order to facilitate this program, any railroad involved in an accident that must be reported to the Federal Railroad Administration shall also notify the Department of Transportation of the occurrence of the accident.

(35) To establish rural planning organizations, as provided in Article 17 of this Chapter.

(36) To oversee the safety of fixed guideway transit systems in the State not regulated by the Federal Railroad Administration, pursuant to the Intermodal Surface Transportation Efficiency Act of 1991 (49 U.S.C. § 5330). The Department shall adopt rules in conformance with 49 U.S.C. § 5330 concerning its oversight of the safety of fixed guideway transit systems.

(37) To permit private use of and encroachment upon the right-of-way of a State highway or road for the purpose of construction and maintenance of a privately owned bridge for pedestrians or motor vehicles, if the bridge shall not unreasonably interfere with or obstruct the public use of the right-of-way. Any agreement for an encroachment authorized by this subdivision shall be approved by the Board of Transportation, upon a finding that the encroachment is necessary and appropriate, in the sole discretion of the Board. Locations, plans, and specifications for any pedestrian or vehicular bridge authorized by the Board for construction pursuant to this subdivision shall be approved by the Department of Transportation. For any bridge subject to this subdivision, the Department shall retain the right to reject any plans, specifications, or materials used or proposed to be used, inspect and approve all materials to be used, inspect the construction, maintenance, or repair, and require the replacement, reconstruction, repair, or demolition of any partially or wholly completed bridge that, in the sole discretion of the Department, is unsafe or substandard in design or construction. An encroachment agreement authorized by this subdivision may include a requirement to purchase and maintain liability insurance in an amount determined by the Department of Transportation. The Department shall ensure that any bridge constructed pursuant to this subdivision is regularly inspected for safety. The owner shall have the bridge inspected every two years by a qualified private engineering firm based on National Bridge Inspection Standards and shall provide the Department copies of the Bridge Inspection Reports where they shall be kept on file. Any bridge authorized and constructed pursuant to this subdivision shall be subject to all other rules and conditions of the Department of Transportation for encroachments.

(38) To enter into agreements with municipalities, counties, governmental entities, or nonprofit corporations to receive funds for the purposes of advancing right-of-way acquisition or the construction schedule of a project identified in the Transportation Improvement Program. If these funds are subject to repayment by the Department, prior to receipt of funds, reimbursement of all funds received by the Department shall be shown in the existing Transportation Improvement

Program and shall be reimbursed within the period of the existing Transportation Improvement Program.

(39) To enter into partnership agreements with private entities, and authorized political subdivisions to finance, by tolls, contracts, and other financing methods authorized by law, the cost of acquiring, constructing, equipping, maintaining, and operating transportation infrastructure in this State, and to plan, design, develop, acquire, construct, equip, maintain, and operate transportation infrastructure in this State. An agreement entered into under this subdivision requires the concurrence of the Board of Transportation. The Department shall report to the Chairs of the Joint Legislative Transportation Oversight Committee, the Chairs of the House of Representatives Appropriations Subcommittee on Transportation, and the Chairs of the Senate Appropriations Committee on the Department of Transportation, at the same time it notifies the Board of Transportation of any proposed agreement under this subdivision. No contract for transportation infrastructure subject to such an agreement that commits the Department to make nonretainage payments for undisputed capital costs of a completed transportation infrastructure to be made later than 18 months after final acceptance by the Department of such transportation infrastructure shall be executed without approval of the Local Government Commission. Any contracts for construction of highways, roads, streets, and bridges which are awarded pursuant to an agreement entered into under this section shall comply with the competitive bidding requirements of Article 2 of this Chapter.

(39a) a. The Department of Transportation or Turnpike Authority, as applicable, may enter into up to three agreements with a private entity as provided under subdivision (39) of this section for which the provisions of this section apply.

b. A private entity or its contractors must provide performance and payment security in the form and in the amount determined by the Department of Transportation. The form of the performance and payment security may consist of bonds, letters of credit, parent guaranties, or other instruments acceptable to the Department of Transportation.

c. Notwithstanding the provisions of G.S. 143B-426.40A, an agreement entered into under this subdivision may allow the private entity to assign, transfer, sell, hypothecate, and otherwise convey some or all of its right, title, and interest in and to such agreement, and any rights and remedies thereunder, to a lender, bondholder, or any other party. However, in no event shall any such assignment create additional debt or debt-like obligations of the State of North Carolina, the Department, or any other agency, authority, commission, or similar subdivision of the State to any lender, bondholder, entity purchasing a participation in the right to receive the payment, trustee, trust, or any other party providing financing or funding of projects described in this section. The foregoing shall not preclude the Department from making any payments due and owing pursuant to an agreement entered into under this section.

    d.   Article 6H of Chapter 136 of the General Statutes shall apply to the Department of Transportation and to projects undertaken by the Department of Transportation under subdivision (39) of this section. The Department may assign its authority under that Article to fix, revise, charge, retain, enforce, and collect tolls and fees to the private entity.

    e.   Any contract under this subdivision or under Article 6H of this Chapter for the development, construction, maintenance, or operation of a project shall provide for revenue sharing, if applicable, between the private party and the Department, and revenues derived from such project may be used as set forth in G.S. 136-89.188(a), notwithstanding the provisions of G.S. 136-89.188(d). Excess toll revenues from a Turnpike project shall be used for the funding or financing of transportation projects within the corridor where the Turnpike Project is located. For purposes of this subdivision, the term "excess toll revenues" means those toll revenues derived from a Turnpike Project that are not otherwise used or allocated to the Authority or a private entity pursuant to this subdivision, notwithstanding the provisions of G.S. 136-89.188(d). For purposes of this subdivision, the term "corridor" means (i) the right-of-way limits of the Turnpike Project and any facilities related to the Turnpike Project or any facility or improvement necessary for the use, design, construction, operation, maintenance, repair, rehabilitation, reconstruction, or financing of a Turnpike Project; (ii) the right-of-way limits of any subsequent improvements, additions, or extension to the Turnpike Project and facilities related to the Turnpike projects, including any improvements necessary for the use, design, construction, operation, maintenance, repair, rehabilitation, reconstruction, or financing of those subsequent improvements, additions, or extensions to the Turnpike Project; and (iii) roads used for ingress or egress to the toll facility or roads that intersect with the toll facility, whether by ramps or separated grade facility, and located within one mile in any direction.

    f.   Agreements entered into under this subdivision shall comply with the following additional provisions:

1. The Department shall solicit proposals for agreements.

2. Agreement shall be limited to no more than 50 years from the date of the beginning of operations on the toll facility.

3. Notwithstanding the provisions of G.S. 136-89.183(a)(5), all initial tolls or fees to be charged by a private entity shall be reviewed by the Turnpike Authority Board. Prior to setting toll rates, either a set rate or a minimum and maximum rate set by the private entity, the private entity shall hold a public hearing on the toll rates, including an explanation of the toll setting methodology, in accordance with guidelines for the hearing developed by the Department. After tolls go into effect, the private entity shall report to the Turnpike Authority Board 30 days prior to any increase in toll rates or change in the toll setting methodology by the private entity from the previous toll rates or toll setting methodology last reported to the Turnpike Authority Board.

4. Financial advisors and attorneys retained by the Department on contract to work on projects pursuant to this subsection shall be subject to State law governing conflicts of interest.

5. 60 days prior to the signing of a concession agreement subject to this subdivision, the Department shall report to the Joint Legislative Transportation Oversight Committee on the following for the presumptive concessionaire:

I. Project description.

II. Number of years that tolls will be in place.

III. Name and location of firms and parent companies, if applicable, including firm responsibility and stake, and assessment of audited financial statements.

IV. Analysis of firm selection criteria.

V. Name of any firm or individual under contract to provide counsel or financial analysis to the Department or Authority. The Department shall disclose payments to these contractors related to completing the agreement under this subdivision.

VI. Demonstrated ability of the project team to deliver the project, by evidence of the project team's prior experience in delivering a project on schedule and budget, and disclosure of any unfavorable outcomes on prior projects.

VII. Detailed description of method of finance, including sources of funds, State contribution amounts, including schedule of availability payments and terms of debt payments.

VIII. Information on assignment of risk shared or assigned to State and private partner.

IX. Information on the feasibility of finance as obtained in traffic and revenue studies.

6. The Turnpike Authority annual report under G.S. 136-89.193 shall include reporting on all revenue collections associated with projects subject to this subdivision under the Turnpike Authority.

7. The Department shall develop standards for entering into comprehensive agreements with private entities under the authority of this subdivision and report those standards to the Joint Legislative Transportation Oversight Committee on or before October 1, 2013.

(40) To expand public access to coastal waters in its road project planning and construction programs. The Department shall work with the Wildlife Resources Commission, other State agencies, and other government entities to address public access to coastal waters along the roadways, bridges, and other transportation infrastructure owned or maintained by the Department. The Department shall adhere to all applicable design standards and guidelines in implementation of this enhanced access.

(41) The Department shall, prior to the beginning of construction, determine whether all sidewalks and other facilities primarily intended for the use of pedestrians and bicycles that are to be constructed within the right-of-way of a public street or highway that is a part of the State highway system or an urban highway system must be constructed of permeable pavement. "Permeable pavement" means paving material that absorbs water or allows water to infiltrate through the paving material. Permeable pavement materials include porous concrete, permeable interlocking concrete pavers, concrete grid pavers, porous asphalt, and any other material with similar characteristics. Compacted gravel shall not be considered permeable pavement.

(42) The Department shall develop and utilize a process for selection of transportation projects that is based on professional standards in order to most efficiently use limited resources to benefit all citizens of the State. The strategic prioritization process should be a systematic, data-driven process that includes a combination of quantitative data, qualitative input, and multimodal characteristics, and should include local input. The Department shall develop a process for standardizing or approving local methodology used in Metropolitan Planning Organization and Rural Transportation Planning Organization prioritization.

(43) For the purposes of financing an agreement under subdivision (39a) of this section, the Department of Transportation may act as a conduit issuer for private activity bonds to the extent the bonds do not constitute a debt obligation of the State. The issuance of private activity bonds under this subdivision and any related actions shall be governed by The State and Local Government Revenue Bond Act, Article 5 of Chapter 159 of the General Statutes, with G.S. 159-88 satisfied by adherence to the requirements of subdivision (39a) of this section. (1921, c. 2, s. 10; 1923, c. 160, s. 1; c. 247; C.S., s. 3846(j); 1929, c. 138, s. 1; 1931, c. 145, ss. 21, 25; 1933, c. 172; c. 517, c. 1; 1935, c. 213, s. 1; c. 301; 1937, c. 297, s. 2; c. 407, s. 80; 1941, c. 47; c. 217, s. 6; 1943, c. 410; 1945, c. 842; 1951, c. 372; 1953, c. 437; 1957, c. 65, s. 11; c. 349, s. 9; 1959, c. 557; 1963, cc. 520, 1155; 1965, c. 879, s. 1; 1967, c. 1129; 1969, c. 794, s. 2; 1971, cc. 289, 291, 292, 977; 1973, c. 507, s. 5; 1977, c. 460, ss. 1, 2; c. 464, ss. 7.1, 14, 42; 1981, c. 682, s. 19; 1983, c. 84; c. 102; 1985, c. 718, ss. 1, 6; 1987, c. 311; c. 417, ss. 1, 2; 1989, c. 158; 1989 (Reg. Sess. 1990), c. 962, s. 1; 1993, c. 197, s. 2; c. 488, s. 1; c. 524, s. 4; c. 539, ss. 974-977; 1994, Ex. Sess., c. 24, s. 14(c); 1995, c. 247, s. 1; c. 507, s. 18.2; 1995 (Reg. Sess., 1996), c. 673, s. 4; 1996, 2nd Ex. Sess., c. 18, s. 19.10(a); 1997-428, s. 1; 1997-443, s. 11A.118(a); 2000-123, s. 1; 2000-140, s. 102; 2001-424, s. 27.27; 2003-184, s. 1; 2003-267, s. 1; 2004-168, s. 1; 2005-403, s. 2; 2006-230, s. 1(a); 2007-428, s. 1; 2007-439, s. 1; 2007-485, s. 3.1; 2008-164, s. 1; 2008-180, ss. 2, 8; 2009-266, s. 6; 2009-451, s. 25.6(a); 2010-97, s. 14; 2010-165, ss. 4, 4(a), 5-8; 2012-84, s. 2; 2012-184, s. 1; 2013-137, ss. 1, 2; 2013-183, ss. 4.2, 5.2; 2013-266, s. 1.)

§ 136-18.01. Consultation required for welcome and visitor centers.

The Department of Commerce and the Department of Transportation shall consult with the Joint Legislative Commission on Governmental Operations and the House and Senate Appropriations Subcommittees on Natural and Economic Resources before beginning the design or construction of any new welcome center or visitor center buildings. (2007-356, s. 1.)

§ 136-18.02. Operation of electric vehicle charging stations at rest stops; report.

(a) The Department of Transportation may operate an electric vehicle charging station at State-owned rest stops along the highways only if all of the following conditions are met:

(1) The electric vehicle charging station is accessible by the public.

(2) The Department has developed a mechanism to charge the user of the electric vehicle charging station a fee in order to recover the cost of electricity consumed, the cost of processing the user fee, and a proportionate cost of the operation and maintenance of the electric vehicle charging station.

(b) If the cost of the electricity consumed at the electric vehicle charging stations cannot be calculated as provided by subsection (a) of this section, the Department shall develop an alternative mechanism, other than electricity metering, to recover the cost of the electricity consumed at the vehicle charging station.

(c) The Department may consult with other State agencies and industry representatives in order to develop the mechanisms for cost recovery required pursuant to subsection (a) of this section.

(d) Beginning January 1, 2014, and annually thereafter, the Department of Transportation shall report to the Joint Legislative Commission on Energy Policy, the Joint Legislative Transportation Oversight Committee, the House Appropriations Subcommittee on Transportation, and the Senate Appropriations Subcommittee on Department of Transportation on the implementation of this section. (2012-186, s. 2.)

§ 136-18.1. Repealed by Session Laws 1999-29, s. 1.

§ 136-18.2. Seed planted by Department of Transportation to be approved by Department of Agriculture and Consumer Services.

The Department of Transportation shall not cause any seed to be planted on or along any highway or road right-of-way unless and until such seed has been approved by the Department of Agriculture and Consumer Services as provided for in the rules and regulations of the Department of Agriculture and Consumer Services for such seed. (1957, c. 1002; 1973, c. 507, s. 5; 1977, c. 464, s. 7.1; 1997-261, ss. 88, 109.)

§ 136-18.3. Location of garbage collection containers by counties and municipalities.

(a) The Department of Transportation is authorized to issue permits to counties and municipalities for the location of containers on rights-of-way of state-maintained highways for the collection of garbage. Such containers may be located on highway rights-of-way only when authorized in writing by the Chief Engineer in accordance with rules and regulations promulgated by the Department of Transportation. Such rules and regulations shall take into consideration the safety of travelers on the highway and the elimination of unsightly conditions and health hazards. Such containers shall not be located on fully controlled-access highways.

(b) The provisions of G.S. 14-399, which make it a misdemeanor to place garbage on highway rights-of-way, shall not apply to persons placing garbage in containers in accordance with rules and regulations promulgated by the Department of Transportation.

(c) The written authority granted by the Department of Transportation shall be no guarantee that the State system highway rights-of-way on which the containers are authorized to be located is owned by the Department of Transportation, and the issuance of such written authority shall be granted only when the county or municipality certifies that written permission to locate the refuse container has been obtained from the owner of the underlying fee if the owner can be determined and located.

(d) Whenever any municipality or county fails to comply with the rules and regulations promulgated by the Department of Transportation or whenever they fail or refuse to comply with any order of the Department of Transportation for the removal or change in the location of a container, then the permit of such county or municipality shall be revoked. The location of such garbage containers on highway rights-of-way after such order for removal or change is unauthorized and illegal; the Department of Transportation shall have the authority to remove such unauthorized or illegal containers and charge the expense of such removal to the county or municipality failing to comply with the order of the Department of Transportation. (1973, c. 1381; 1977, c. 464, s. 7.1; 2012-85, s. 5.)

§ 136-18.4. Provision and marking of "pull-off" areas.

The Department of Transportation is hereby authorized and directed (i) to provide as needed within its right-of-way, adjacent to long sections of two-lane primary highway having a steep uphill grade or numerous curves, areas on which buses, trucks and other slow-moving vehicles can pull over so that faster moving traffic may proceed unimpeded and (ii) to erect appropriate and adequate signs along such sections of highway and at the pull-off areas. A driver of a truck, bus, or other slow-moving vehicle who fails to use an area so provided and thereby impedes faster moving traffic following his vehicle shall be guilty of a Class 3 misdemeanor. (1975, c. 704; 1977, c. 464, s. 7.1; 1993, c. 539, s. 978; 1994, Ex. Sess., c. 24, s. 14(c).)

§ 136-18.5. Wesley D. Webster Highway.

State Highway 704 shall be known as the "Wesley D. Webster Highway". (1983 (Reg. Sess., 1984), c. 974.)

§ 136-18.5A. Purple Heart Memorial Highway.

Interstate Highway 95 in North Carolina is designated as the "Purple Heart Memorial Highway" to pay tribute to the many North Carolinians who have been awarded the Purple Heart medal after being wounded or killed in action against the enemy. (2002-86, s. 2(a).)

§ 136-18.5B. Dale Earnhardt Highway.

The Board of Transportation shall designate State Highway 136 in Iredell and Cabarrus counties as State Highway 3, which shall be known as the "Dale Earnhardt Highway". (2002-170, s. 4.)

§ 136-18.5C. The U.S. Marine Corps Highway: Home of Carolina-Based Marines since 1941.

U.S. Highway 17 running between the Town of Holly Ridge and the Town of Edenton, and the portion of U.S. Highway 70 running between the intersection of U.S. Highway 70 and N.C. Highway 101 near Cherry Point Marine Corps Air Station and the intersection of U.S. Highway 70 and U.S. Highway 17 is designated as "The U.S. Marine Corps Highway: Home of Carolina-Based Marines since 1941" in light of the historical contributions of the United States Marine Corps. (2009-198, s. 1.)

§ 136-18.6. Cutting down trees.

Except in the process of an authorized construction, maintenance or safety project, the Department shall not cut down trees unless:

(1)   The trees pose a potential danger to persons or property; or

(2)   The cutting down of the trees is approved by the appropriate District Engineer. (1989, c. 63.)

§ 136-18.7. Fees.

The fee for a selective vegetation removal permit issued pursuant to G.S. 136-18(5), (7), and (9) is two hundred dollars ($200.00). (1999-404, s. 5.)

§ 136-19. Acquisition of land and deposits of materials; condemnation proceedings; federal parkways.

(a) The Department of Transportation is vested with the power to acquire either in the nature of an appropriate easement or in fee simple such rights-of-way and title to such land, gravel, gravel beds or bars, sand, sand beds or bars, rock, stone, boulders, quarries, or quarry beds, lime or other earth or mineral deposits or formations, and such standing timber as it may deem necessary and suitable for transportation infrastructure construction, including road construction, maintenance, and repair, and the necessary approaches and ways through, and a sufficient amount of land surrounding and adjacent thereto, as it may determine to enable it to properly prosecute the work, by purchase, donation, or condemnation, in the manner hereinafter set out. If the Department of Transportation acquires by purchase, donation, or condemnation part of a tract of land in fee simple for highway right-of-way as authorized by this section and the Department of Transportation later determines that the property acquired for transportation infrastructure, including highway right-of-way, or a part of that property, is no longer needed for infrastructure right-of-way, then the Department shall give first consideration to any offer to purchase the property made by the former owner. The Department may refuse any offer that is less than the current market value of the property, as determined by the Department. Unless the Department acquired an entire lot, block, or tract of land belonging to the former owner, the former owner must own the remainder of the lot, block, or tract of land from which the property was acquired to receive first consideration by the Department of their offer to purchase the property.

(b) Notwithstanding the provisions of subsection (a), if the Department acquires the property by condemnation and determines that the property or a part of that property is no longer needed for highway right-of-way or other transportation projects, the Department of Transportation may reconvey the property to the former owner upon payment by the former owner of the full price paid to the owner when the property was taken, the cost of any improvements, together with interest at the legal rate to the date when the decision was made to offer the return of the property. Unless the Department acquired an entire lot, block, or tract of land belonging to the former owner, the former owner must own the remainder of the lot, block, or tract of land from which the property was acquired to purchase the property pursuant to this subsection.

(c) The requirements of this section for reconveying property to the former owner, regardless of whether such property was acquired by purchase, donation, or condemnation, shall not apply to property acquired outside the right-of-way as an "uneconomic remnant" or "residue".

(d) The Department of Transportation is also vested with the power to acquire such additional land alongside of the rights-of-way for transportation projects, including roads as in its opinion may be necessary and proper for the protection of the transportation projects, including roads and roadways, and such additional area as may be necessary as by it determined for approaches to and from such material and other requisite area as may be desired by it for working purposes. The Department of Transportation may, in its discretion, with the consent of the landowner, acquire in fee simple an entire lot, block or tract of land, if by so doing, the interest of the public will be best served, even though said entire lot, block or tract is not immediately needed for right-of-way purposes.

(e) Notwithstanding any other provisions of law or eminent domain powers of utility companies, utility membership corporations, municipalities, counties, entities created by political subdivisions, or any combination thereof, and in order to prevent undue delay of highway projects because of utility conflicts, the Department of Transportation may condemn or acquire property in fee or appropriate easements necessary to provide transportation project rights-of-way for the relocation of utilities when required in the construction, reconstruction, or rehabilitation of a State transportation project. The Department of Transportation shall also have the authority, subject to the provisions of G.S. 136-19.5(a) and (b), to, in its discretion, acquire rights-of-way necessary for the present or future placement of utilities as described in G.S. 136-18(2).

(f) Whenever the Department of Transportation and the owner or owners of the lands, materials, and timber required by the Department of Transportation to carry on the work as herein provided for, are unable to agree as to the price thereof, the Department of Transportation is hereby vested with the power to condemn the lands, materials, and timber and in so doing the ways, means, methods, and procedure of Article 9 of this Chapter shall be used by it exclusively.

(g) The Department of Transportation shall have the same authority, under the same provisions of law provided for construction of State transportation projects, for acquirement of all rights-of-way and easements necessary to comply with the rules and regulations of the United States government for the construction of federal parkways and entrance roads to federal parks in the State of North Carolina. The acquirement of a total of 125 acres per mile of said parkways, including roadway and recreational, and scenic areas on either side thereof, shall be deemed a reasonable area for said purpose. The right-of-way acquired or appropriated may, at the option of the Department of Transportation, be a fee-simple title. The said Department of Transportation is hereby authorized to convey such title so acquired to the United States government, or its appropriate agency, free and clear of all claims for compensation. All compensation contracted to be paid or legally assessed shall be a valid claim against the Department of Transportation, payable out of the State Highway Fund. Any conveyance to the United States Department of Interior of land acquired as provided by this section shall contain a provision whereby the State of North Carolina shall retain concurrent jurisdiction over the areas conveyed. The Governor is further authorized to grant concurrent jurisdiction to lands already conveyed to the United States Department of Interior for parkways and entrances to parkways.

(h)   The action of the Department of Transportation heretofore taken in the acquirement of areas for the Blue Ridge Parkway in accordance with the rules and regulations of the United States government is hereby ratified and approved and declared to be a reasonable exercise of the discretion vested in the said Department of Transportation in furtherance of the public interest.

(i)   When areas have been tentatively designated by the United States government to be included within a parkway, but the final survey necessary for the filing of maps as provided in this section has not yet been made, no person shall cut or remove any timber from said areas pending the filing of said maps after receiving notice from the Department of Transportation that such area is under investigation; and any property owner who suffers loss by reason of the restraint upon his right to use the said timber pending such investigation shall be entitled to recover compensation from the Department of Transportation for the temporary appropriation of his property, in the event the same is not finally included within the appropriated area, and the provisions of this section may be enforced under the same law now applicable for the adjustment of compensation in the acquirement of rights-of-way on other property by the Department of Transportation. (1921, c. 2, s. 22; 1923, c. 160, s. 6; C.S., s. 3846(bb); 1931, c. 145, s. 23; 1933, c. 172, s. 17; 1935, c. 2; 1937, c. 42; 1949, c. 1115; 1953, c. 217; 1957, c. 65, s. 11; 1959, c. 1025, s. 1; cc. 1127, 1128; 1963, c. 638; 1971, c. 1105; 1973, c. 507, ss. 5, 11; 1977, c. 464, s. 7.1; 1989 (Reg. Sess., 1990), c. 962, s. 2; 1991 (Reg. Sess., 1992), c. 979, s. 1; 2009-266, s. 7.)

§ 136-19.1. Repealed by Session Laws 1977, c. 338, s. 1.

§ 136-19.2. Repealed by Session Laws 1969, c. 733, s. 13.

§ 136-19.3. Acquisition of buildings.

Where the right-of-way of a proposed highway or other transportation project necessitates the taking of a portion of a building or structure, the Department of Transportation may acquire, by condemnation or purchase, the entire building or structure, together with the right to enter upon the surrounding land for the purpose of removing said building or structure, upon a determination by the Department of Transportation based upon an affidavit of an independent real estate appraiser that the partial taking will substantially destroy the economic value or utility of the building or structure and (i) that an economy in the expenditure of public funds will be promoted thereby; or (ii) that it is not feasible to cut off a portion of the building without destroying the entire building; or (iii) that the convenience, safety or improvement of the transportation project will be promoted thereby; provided, nothing herein contained shall be deemed to give the Department of Transportation authority to condemn the underlying fee of the portion of any building or structure which lies outside the right-of-way of any existing or proposed transportation project, including a public road, street or highway. (1965, c. 660; 1973, c. 507, s. 5; 1977, c. 464, s. 7.1; 2009-266, s. 8.)

§ 136-19.4. Registration of right-of-way plans.

(a) A copy of the cover sheet and plan and profile sheets of the final right-of-way plans for all Department of Transportation projects, on those projects for which plans are prepared, under which right-of-way or other interest in real property is acquired or access is controlled shall be certified by the Department of Transportation to the register of deeds of the county or counties within which the project is located. The Department shall certify said plan sheets to the register of deeds within two weeks from their formal approval by the Board of Transportation.

(b) The copy of the plans certified to the register of deeds shall consist of a Xerox, photographic, or other permanent copy, except for plans electronically transmitted pursuant to subsection (b1) of this section, and shall measure approximately 17 inches by 11 inches including no less than one and one-half inches binding space on the left-hand side.

(b1) With the approval of the county in which the right-of-way plans are to be filed, the Department may transmit the plans electronically.

(c) Notwithstanding any other provision in the law, upon receipt of said original certified copy of the right-of-way plans, the register of deeds shall record said right-of-way plans and place the same in a book maintained for that purpose, and the register of deeds shall maintain a cross-index to said right-of-way plans by number of road affected, if any, and by identification number. No probate before the clerk of the superior court shall be required.

(d) If after the approval of said final right-of-way plans the Board of Transportation shall by resolution alter or amend said right-of-way or control of access, the Department of Transportation, within two weeks from the adoption by the Board of Transportation of said alteration or amendment, shall certify to the register of deeds in the county or counties within which the project is located a copy of the amended plan and profile sheets approved by the Board of Transportation and the register of deeds shall remove the original plan sheets and record the amended plan sheets in lieu thereof.

(e) The register of deeds in each county shall collect a fee from the Department of Transportation for recording right-of-way plans and profile sheets in the amount set out in G.S. 161-10. (1967, c. 228, s. 1; 1969, c. 80, s. 13; 1973, c. 507, ss. 5, 12-15; 1975, c. 716, s. 7; 1977, c. 464, s. 7.1; 1999-422, s. 1; 2000-68, s. 1; 2001-390, s. 6.)

§ 136-19.5. Utility right-of-way agreements.

(a) Before the Department of Transportation acquires or proposes to acquire additional rights-of-way for the purpose of accommodating the installation of utilities as authorized by G.S. 136-18 and G.S. 136-19, there shall first be voluntary agreements with the appropriate utilities regarding the acquisition and use of the particular right-of-way and requiring the payment to the Department of Transportation for or recapture of all of its costs associated with that acquisition, including the use of funds allocated to such acquisition. Such agreements may take into account the fact that more than one utility can make use of the right-of-way. No such agreement shall constitute a sale of the right-of-way and all such rights-of-way shall remain under the control of the Department of Transportation.

(b)   A prior agreement between the Department of Transportation and the affected utilities may be entered into but is not required when the acquisition of right-of-way is for the purpose of relocation of utilities due to construction, reconstruction, or rehabilitation of a State transportation project. The Department of Transportation shall notify the affected utility whose facilities are being relocated and the affected utility may choose not to participate in the proposed plan for right-of-way acquisition. The decision not to participate in the proposed plan of right-of-way acquisition shall not affect any other rights the utility may have as a result of the relocation of its lines or pipelines.

(c)   Whenever the Department of Transportation requires the relocation of utilities located in a right-of-way for which the utility owner contributed to the cost of acquisition, the Department of Transportation shall reimburse the utility owner for the cost of moving those utilities.

(d)   Any additional right-of-way obtained pursuant to this section which is part of a railroad right-of-way shall be returned to the railroad or its successor in interest when the Department of Transportation and the affected utilities agree that the additional right-of-way is no longer useful for utility purposes and the Department of Transportation determines that it is no longer useful for transportation purposes. (1989 (Reg. Sess., 1990), c. 962, s. 3; 2009-266, s. 9.)

§ 136-20. Elimination or safeguarding of grade crossings and inadequate underpasses or overpasses.

(a)   Whenever any road or street forming a link in or a part of the State highway system, whether under construction or heretofore or hereafter constructed, shall cross or intersect any railroad at the same level or grade, or by an underpass or overpass, and in the opinion of the Secretary of Transportation such crossing is dangerous to the traveling public, or unreasonably interferes with or impedes traffic on said State highway, the Department of Transportation shall issue notice requiring the person or company operating such railroad to appear before the Secretary of Transportation, at his office in Raleigh, upon a day named, which shall not be less than 10 days or more than 20 days from the date of said notice, and show cause, if any it has, why such railroad company shall not be required to alter such crossing in such way as to remove such dangerous condition and to make such changes and improvements thereat as will safeguard and secure the safety and convenience of the traveling public thereafter. Such notice shall be served on such railroad company as is now provided by law for the service of summons on domestic corporations, and officers serving such notice shall receive the same fees as now provided by law for the service of such summons.

(b)   Upon the day named, the Secretary of Transportation shall hear said matter and shall determine whether such crossing is dangerous to public safety, or unreasonably interferes with traffic thereon. If he shall determine that said crossing is, or upon the completion of such highway will be, dangerous to public safety and its elimination or safeguarding is necessary for the proper protection of the traffic on said State highway, the Secretary of Transportation shall thereupon order the construction of an adequate underpass or overpass at said crossing or he may in his discretion order said railroad company to install and maintain gates, alarm signals or other approved safety devices if and when in the opinion of said Secretary of Transportation upon the hearing as aforesaid the public safety and convenience will be secured thereby. And said order shall specify that the cost of construction of such underpass or overpass or the installation of such safety device shall be allocated between the railroad company and the Department of Transportation in the same ratio as the net benefits received by such railroad company from the project bear to the net benefits accruing to the public using the highway, and in no case shall the net benefit to any railroad company or companies be deemed to be more than ten percent (10%) of the total benefits resulting from the project. The Secretary of Transportation shall be responsible for determining the proportion of the benefits derived by the railroad company from the project, and shall fix standards for the determining of said benefits which shall be consistent with the standards adopted for similar purposes by the United States Bureau of Public Roads under the Federal-Aid Highway Act of 1944.

(c)   Upon the filing and issuance of the order as hereinbefore provided for requiring the construction of any underpass or overpass or the installation and maintenance of gates, alarm signals or other safety devices at any crossing upon the State highway system, it shall be the duty of the railroad company operating the railroad with which said public road or street intersects or crosses to construct such underpass or overpass or to install and maintain such safety device as may be required in said order. The work may be done and material furnished either by the railroad company or the Department of Transportation, as may be agreed upon, and the cost thereof shall be allocated and borne as set out in subsection (b) hereof. If the work is done and material furnished by the railroad company, an itemized statement of the total amount expended therefor shall, at the completion of the work, be furnished the Department of Transportation, and the Department of Transportation shall pay such amount to the railroad company as may be shown on such statement after deducting the amount for which the railroad company is responsible; and if the work is done by the Department of Transportation, an itemized statement of the total amount expended shall be furnished to the railroad company, and the railroad company shall pay to the Department of Transportation such part thereof as the railroad company may be responsible for as herein provided; such payment by the railroad company shall be under such rules and regulations and by such methods as the Department of Transportation may provide.

(d) Within 60 days after the issuance of the order for construction of an underpass or overpass or the installation of other safety devices as herein provided for, the railroad company against which such order is issued shall submit to the Department of Transportation plans for such construction or installation, and within 10 days thereafter said Department of Transportation, through its chairman of the Department of Transportation, shall notify such railroad company of its approval of said plan or of such changes and amendments thereto as to it shall seem advisable. If such plans are not submitted to the Department of Transportation by said railroad company within 60 days as aforesaid, the chairman of the Department of Transportation shall have plans prepared and submit them to the railroad company. The railroad company shall within 10 days notify the chairman of the Department of Transportation of its approval of the said plans or shall have the right within such 10 days to suggest such changes and amendments in the plans so submitted by the chairman of the Department of Transportation as to it shall seem advisable. The plans so prepared and finally approved by the chairman of the Department of Transportation shall have the same force and effect, and said railroad company shall be charged with like liability, and said underpass or overpass shall be constructed or such safety device installed in accordance therewith, as if said plans had been originally prepared and submitted by said railroad company. If said railroad company shall fail or neglect to begin or complete the construction of said underpass or overpass, or the installation of such safety device, as required by the order of the Secretary of Transportation, said Secretary of Transportation is authorized and directed to prepare the necessary plans therefor, which plans shall have the same force and effect, and shall fix said railroad company with like liability, as if said plans had been originally prepared and submitted by said railroad company, and the Department of Transportation shall proceed to construct said underpass or overpass or install such safety device in accordance therewith. An accurate account of the cost of said construction or installation shall be kept by the Department of Transportation and upon the completion of such work a statement of that portion thereof chargeable to such railroad company as set out in the order of the Department of Transportation shall be rendered said railroad company. Upon the failure or refusal of said company to pay the bill so rendered, the Department of Transportation shall recover the amount thereof by suit therefor against said company in the Superior Court of Wake County: Provided, that the payment by such railroad company of said proportionate part may be made under such rules and regulations and by such methods as the Department of Transportation may provide. If the Department of Transportation shall undertake to do the work, it shall not obstruct or impair the operation of the railroad and shall keep the roadbed and track safe for the operation of trains at every stage of work. If said railroad company shall construct such underpass or overpass or shall install such safety devices in accordance with the order of the Secretary of Transportation, the proportionate share of the cost thereof as set out in subsection (b) hereof shall upon the completion of said work be paid to the railroad company by the Department of Transportation. The Department of Transportation may inspect and check the expenditures for such construction or installation so made by the railroad company and an accurate account of the cost thereof shall upon the completion of said work be submitted to the Department of Transportation by the railroad company. If the Department of Transportation shall neglect or refuse to pay that portion of the cost of said construction or installation chargeable to it, the railroad company shall recover the amount thereof by suit therefor against the Department of Transportation in the Superior Court of Wake County.

(e) If any railroad company so ordered by the Secretary of Transportation to construct an underpass or overpass or to install safety devices at grade crossings as hereinbefore provided for shall fail or refuse to comply with the order of the Secretary of Transportation requiring such construction or installation, said railroad company shall be guilty of a Class 3 misdemeanor and shall only be fined not less than fifty dollars ($50.00) nor more than one hundred dollars ($100.00) in the discretion of the court for each day such failure or refusal shall continue, each said day to constitute a separate offense.

(f) The jurisdiction over and control of said grade crossings and safety devices upon the State highway system herein given the Department of Transportation shall be exclusive.

(g) From any order or decision so made by the Secretary of Transportation the railroad company may appeal to the superior court of the county wherein is located the crossing affected by said order. Such appeal shall not defer or delay the construction of such underpass or overpass or the installation of such safety device as required by the order of the Secretary of Transportation, but the railroad company shall proceed to comply with such order in accordance with his terms. The action of the railroad company in complying with and carrying out such order pending said appeal shall not prejudice or affect the right or remedies of such railroad company on such appeal. Upon such appeal the court shall determine only whether the order of the Secretary of Transportation for such construction or installation is unreasonable and unnecessary for the protection of the traveling public and the apportionment of the cost to the extent hereinafter provided in this subsection, and if upon the hearing of said appeal it shall be determined that said order was unnecessary for the protection of the traveling public, the Department of Transportation shall bear the total cost of the construction of such underpass or overpass or the installation of such safety device. In the event the decision on appeal should be that the construction or installation was necessary but the cost or apportionment thereof unreasonable, then the railroad company shall bear its proportion as provided in this section of such cost as may be determined on appeal to have been reasonable to meet the necessity of the case. Upon said appeal from an order of the Secretary of Transportation, the burden of proof shall be upon the railroad company, and if it shall not be found and determined upon said appeal that said order was unreasonable or unnecessary for the protection of the traveling public at said crossing, then such railroad company shall bear its proportion of the cost of such construction or installation in accordance with this section.

(h) The Department of Transportation shall pay the cost of maintenance of all overpasses and the railroad company shall pay the cost of maintenance of all underpasses constructed in accordance with this section. The cost of maintenance of safety devices at all intersections of any railroad company and any street or road forming a link in or a part of the State highway system which have been constructed prior to July 1, 1959, or which shall be constructed thereafter shall be borne fifty percent (50%) by the railroad company and fifty percent (50%) by the Department of Transportation. The maintenance of said overpasses and underpasses shall be performed by the railroad company or the Department of Transportation as may be agreed upon and reimbursement for the cost thereof, in accordance with this section, shall be made annually. The maintenance of such safety devices shall be performed by the railroad company and reimbursement for the cost thereof, in accordance with this section, shall be made annually by the Department of Transportation. (1921, c. 2, s. 19; 1923, c. 160, s. 5; C.S., s. 3846(y); 1925, c. 277; 1929, c. 74; 1933, c. 172, s. 17; 1957,

c. 65, s. 11; 1959, c. 1216; 1973, c. 507, s. 5; 1977, c. 464, ss. 7.1, 11, 15; 1993, c. 539, s. 979; 1994, Ex. Sess., c. 14, s. 60, c. 24, s. 14(c).)

§ 136-20.1. To require installation and maintenance of block system and safety devices; automatic signals at railroad intersections.

(a) The Department of Transportation is empowered and directed to require any railroad company to install and put in operation and maintain upon the whole or any part of its road a block system of telegraphy or any other reasonable safety device, but no railroad company shall be required to install a block system upon any part of its road unless at least eight trains each way per day are operated on that part.

(b) The Department of Transportation is empowered and directed to require, when public safety demands, where two or more railroads cross each other at a common grade, or any railroad crosses any stream or harbor by means of a bridge, to install and maintain such a system of interlocking or automatic signals as will render it safe for engines and trains to pass over such crossings or bridge without stopping, and to apportion the cost of installation and maintenance between said railroads as may be just and proper. (1907, c. 469, s. 1b; 1911, c. 197, s. 2; Ex. Sess. 1913, c. 63, s. 1; C.S., ss. 1047, 1049; 1933, c. 134, s. 8; 1941, c. 97; 1963, c. 1165, s. 1; 1995 (Reg. Sess., 1996), c. 673, s. 5.)

§ 136-21. Drainage of highway; application to court; summons; commissioners.

Whenever in the establishment, construction, improvement or maintenance of any public highway it shall be necessary to drain said highway, and to accomplish such purpose it becomes necessary to excavate a canal or canals for carrying the surplus water to some appropriate outlet, either along the right-of-way of said highway or across the lands of other landowners, and by the construction, enlargement or improvement of such canal or canals, lands other than said highway will be drained and benefited, then, and in such event, the Department of Transportation, if said highway be a part of the State highway system, or the county commissioners, if said road is not under State supervision, may, by petition, apply to the superior court of the county in which, in whole or in part, said highway lies or said canal is to be constructed, setting forth the necessity for the construction, improvement or maintenance of said canal, the lands which will be drained thereby, with such particularity as to enable same to be identified, the names of the owners of said land and the particular circumstances of the case; whereupon a summons shall be issued for and served upon each of the proprietors, requiring them to appear before the court at a time to be named in the summons, which shall not be less than 10 days from the service thereof, and upon such day the petition shall be heard, and the court shall appoint three disinterested persons, one of whom shall be a competent civil and drainage engineer recommended by the Department of Environment and Natural Resources, and the other two of whom shall be resident freeholders of the county or counties in which the road and lands are, in whole or in part, located, as commissioners, who shall, before entering upon the discharge of their duties, be sworn to do justice between the parties. (1925, c. 85, s. 3; c. 122, s. 44; 1933, c. 172, s. 17; 1957, c. 65, s. 11; 1973, c. 507, s. 5; c. 1262, s. 86; 1977, c. 464, s. 7.1; c. 771, s. 4; 1989, c. 727, s. 218(88); 1997-443, s. 11A.119(a).)

§ 136-22. View by commissioners; report; judgment.

The commissioners, or a majority of them, one of whom must be the engineer aforesaid, shall, on a day of which each party is to be notified at least five days in advance, meet on the premises, and view the highway, or proposed highway, and also the lands which may be drained by the proposed canal, and shall determine and report what lands will be drained and benefited by the construction, enlargement or improvement of such canal, and whether said drainage ought to be done exclusively by said highway authorities, and if they are of opinion that the same ought not to be drained exclusively at their expense, then they shall decide and determine the route of the canal, the dimensions and character thereof, and the manner in which the same shall be cut or thrown up, considering all the circumstances of the case, the extent, area and identity of lands which shall be permitted to drain therein, and providing as far as possible for the effectual drainage of said highway, and the protection and benefit of the lands of all the parties; and they shall apportion the cost of the construction, repair and maintenance of said canal among said highway authorities and said landowners, and report the same to the court, which when confirmed by the clerk shall stand as a judgment of the court against each of the parties, his or its executors, administrators, heirs, assigns or successors. (1925, c. 85, s. 4.)

§ 136-23. Appeal.

Upon the entry of the judgment or decree aforesaid the parties to said action, or any of them, shall have the right to appeal to the superior court in term time under the same rules and regulations as apply to other special proceedings. (1925, c. 85, s. 5.)

§ 136-24. Rights of parties.

The parties to such special proceeding shall have all the rights which are secured to similar parties by Article 1 of Chapter 146 of this Code and shall be regulated by the provisions thereof and amendments thereto, insofar as the same are not inconsistent herewith. (1925, c. 85, s. 6.)

§ 136-25. Repair of road detour.

It shall be mandatory upon the Department of Transportation, its officers and employees, or any contractor or subcontractor employed by the said Department of Transportation, to select, lay out, maintain and keep in as good repair as possible suitable detours by the most practical route while said highways or roads are being improved or constructed, and it shall be mandatory upon the said Department of Transportation and its employees or contractors to place or cause to be placed explicit directions to the traveling public during repair of said highway or road under the process of construction. All expense of laying out and maintaining said detours shall be paid out of the State Highway Fund. (1921, c. 2, s. 11; C.S., s. 3846(s); 1933, c. 172, s. 17; 1957, c. 65, s. 11; 1973, c. 507, s. 5; 1977, c. 464, s. 7.1.)

§ 136-26. Closing of State transportation infrastructure during construction; injury to barriers, warning signs, etc.

If it shall appear necessary to the Department of Transportation, its officers, or appropriate employees, to close any transportation infrastructure coming under its jurisdiction so as to permit proper completion of work which is being performed, the Department of Transportation, its officers or employees, may close, or cause to be closed, the whole or any portion of transportation infrastructure deemed necessary to be excluded from public travel. While any transportation infrastructure, or portion thereof, is so closed, or while any transportation infrastructure, or portion thereof, is in process of construction or maintenance, the Department of Transportation, its officers or appropriate employees, or its contractor, under authority from the Department of Transportation, may erect, or cause to be erected, suitable barriers or obstruction thereon; may post, or cause to be posted, conspicuous notices to the effect that the transportation infrastructure, or portion thereof, is closed; and may place warning signs, lights and lanterns on transportation infrastructure, or portions thereof. When infrastructure is closed to the public or in process of construction or maintenance, as provided herein, any person who willfully drives into new construction work, breaks down, removes, injures or destroys any such barrier or barriers or obstructions on the road closed or being constructed, or tears down, removes or destroys any such notices, or extinguishes, removes, injures or destroys any such warning lights or lanterns so erected, posted or placed, shall be guilty of a Class 1 misdemeanor. (1921, c. 2, s. 12; C.S., s. 3846(t); 1933, c. 172, s. 17; 1957, c. 65, s. 11; 1973, c. 507, s. 5; 1977, c. 464, s. 7.1; 1993, c. 539, s. 980; 2009-266, s. 10.)

§ 136-27. Connection of highways with improved streets; pipelines and conduits; cost.

When any portion of the State highway system shall run through any city or town and it shall be found necessary to connect the State highway system with improved streets of such city or town as may be designated as part of such system, the Department of Transportation shall build such connecting links, the same to be uniform in dimensions and materials with such State highways: Provided, however, that whenever any city or town may desire to widen its streets which may be traversed by the State highway, the Department of Transportation may make such arrangements with said city or town in connection with the construction of said road as, in its discretion, may seem wise and just under all the facts and circumstances in connection therewith: Provided further, that such city or town shall save the Department of Transportation harmless from any claims for damage arising from the construction of said road through such city or town and including claims for rights-of-way, change of grade line, and interference with public-service structures. And the Department of Transportation may require such city or town to cause to be laid all water, sewer, gas or other pipelines or conduits, together with all necessary house or lot connections or services, to the curb line of such road or street to be constructed: Provided further, that whenever by agreement with the road governing body of any city or town any street designated as a part of the State highway system shall be surfaced by order of the Department of Transportation at the expense, in whole or in part, of a city or town it shall be lawful for the governing body of such city or town to declare an assessment district as to the street to be improved, without petition by the owners of property abutting thereon, and the costs thereof, exclusive of so much of the cost as is incurred at street intersections and the share of railroads or street railways whose tracks are laid in said street, which shall be assessed under their franchise, shall be specially assessed upon the lots or parcels of land abutting directly on the improvements, according to the extent of their respective frontage thereon by an equal rate per foot of such frontage. (1921, c. 2, s. 16; 1923, c. 160, s. 4; C.S., s. 3846(ff); 1933, c. 172, s. 17; 1957, c. 65, s. 11; 1973, c. 507, s. 5; 1977, c. 464, s. 7.1.)

§ 136-27.1. Relocation of water and sewer lines of municipalities and nonprofit water or sewer corporations or associations.

The Department of Transportation shall pay the nonbetterment cost for the relocation of water and sewer lines, located within the existing State transportation project right-of-way, that are necessary to be relocated for a State transportation improvement project and that are owned by: (i) a municipality with a population of 5,500 or less according to the latest decennial census; (ii) a nonprofit water or sewer association or corporation; (iii) any water or sewer system organized pursuant to Chapter 162A of the General Statutes; (iv) a rural water system operated by a County as an enterprise system; (v) any sanitary district organized pursuant to Part 2 of Article 2 of Chapter 130A of the General Statutes; or (vi) constructed by a water or sewer system organized pursuant to Chapter 162A of the General Statutes and then sold or transferred to a municipality with a population of greater than 5,500 according to the latest decennial census. (1983 (Reg. Sess., 1984), c. 1090; 1985, c. 479, s. 186(a); 1985 (Reg. Sess., 1986), c. 1018, s. 11; 1993 (Reg. Sess., 1994), c. 736, s. 1; 1995, c. 33, s. 1; c. 266, s. 1.1; 2009-266, s. 11.)

§ 136-27.2. Relocation of county-owned natural gas lines located on Department of Transportation right-of-way.

The Department of Transportation shall pay the nonbetterment cost for the relocation of county-owned natural gas lines, located within the existing State transportation project right-of-way, that the Department needs to relocate due to a State transportation improvement project. (2002-126, s. 26.18(a); 2009-266, s. 12.)

§ 136-27.3. Relocation of municipalities' utilities by Department; repayment by municipalities.

When requiring municipalities to relocate utilities under its power granted in G.S. 136-18(10), the Department may enter into agreements with municipalities to provide that the necessary engineering and utility construction be accomplished by the Department on a reimbursement basis as follows:

(1) Reimbursement to the Department shall be due after completion of the work and within 60 days after date of invoice.

(2) Interest shall be paid on any unpaid balance due at a variable rate of the prime rate plus one percent (1%). (2012-142, s. 24.22; 2012-145, s. 6.1.)

§ 136-27.4. Use of certain right-of-way for sidewalk dining.

(a) The Department may enter into an agreement with any local government permitting use of the State right-of-way associated with components of the State highway system and located within the zoning jurisdiction of the local government for sidewalk dining activities. For purposes of this section, "sidewalk dining activities" means serving food and beverages from a restaurant abutting State right-of-way to customers seated in the State right-of-way. The agreement between the Department and the local government shall provide that the local government is granted the administrative right to permit sidewalk dining activities that, at a minimum, comply with all of the following requirements and conditions:

(1) Tables, chairs, and other furnishings shall be placed a minimum of six feet from any travel lane.

(2)   Tables, chairs, and other furnishings shall be placed in such a manner that at least five feet of unobstructed paved space of the sidewalk, measured from any permanent or semi-permanent object, remains clear for the passage of pedestrians and provides adequate passing space that complies with the Americans with Disabilities Act.

(3)   Tables, chairs, and other furnishings shall not obstruct any driveway, alleyway, building entrance or exit, emergency entrance or exit, fire hydrant or standpipe, utility access, ventilations areas, or ramps necessary to meet accessibility requirements under the Americans with Disabilities Act.

(4)   The maximum posted speed permitted on the roadway adjacent to the right-of-way to be used for sidewalk dining activities shall not be greater than 45 miles per hour.

(5)   The restaurant operator shall provide evidence of adequate liability insurance in an amount satisfactory to the local government, but in no event in an amount less than the amount specified by the local government under G.S. 160A-485 as the limit of the local government's waiver of immunity or the amount of Tort Claim liability specified in G.S. 143-299.2, whichever is greater. The insurance shall protect and name the Department and the local government as additional insureds on any policies covering the business and the sidewalk activities.

(6)   The restaurant operator shall provide an agreement to indemnify and hold harmless the Department or the local government from any claim resulting from the operation of sidewalk dining activities.

(7)   The restaurant operator shall provide a copy of all permits and licenses issued by the State, county or city, including health and ABC permits, if any, necessary for the operation of the restaurant or business, or a copy of the application for the permit if no permit has been issued. This requirement includes any permits or certificates issued by the county or city for exterior alterations or improvements to the restaurant.

(8)   The restaurant operator shall cease part or all sidewalk dining activities in order to allow construction, maintenance, or repair of any street, sidewalk, utility, or public building, by the Department, the local government, its agents or employees, or by any other governmental entity or public utility.

(9) Any other requirements deemed necessary by the Department, either for a particular local government or a particular component of the State highway system.

A local government given the administrative right to permit sidewalk dining activities under this section may impose additional requirements on a case-by-case basis, and nothing in this section requires the local government to issue or maintain any permit for sidewalk dining activities if, in the opinion of the local government, such activities cannot be conducted in a safe manner. Nothing in this section requires the Department to give a local government the right to establish a permit program for sidewalk dining activities if, in the opinion of the Department, such activities cannot be conducted in a safe manner.

(b) A municipality applying to the Department for administrative rights under this section shall:

(1) Enact an ordinance consistent with, but not necessarily limited to, the requirements of this section.

(2) For applications along a federal-aid route or where the laws of the United States otherwise require, obtain permission from the Federal Highway Administration to permit the right-of-way to be used for the sidewalk dining. (2013-266, s. 2.)

§ 136-28. Repealed by Session Laws 1971, c. 972, s. 6.

§ 136-28.1. Letting of contracts to bidders after advertisement; exceptions.

(a) All contracts over two million five hundred thousand dollars ($2,500,000) that the Department of Transportation may let for construction, maintenance, operations, or repair necessary to carry out the provisions of this Chapter shall be let to a responsible bidder after public advertising under rules and regulations to be made and published by the Department of Transportation. The right to reject any and all bids shall be reserved to the Board of Transportation. Contracts for construction or repair for federal aid projects entered into pursuant to this section shall not contain the standardized contract clauses prescribed by 23 U.S.C. § 112(e) and 23 C.F.R. § 635.109 for differing site conditions, suspensions of work ordered by the engineer or significant changes in the character of the work. For those federal aid projects, the Department of

Transportation shall use only the contract provisions for differing site conditions, suspensions of work ordered by the engineer, or significant changes in the character of the work developed by the North Carolina Department of Transportation and approved by the Board of Transportation.

(b) For contracts let to carry out the provisions of this Chapter in which the amount of work to be let to contract for transportation infrastructure construction or repair is two million five hundred thousand dollars ($2,500,000) or less, and for transportation infrastructure maintenance, excluding resurfacing, that is two million five hundred thousand dollars ($2,500,000) per year or less, at least three informal bids shall be solicited. The term "informal bids" is defined as bids in writing, received pursuant to a written request, without public advertising. All such contracts shall be awarded to the lowest responsible bidder. The Secretary of Transportation shall keep a record of all bids submitted, which record shall be subject to public inspection at any time after the bids are opened.

(c) The construction, maintenance, and repair of ferryboats and all other marine floating equipment and the construction and repair of all types of docks by the Department of Transportation shall be deemed highway construction, maintenance, or repair for the purpose of G.S. 136-28.1 and Chapter 44A and Chapter 143C of the General Statutes, the State Budget Act. In cases of a written determination by the Secretary of Transportation that the requirement for compatibility does not make public advertising feasible for the repair of ferryboats, the public advertising as well as the soliciting of informal bids may be waived.

(d) The construction, maintenance, and repair of the highway rest area buildings and facilities, weight stations and the Department of Transportation's participation in the construction of welcome center buildings shall be deemed highway construction, maintenance, or repair for the purpose of G.S. 136-28.1 and 136-28.3 and Chapter 143C of the General Statutes, the State Budget Act.

(e) The Department of Transportation may enter into contracts for construction, maintenance, or repair without complying with the bidding requirements of this section upon a determination of the Secretary of Transportation or the Secretary's designee that an emergency exists and that it is not feasible or not in the public interest for the Department of Transportation to comply with the bidding requirements.

(f) Notwithstanding any other provision of law, the Department of Transportation may solicit proposals under rules and regulations adopted by the

Department of Transportation for all contracts for professional engineering services and other kinds of professional or specialized services necessary in connection with the planning, design, maintenance, repair, and construction of transportation infrastructure. In order to promote engineering and design quality and ensure maximum competition by professional firms of all sizes, the Department may establish fiscal guidelines and limitations necessary to promote cost-efficiencies in overhead, salary, and expense reimbursement rates. The right to reject any and all proposals is reserved to the Board of Transportation.

(g) The Department of Transportation may enter into contracts for research and development with educational institutions and nonprofit organizations without soliciting bids or proposals.

(h) The Department of Transportation may enter into contracts for applied research and experimental work without soliciting bids or proposals; provided, however, that if the research or work is for the purpose of testing equipment, materials, or supplies, the provisions of Article 3 of Chapter 143 of the General Statutes shall apply. However, the Department of Transportation shall: (i) submit all proposed contracts for supplies, materials, printing, equipment, and contractual services that exceed one million dollars ($1,000,000) authorized by this subsection to the Attorney General or the Attorney General's designee for review as provided in G.S. 114-8.3; and (ii) include in all proposed contracts to be awarded by the Department of Transportation under this subsection a standard clause which provides that the State Auditor and internal auditors of the Department of Transportation may audit the records of the contractor during and after the term of the contract to verify accounts and data affecting fees and performance. The Department of Transportation shall not award a cost plus percentage of cost agreement or contract for any purpose. The Department of Transportation is encouraged to solicit proposals when contracts are entered into with private firms when it is in the public interest to do so.

(i) The Department of Transportation may negotiate and enter into contracts with public utility companies for the lease, purchase, installation, and maintenance of generators for electricity for its ferry repair facilities.

(j) Repealed by Session Laws 2002-151, s. 1, effective October 9, 2002.

(k) The Department of Transportation may accept bids under this section by electronic means and may issue rules governing the acceptance of these bids. For purposes of this subsection "electronic means" is defined as means relating to technology having electrical, digital, magnetic, wireless, optical, electromagnetic, or similar capabilities.

(l) The Department of Transportation may enter into contracts for public-private participation in providing litter removal from State right-of-way. Selection of firms to perform this work shall be made using a best value procurement process and shall be without regard to other provisions of law regarding the Adopt-A-Highway Program administered by the Department. Acknowledgement of sponsors may be indicated by appropriate signs that shall be owned by the Department of Transportation. The size, style, specifications, and content of the signs shall be determined in the sole discretion of the Department of Transportation. The Department of Transportation may issue guidelines, rules, and policies necessary to administer this subsection.

(m) The Department of Transportation may enter into contracts for public-private participation at State-owned rest areas. Selection of firms shall be made using a best value procurement process. Recognition of sponsors in the program may be indicated by appropriate acknowledgment for any services provided. The size, style, specifications, and content of the acknowledgment shall be determined in the sole discretion of the Department. Revenues generated pursuant to a contract initiated under this subsection shall be shared with Department of Transportation at a predetermined percentage or rate, and shall be earmarked by the Department to maintain the State owned rest areas from which the revenues are generated. The Department of Transportation may issue guidelines, rules, and policies necessary to administer this subsection. (1971, c. 972, s. 1; 1973, c. 507, ss. 5, 16; c. 1194, ss. 4, 5; 1977, c. 464, ss. 7.1, 16; 1979, c. 174; 1981, c. 200, ss. 1, 2; c. 859, s. 68; 1985, c. 122, s. 2; 1985 (Reg. Sess., 1986), c. 955, s. 46; c. 1018, s. 2; 1987, c. 400; 1989, c. 78; c. 749, ss. 2, 3; 1995, c. 167, s. 1; 1997-196, s. 1; 1999-25, ss. 2, 3; 2001-424, ss. 27.9(a), 27.9(b); 2002-151, s. 1; 2006-68, s. 1; 2006-203, s. 75; 2007-439, ss. 3, 4; 2009-266, s. 1; 2009-475, s. 12; 2010-194, s. 19; 2011-145, s. 28.3; 2011-326, s. 15(t); 2013-340, s. 2.1.)

§ 136-28.2. Relocated transportation infrastructure; contracts let by others.

The Department of Transportation is authorized to permit power companies and governmental agencies, including agencies of the federal government, when it is necessary to relocate transportation infrastructure by reason of the construction of a dam, to let contracts for the construction of the relocated transportation infrastructure. The construction shall be in accordance with the Department of Transportation standards and specifications. The Department of Transportation is further authorized to reimburse the power company or governmental agency for betterments arising out of the construction of the relocated transportation infrastructure, provided the bidding and the award is in accordance with the Department of Transportation's regulations and the Department of Transportation approves the award of the contract. (1971, c. 972, s. 2; 1973, c. 507, s. 5; 1977, c. 464, s. 7.1; 2009-266, s. 13.)

§ 136-28.3. Repealed by Session Laws 1973, c. 1194, s. 6.

§ 136-28.4. (Expires August 31, 2014) State policy concerning participation by disadvantaged minority-owned and women-owned businesses in transportation contracts.

(a)   It is the policy of this State, based on a compelling governmental interest, to encourage and promote participation by disadvantaged minority-owned and women-owned businesses in contracts let by the Department pursuant to this Chapter for the planning, design, preconstruction, construction, alteration, or maintenance of State transportation infrastructure and in the procurement of materials for these projects. All State agencies, institutions, and political subdivisions shall cooperate with the Department of Transportation and among themselves in all efforts to conduct outreach and to encourage and promote the use of disadvantaged minority-owned and women-owned businesses in these contracts.

(b)   At least every five years, the Department shall conduct a study on the availability and utilization of disadvantaged minority-owned and women-owned business enterprises and examine relevant evidence of the effects of race-based or gender-based discrimination upon the utilization of such business enterprises in contracts for planning, design, preconstruction, construction, alteration, or maintenance of State transportation infrastructure and in the procurement of materials for these projects. Should the study show a strong basis in evidence of ongoing effects of past or present discrimination that prevents or limits disadvantaged minority-owned and women-owned businesses from participating in the above contracts at a level which would have existed absent such discrimination, such evidence shall constitute a basis for the State's continued compelling governmental interest in remedying such race and gender discrimination in transportation contracting. Under such circumstances, the Department shall, in conformity with State and federal law, adopt by rule and contract provisions a specific program to remedy such discrimination. This specific program shall, to the extent reasonably practicable, address each barrier identified in such study that adversely affects contract participation by disadvantaged minority-owned and women-owned businesses.

(b1) Based upon the findings of the Department's 2009 study entitled "Measuring Business Opportunity: A Disparity Study of NCDOT's State and Federal Programs" hereinafter referred to as "Study", the program design shall, to the extent reasonably practicable, incorporate narrowly tailored remedies identified in the Study, and the Department shall implement a comprehensive antidiscrimination enforcement policy. As appropriate, the program design shall be modified by rules adopted by the Department that are consistent with findings made in the Study and in subsequent studies conducted in accordance with subsection (b) of this section. As part of this program, the Department shall review its budget and establish aspirational goals every three years, not mandatory goals, in percentages, for the overall participation in contracts by disadvantaged minority-owned and women-owned businesses. These aspirational goals for disadvantaged minority-owned and women-owned businesses shall be established consistent with federal methodology, and they shall not be applied rigidly on specific contracts or projects. Instead, the Department shall establish contract-specific goals or project-specific goals for the participation of such firms in a manner consistent with availability of disadvantaged minority-owned and women-owned businesses, as appropriately defined by its most recent Study, for each disadvantaged minority-owned and women-owned business category that has demonstrated significant disparity in contract utilization. Nothing in this section shall authorize the use of quotas. Any program implemented as a result of the Study conducted in accordance with this section shall be narrowly tailored to eliminate the effects of historical and continuing discrimination and its impacts on such disadvantaged minority-owned and women-owned businesses without any undue burden on other contractors. The Department shall give equal opportunity for contracts it lets without regard to race, religion, color, creed, national origin, sex, age, or handicapping condition, as defined in G.S. 168A-3, to all contractors and businesses otherwise qualified.

(c) The following definitions apply in this section:

(1)   "Contract" includes, but is not limited to, contracts let under the procedures set forth in G.S. 136-28.1(a) and (b).

(1a)   "Disadvantaged Business" has the same meaning as "disadvantaged business enterprise" in 49 C.F.R. § 26.5 Subpart A or any subsequently promulgated replacement regulation.

(2)   "Minority" includes only those racial or ethnicity classifications identified by a study conducted in accordance with this section that have been subjected to discrimination in the relevant marketplace and that have been adversely affected in their ability to obtain contracts with the Department.

(3)   "Women" means nonminority persons born of the female sex.

(d)   The Department shall report annually to the Joint Legislative Transportation Oversight Committee on the utilization of disadvantaged minority-owned businesses and women-owned businesses and any program adopted to promote contracting opportunities for those businesses. Following each study of availability and utilization, the Department shall report to the Joint Legislative Transportation Oversight Committee on the results of the study for the purpose of determining whether the provisions of this section should continue in force and effect.

(e)   This section expires August 31, 2014. (1983, c. 692, s. 3; 1989, c. 692, s. 1.5; 1989 (Reg. Sess., 1990), c. 1066, s. 143(a); 2006-261, s. 4; 2009-266, s. 3; 2010-165, s. 9; 2013-340, s. 2.2.)

§ 136-28.5. Construction diaries; bid analysis and management system.

(a)   Diaries kept in connection with construction or repair contracts entered into pursuant to G.S. 136-28.1 shall not be considered public records for the purposes of Chapter 132 of the General Statutes until the final estimate has been paid.

(b)   Analyses generated by the Department of Transportation's Bid Analysis and Management System, including work papers, documents and the output of automated systems associated with the analyses of bids made by the Bid Analysis and Management System, are confidential and are not subject to the public records provisions of Chapter 132 of the General Statutes.

(c) Notwithstanding G.S. 132-1, bids and documents submitted in response to an advertisement or request for proposal under this Chapter shall not be public record until the Department issues a decision to award or not to award the contract. (1987, c. 380, s. 1; 1991, c. 716, s. 1; 2012-78, s. 11.)

§ 136-28.6. Participation by the Department of Transportation with private developers.

(a) The Department of Transportation may participate in private engineering and construction contracts for State transportation systems.

(b) In order to qualify for State participation, the project must be:

(1) The construction of a transportation project on the Transportation Improvement Plan adopted by the Department of Transportation; or

(2) The construction of a transportation project on a mutually adopted transportation plan that is designated a Department of Transportation responsibility.

(c) Only those projects in which the right-of-way is furnished without cost to the Department of Transportation are eligible.

(d) The Department's participation shall be limited to fifty percent (50%) of the amount of any engineering contract and/or any construction contract let for the project.

(e) Department of Transportation participation in the contracts shall be limited to cost associated with normal practices of the Department of Transportation.

(f) Plans for the project must meet Department of Transportation standards and shall be approved by the Department of Transportation.

(g) Projects shall be constructed in accordance with the plans and specifications approved by the Department of Transportation.

(h) The Secretary shall report in writing, on a quarterly basis, to the Joint Legislative Commission on Governmental Operations on all agreements entered into between a private developer and the Department of Transportation for participation in private engineering and construction contracts under this section.

(i) Counties and municipalities may participate financially in private engineering, land acquisition, and construction contracts for transportation projects which meet the requirements of subsection (b) of this section within their jurisdiction.

(j) The Department is authorized to create a statewide pilot program for participation in cost-sharing for transportation improvements in connection with driveway permits. The Department may create a fair share allocation formula and other procedures to facilitate the pilot program. The formula shall uniformly determine the value of transportation improvements and apportion these costs, on a project-by-project basis, among applicable parties, including the Department and private property developers. Transportation improvement projects developed under the pilot program may include the provision of ingress and egress to new private development prior to acceptance of the improved portion of the roads constructed providing access to the development by the State or local government for maintenance as a public street or highway. Nothing in this section shall require a private developer to participate in the pilot program to obtain a driveway permit or other approval from the Department or any local government.

(k) Nothing in this section shall obligate the Department to custodial responsibility for managing or distributing monies in the application of this program.

(l) The Department shall report on the pilot program to the Joint Legislative Commission on Governmental Operations and the Fiscal Research Division of the Legislative Services Commission no later than the convening date of the 2021 Regular Session of the General Assembly. (1987, c. 860, ss. 1, 2; 1989, c. 749, s. 1; 1991, c. 272, s. 1; 1993, c. 183, s. 1; 1995, c. 358, s. 5; c. 437, s. 3; c. 447, ss. 1, 2; 2002-170, s. 1; 2008-164, s. 2; 2009-266, s. 14; 2013-245, s. 1.)

§ 136-28.6A. Expired, pursuant to Session Laws 2009-235, s. 2, effective December 31, 2011.

§ 136-28.7. Contract requirements relating to construction materials.

(a) The Department of Transportation shall require that every contract for construction or repair necessary to carry out the provisions of this Chapter shall contain a provision requiring that all steel and iron permanently incorporated into the construction or repair project be produced in the United States.

(b) Subsection (a) shall not apply whenever the Department of Transportation determines in writing that this provision required by subsection (a) cannot be complied with because such products are not produced in the United States in sufficient quantities to meet the requirements of such contracts or cannot be complied with because the cost of such products produced in the United States unreasonably exceeds other such products.

(c) The Department of Transportation shall apply this section consistent with the requirements in 23 C.F.R. § 635.410(b)(4).

(d) The Department of Transportation shall not authorize, provide for, or make payments to any person pursuant to any contract containing the provision required by subsection (a) unless such person has fully complied with such provision. (1989, c. 692, s. 1.18; c. 770, ss. 74.12, 74.14, 74.15; 2002-151, s. 3.)

§ 136-28.8. Use of recycled materials in construction.

(a) It is the intent of the General Assembly that the Department of Transportation continue to expand its use of recycled materials in its construction and maintenance programs.

(b) The General Assembly declares it to be in the public interest to find alternative ways to use certain recycled materials that currently are part of the solid waste stream and that contribute to problems of declining space in landfills. The Department shall, consistent with economic feasibility and applicable engineering and environmental quality standards, use:

(1) Rubber from tires in road pavements, subbase materials, or other appropriate applications.

(2) Recycled materials for guard rail posts, right-of-way fence posts, and sign supports.

(3) Recycling technology, including, but not limited to, hot in-place recycling, in road and highway maintenance.

(4) Recycled asphalt, provided that minimum content standards are met and the material meets minimum specifications for the project.

(c) As a part of its scheduled projects, the Department shall conduct additional research, which may include demonstration projects, on the use of recycled materials in construction and maintenance.

(d) The Department shall review and revise existing bid procedures and specifications to eliminate any procedures and specifications that explicitly discriminate against recycled materials in construction and maintenance, except where the procedures and specifications are necessary to protect the health, safety, and welfare of the people of this State.

(e) The Department shall review and revise its bid procedures and specifications on a continuing basis to encourage the use of recycled materials in construction and maintenance and shall, to the extent economically practicable, require the use of recycled materials.

(f) All agencies shall cooperate with the Department in carrying out the provisions of this section.

(g) On or before October 1 of each year, the Department shall report to the Division of Environmental Assistance and Outreach of the Department of Environment and Natural Resources as to the amounts and types of recycled materials that were specified or used in contracts that were entered into during the previous fiscal year. On or before January 15 of each year, the Division of Environmental Assistance and Outreach shall prepare a summary of this report and submit the summary to the Joint Legislative Commission on Governmental Operations and the Joint Legislative Transportation Oversight Committee. The summary of this report shall also be included in the report required by G.S. 130A-309.06(c).

(h) The Department, in consultation with the Department of Environment and Natural Resources, shall determine minimum content standards for recycled materials.

(i) This section is broadly applicable to all procurements by the Department if the quality of the product is consistent with the requirements of the bid specifications.

(j) The Department may adopt rules to implement this section. (1989, c. 784, s. 6; 1993, c. 256, s. 3; 1995 (Reg. Sess., 1996), c. 743, s. 9; 1997-443, s. 11A.119(a); 1999-237, s. 27.4; 2001-452, s. 3.6; 2010-31, s. 13.1(e); 2012-8, s. 1; 2012-200, s. 25.)

§ 136-28.9. Retainage - construction contracts.

Notwithstanding the provisions of G.S. 147-69.1, 147-77, 147-80, 147-86.10, and 147-86.11, or any other provision of the law, the Department of Transportation is authorized to enter into trust agreements with banks and contractors for the deposit of retainage and for the payment to contractors of income on these deposits, in connection with transportation construction contracts, in trust accounts with banks in accordance with Department of Transportation regulations, including deposit insurance and collateral requirements. The Department of Transportation may contract with those banks without trust departments in addition to those with trust departments. Funds deposited in any trust account shall be invested only in bonds, securities, certificates of deposits, or other forms of investment authorized by G.S. 147-69.1 for the investment of State funds. The trust agreement may also provide for interest to be paid on uninvested cash balances. (1989 (Reg. Sess., 1990), c. 1074, s. 38; 2009-266, s. 15.)

§ 136-28.10. Highway Fund and Highway Trust Fund Small Project Bidding.

(a) Notwithstanding the provisions of G.S. 136-28.4(b), for Highway Fund or Highway Trust Fund construction and repair projects of five hundred thousand dollars ($500,000) or less, and maintenance projects of five hundred thousand dollars ($500,000) or less per year, the Board of Transportation may, after soliciting at least three informal bids in writing from Small Business Enterprises, award contracts to the lowest responsible bidder. The Department of Transportation may identify projects likely to attract increased participation by Small Business Enterprises, and restrict the solicitation and award to those bidders. The Board of Transportation may delegate full authority to award contracts, adopt necessary rules, and administer the provisions of this section to the Secretary of Transportation.

(b)   The letting of contracts under this section is not subject to any of the provisions of G.S. 136-28.1 relating to the letting of contracts. The Department may waive the bonding requirements of Chapter 44A of the General Statutes and the licensing requirements of Chapter 87 for contracts awarded under this section.

(c)   The Secretary of Transportation shall report quarterly to the Joint Legislative Transportation Oversight Committee on the implementation of this section. (1993, c. 561, s. 65; 1999-25, s. 1; 2009-266, s. 2.)

§ 136-28.11. Design-build construction of transportation projects.

(a)   Design-Build Contracts Authorized. - Notwithstanding any other provision of law, the Board of Transportation may award contracts each fiscal year for construction of transportation projects on a design-build basis.

(b)   Design-Build Contract Amounts; Basis of Award. - The Department may award contracts for the construction of transportation projects on a design-build basis of any amount. The Department shall endeavor to ensure design-build projects are awarded on a basis to maximize participation, competition, and cost benefit. On any project for which the Department proposes to use the design-build contracting method, the Department shall attempt to structure and size the contracts for the project in order that contracting firms and engineering firms based in North Carolina have a fair and equal opportunity to compete for the contracts.

(c)   Disadvantaged Business Participation Goals. - The provisions of G.S. 136-28.4 and 49 C.F.R. Part 26 shall apply to the award of contracts under this section.

(d)   Repealed by Session Laws 2013-360, s. 34.2(c), effective July 1, 2013.

(e)   Reporting Requirements. - The Department, for any proposed design-build project projected to have a construction cost in excess of fifty million dollars ($50,000,000), shall present to the Joint Legislative Transportation Oversight Committee information on the scope and nature of the project and the reasons the development of the project on a design-build basis will best serve the public interest. (2001-424, s. 27.2(a); 2002-151, s. 2; 2007-357, s. 1; 2011-145, s. 28.4; 2013-360, s. 34.2(c).)

§ 136-28.12. Litter removal coordinated with mowing of highway rights-of-way.

The Department of Transportation shall, to the extent practicable, schedule the removal of debris, trash, and litter from highways and highway rights-of-way prior to the mowing of highway rights-of-way. The Department of Transportation shall include as a term of any contract that it enters into for the mowing of a highway right-of-way that the contracting party shall, to the extent practicable, coordinate with the scheduled removal of debris, trash, and litter from the highway and highway right-of-way prior to the mowing of the highway right-of-way. (2001-512, s. 3.)

§ 136-28.13. Participation in the energy credit banking and selling program.

The Department of Transportation shall participate in the energy credit banking and selling program under G.S. 143-58.4 and is eligible to receive proceeds from the Alternative Fuel Revolving Fund under G.S. 143-58.5 to purchase alternative fuel, develop alternative fuel refueling infrastructure, or purchase AFVs as defined in G.S. 143-58.4. (2005-413, s. 2.)

§ 136-28.14. Project contractor licensing requirements.

The letting of contracts under this Chapter for the following types of projects shall not be subject to the licensing requirements of Article 1 of Chapter 87 of the General Statutes:

(1)   Routine maintenance and minor repair of pavements, bridges, roadside vegetation and plantings, drainage systems, concrete sidewalks, curbs, gutters, and rest areas.

(2) Installation and maintenance of pavement markings and markers, ground mounted signs, guardrail, fencing, and roadside vegetation and plantings. (2006-261, s. 1.)

§ 136-28.15. Diesel vehicles purchase warranty requirement.

Every new motor vehicle transferred to or purchased by the Department of Transportation that is designed to operate on diesel fuel shall be covered by an express manufacturer's warranty that allows the use of B-20 fuel, as defined in G.S. 143-58.4. This section does not apply if the intended use, as determined by the Department, of the new motor vehicle requires a type of vehicle for which an express manufacturer's warranty allows the use of B-20 fuel is not available. (2007-420, s. 3.)

§ 136-29. Adjustment and resolution of Department of Transportation contract claim.

(a) A contractor who has completed a contract with the Department of Transportation let in accordance with Article 2 of this Chapter and who has not received the amount he claims is due under the contract may submit a verified written claim to the Secretary of Transportation for the amount the contractor claims is due. The claim shall be submitted within 60 days after the contractor receives his final statement from the Department and shall state the factual basis for the claim.

The Secretary or the Secretary's designee shall investigate a submitted claim within 90 days of receiving the claim or within any longer time period agreed to by the Secretary or the Secretary's designee and the contractor. The contractor may appear before the Secretary or the Secretary's designee, either in person or through counsel, to present facts and arguments in support of the claim. The Secretary or the Secretary's designee may allow, deny, or compromise the claim, in whole or in part. The Secretary or the Secretary's designee shall give the contractor a written statement of the decision on the contractor's claim.

(b) A contractor who is dissatisfied with the Secretary or the Secretary's designee's decision on the contractor's claim may commence a contested case on the claim under Chapter 150B of the General Statutes. The contested case shall be commenced within 60 days of receiving the written statement of the decision.

(c) As to any portion of a claim that is denied by the Secretary or the Secretary's designee, the contractor may, in lieu of the procedures set forth in subsection (b) of this section, within six months of receipt of the final decision, institute a civil action for the sum he claims to be entitled to under the contract by filing a verified complaint and the issuance of a summons in the Superior Court of Wake County or in the superior court of any county where the work under the contract was performed. The procedure shall be the same as in all civil actions except that all issues shall be tried by the judge, without a jury.

(d) The provisions of this section shall be part of every contract let in accordance with Article 2 of this Chapter between the Department of Transportation and a contractor. A provision in a contract that conflicts with this section is invalid. (1939, c. 318; 1947, c. 530; 1957, c. 65, s. 11; 1963, c. 667; 1965, c. 55, s. 11; 1967, c. 873; 1973, c. 507, ss. 5, 17, 18; 1977, c. 464, s. 7.1; 1983, c. 761, s. 191; 1987, c. 847, s. 3; 2009-266, s. 16.)

§ 136-30. Uniform signs and other traffic control devices on highways, streets, and public vehicular areas.

(a) State Highway System. - The Department of Transportation may number and mark highways in the State highway system. All traffic signs and other traffic control devices placed on a highway in the State highway system must conform to the Uniform Manual. The Department of Transportation shall have the power to control all signs within the right-of-way of highways in the State highway system. The Department of Transportation may erect signs directing persons to roads and places of importance.

(b) Municipal Street System. - All traffic signs and other traffic control devices placed on a municipal street system street must conform to the appearance criteria of the Uniform Manual. All traffic control devices placed on a highway that is within the corporate limits of a municipality but is part of the State highway system must be approved by the Department of Transportation.

(c) Public Vehicular Areas. - Except as provided in this subsection, all traffic signs and other traffic control devices placed on a public vehicular area, as defined in G.S. 20-4.01, must conform to the Uniform Manual. The owner of private property that contains a public vehicular area may place on the property a traffic control device, other than a sign designating a parking space for handicapped persons, as defined in G.S. 20-37.5, that differs in material from the uniform device but does not differ in shape, size, color, or any other way from the uniform device. The owner of private property that contains a public vehicular area may place on the property a sign designating a parking space for handicapped persons that differs in material and color from the uniform sign but does not differ in shape, size, or any other way from the uniform device.

(d)   Definition. - As used in this section, the term "Uniform Manual" means the Manual on Uniform Traffic Control Devices for Streets and Highways, published by the United States Department of Transportation, and any supplement to that Manual adopted by the North Carolina Department of Transportation.

(e)   Exception for Public Airport Traffic Signs. - Publicly owned airports, as defined in Chapter 63 of the General Statutes, shall be exempt from the requirements of subsections (b) and (c) of this section with respect to informational and directional signs, but not with respect to regulatory traffic signs. (1921, c. 2, ss. 9(a), 9(b); C.S., ss. 3846(q), 3846(r); 1927, c. 148, s. 54; 1933, c. 172, s. 17; 1957, c. 65, s. 11; 1973, c. 507, s. 5; 1977, c. 464, s. 7.1; 1991, c. 530, s. 1; 1991 (Reg. Sess., 1992), c. 818, s. 2; 1993, c. 51.)

§ 136-30.1. Center line and pavement edge line markings.

(a)   The Department of Transportation shall mark with center lines and edge lines all interstate and primary roads and all paved secondary roads having an average traffic volume of 100 vehicles per day or more, and which are traffic service roads forming a connecting link in the State highway system. The Department of Transportation shall not be required to mark with center and edge lines local subdivision roads, loop roads, dead-end roads of less than one mile in length or roads the major purpose of which is to serve the abutting property, nor shall the Department of Transportation be required to mark with edge lines those roads on which curbing has been installed or which are less than 16 feet in width.

(b)   Whenever the Department of Transportation shall construct a new paved road, relocate an existing paved road, resurface an existing paved road, or pave an existing road which under the provisions of subsection (a) hereof is required to be marked with lines, the Department of Transportation shall, within 30 days from the completion of the construction, resurfacing or paving, mark the said road with the lines required in subsection (a) hereof.

(c) Repealed by Session Laws 1991, c. 530, s. 2. (1969, c. 1172, s. 1; 1973, c. 496, ss. 1, 2; c. 507, s. 5; 1977, c. 464, s. 7.1; 1991, c. 530, s. 2.)

§ 136-30.2. Prohibit the use of high content arsenic glass beads in paint used for pavement marking.

No pavement markings shall be placed on or along any road in the State highway system, in any municipal street system, or on any public vehicular area, as defined in G.S. 20-4.01, that is made from paint that has been mixed, in whole or in part, with reflective glass beads containing more than 75 parts per million inorganic arsenic, as determined by the United States Environmental Protection Agency Method 6010B in conjunction with the United States Environmental Protection Agency Method 3052 modified. (2010-180, s. 17(b).)

§ 136-31: Repealed by Session Laws 1991, c. 530, s. 3.

§ 136-32. Regulation of signs.

(a) Commercial Signs. - No unauthorized person shall erect or maintain upon any highway any warning or direction sign, marker, signal or light or imitation of any official sign, marker, signal or light erected under the provisions of G.S. 136-30, except in cases of emergency. No person shall erect or maintain upon any highway any traffic or highway sign or signal bearing thereon any commercial or political advertising, except as provided in subsections (b) through (e) of this section: Provided, nothing in this section shall be construed to prohibit the erection or maintenance of signs, markers, or signals bearing thereon the name of an organization authorized to erect the same by the Department of Transportation or by any local authority referred to in G.S. 136-31. Any person who shall violate any of the provisions of this section shall be guilty of a Class 1 misdemeanor. The Department of Transportation may remove any signs erected without authority or allowed to remain beyond the deadline established in subsection (b) of this section.

(b) Compliant Political Signs Permitted. - During the period beginning on the 30th day before the beginning date of "one-stop" early voting under G.S. 163-227.2 and ending on the 10th day after the primary or election day, persons may place political signs in the right-of-way of the State highway system as provided in this section. Signs must be placed in compliance with subsection (d) of this section and must be removed by the end of the period prescribed in this subsection.

(c) Definition. - For purposes of this section, "political sign" means any sign that advocates for political action. The term does not include a commercial sign.

(d) Sign Placement. - The permittee must obtain the permission of any property owner of a residence, business, or religious institution fronting the right-of-way where a sign would be erected. Signs must be placed in accordance with the following:

(1) No sign shall be permitted in the right-of-way of a fully controlled access highway.

(2) No sign shall be closer than three feet from the edge of the pavement of the road.

(3) No sign shall obscure motorist visibility at an intersection.

(4) No sign shall be higher than 42 inches above the edge of the pavement of the road.

(5) No sign shall be larger than 864 square inches.

(6) No sign shall obscure or replace another sign.

(e) Penalties for Unlawful Removal of Signs. - It is a Class 3 misdemeanor for a person to steal, deface, vandalize, or unlawfully remove a political sign that is lawfully placed under this section.

(f) Application Within Municipalities. - Pursuant to Article 8 of Chapter 160A of the General Statutes, a city may by ordinance prohibit or regulate the placement of political signs on rights-of-way of streets located within the corporate limits of a municipality and maintained by the municipality. In the absence of an ordinance prohibiting or regulating the placement of political signs on the rights-of-way of streets located within a municipality and maintained by the municipality, the provisions of subsections (b) through (e) of this section shall apply. (1921, c. 2, s. 9(b); C.S., s. 3846(r); 1927, c. 148, ss. 56, 58; 1933, c. 172, s. 17; 1957, c. 65, s. 11; 1973, c. 507, s. 5; 1977, c. 464, s. 7.1; 1991 (Reg. Sess., 1992), c. 1030, s. 39; 1993, c. 539, s. 981; 1994, Ex. Sess., c. 24, s. 14(c); 2011-408, s. 1.)

§ 136-32.1. Misleading signs prohibited.

No person shall erect or maintain within 100 feet of any highway right-of-way any warning or direction sign or marker of the same shape, design, color and size of any official highway sign or marker erected under the provisions of G.S. 136-30, or otherwise so similar to an official sign or marker as to appear to be an official highway sign or marker. Any person who violates any of the provisions of this section is guilty of a Class 1 misdemeanor. (1955, c. 231; 1991 (Reg. Sess., 1992), c. 1030, s. 40; 1993, c. 539, s. 982; 1994, Ex. Sess., c. 24, s. 14(c).)

§ 136-32.2. Placing blinding, deceptive or distracting lights unlawful.

(a) If any person, firm or corporation shall place or cause to be placed any lights, which are flashing, moving, rotating, intermittent or steady spotlights, in such a manner and place and of such intensity:

(1) Which, by the use of flashing or blinding lights, blinds, tends to blind and effectively hampers the vision of the operator of any motor vehicle passing on a public highway; or

(2) Which involves red, green or amber lights or reflectorized material and which resembles traffic signal lights or traffic control signs; or

(3) Which, by the use of lights, reasonably causes the operator of any motor vehicle passing upon a public highway to mistakenly believe that there is approaching or situated in his lane of travel some other motor vehicle or obstacle, device or barricade, which would impede his traveling in such lane;

[he or it] shall be guilty of a Class 3 misdemeanor.

(b) Each 10 days during which a violation of the provisions of this section is continued after conviction therefor shall be deemed a separate offense.

(c) The provisions of this section shall not apply to any lights or lighting devices erected or maintained by the Department of Transportation or other properly constituted State or local authorities and intended to effect or implement traffic control and safety. Nothing contained in this section shall be deemed to prohibit the otherwise reasonable use of lights or lighting devices for advertising or other lawful purpose when the same do not fall within the provisions of subdivisions (1) through (3) of subsection (a) of this section.

(d) The enforcement of this section shall be the specific responsibility and duty of the State Highway Patrol in addition to all other law-enforcement agencies and officers within this State; provided, however, no warrant shall issue charging a violation of this section unless the violation has continued for 10 days after notice of the same has been given to the person, firm or corporation maintaining or owning such device or devices alleged to be in violation of this section. (1959, c. 560; 1973, c. 507, s. 5; 1975, c. 716, s. 5; 1977, c. 464, ss. 7.1, 17; 1993, c. 539, s. 983; 1994, Ex. Sess., c. 24, s. 14(c).)

§ 136-32.3. Litter enforcement signs.

The Department of Transportation shall place signs on the Interstate Highway System notifying motorists of the penalties for littering. The signs shall include the amount of the maximum penalty for littering. The Department of Transportation shall determine the locations of and distance between the signs. (2001-512, s. 4.)

§ 136-33. Damaging or removing signs; rewards.

(a) No person shall willfully deface, damage, knock down or remove any sign posted as provided in G.S. 136-26 or G.S. 136-30.

(b) No person, without just cause or excuse, shall have in his possession any highway sign as provided in G.S. 136-26 or G.S. 136-30.

(b1) Any person violating the provisions of this section shall be guilty of a Class 2 misdemeanor.

(c) The Department of Transportation is authorized to offer a reward not to exceed five hundred dollars ($500.00) for information leading to the arrest and conviction of persons who violate the provisions of this section, such reward to be paid from funds of the Department of Transportation.

(d) The enforcement of this section shall be the specific responsibility and duty of the State Highway Patrol in addition to all other law-enforcement agencies and officers within this State. (1927, c. 148, s. 57; 1971, c. 671; 1973, c. 507, s. 5; 1975, cc. 11, 93, c. 716, s. 7; 1977, c. 464, ss. 7.1, 18; 1991 (Reg. Sess., 1992), c. 1030, s. 41; 1993, c. 539, s. 984; 1994, Ex. Sess., c. 24, s. 14(c).)

§ 136-33.1. Signs for protection of cattle.

Upon written request of any owner of more than five head of cattle, the Department of Transportation shall erect appropriate and adequate signs on any road or highway under the control of the Department of Transportation, such signs to be so worded, designed and located as to give adequate warning of the presence and crossing of cattle. Such signs shall be located at points agreed upon by the owner and the Department of Transportation at points selected to give reasonable warning of places customarily or frequently used by the cattle of said owner to cross said road or highway, and no one owner shall be entitled to demand the placing of signs at more than one point on a single or abutting tracts of land. (1949, c. 812; 1957, c. 65, s. 11; 1973, c. 507, s. 5; 1977, c. 464, s. 7.1.)

§ 136-33.2: Repealed by Session Laws 2007-164, s. 2, effective July 1, 2007.

§ 136-33.2A. Signs marking beginning of reduced speed zones.

If a need to reduce speed in a speed zone is determined to exist by an engineer of the Department, there shall be a sign erected, of adequate size, at least 600 feet in advance of the beginning of any speed zone established by any agency of the State authorized to establish the same, which shall indicate a change in the speed limit. (2007-164, s. 3.)

§ 136-34. Department of Transportation authorized to furnish road equipment to municipalities.

The Department of Transportation is hereby authorized to furnish municipalities road maintenance equipment to aid such municipalities in the maintenance of streets upon such rental agreement as may be agreed upon by the Department of Transportation and the said municipality. Such rental, however, is to be at least equal to the cost of operation, plus wear and tear on such equipment; and the Department of Transportation shall not be required to furnish equipment when to do so would interfere with the maintenance of the streets and highways under the control of the Department of Transportation. (1941, c. 299; 1957, c. 65, s. 11; 1973, c. 507, s. 5; 1977, c. 464, ss. 7.1, 19.)

§ 136-34.1. Department of Transportation authorized to furnish road maintenance materials to municipalities.

The Department of Transportation is authorized, in its discretion, to furnish municipalities road maintenance materials to aid municipalities in the maintenance of streets upon agreement for reimbursement, as may be required by the Department and agreed to by the municipality. The agreement shall provide for reimbursement in an amount at least equal to the cost of the materials, together with the actual reasonable cost of any handling and storage of the materials and of administering the reimbursement agreement, all as solely determined by the Department. In no event shall the Department of Transportation be required to furnish road maintenance materials when, in the sole determination of the Department of Transportation, to do so would interfere with the maintenance of the streets and highways under its control. Notwithstanding any other provision of law, the provision of and reimbursement for materials under this section shall not be deemed a sale for any purpose. (2009-332, s. 3.)

§ 136-35. Cooperation with other states and federal government.

It shall also be the duty of the Department of Transportation, where possible, to cooperate with the state highway commissions of other states and with the federal government in the correlation of roads and other transportation systems so as to form a system of intercounty, interstate, and national highways and transportation systems. The Department of Transportation may enter into reciprocal agreements with other states and the United States Department of Transportation to perform inspection work and to pay reasonable fees for inspection work performed by others in connection with supplies and materials used in transportation construction and repair. (1915, c. 113, s. 12; C.S., s. 3584; 1933, c. 172, s. 17; 1957, c. 65, s. 11; 1973, c. 507, s. 5; 1977, c. 464, s. 7.1; 1985, c. 127; c. 689, s. 31; 2009-266, s. 17.)

§ 136-36. Repealed by Session Laws 1951, c. 260, s. 4.

§ 136-37. Repealed by Session Laws 1959, c. 687, s. 5.

§§ 136-38 through 136-41. Repealed by Sessions Laws 1951, c. 260, s. 4.

§ 136-41.1. Appropriation to municipalities; allocation of funds generally; allocation to Butner.

(a) There is annually appropriated out of the State Highway Fund a sum equal to ten and four-tenths percent (10.4%) of the net amount after refunds that was produced during the fiscal year by the tax imposed under Article 36C of Chapter 105 of the General Statutes and on the equivalent amount of alternative fuel taxed under Article 36D of that Chapter. One-half of the amount appropriated shall be allocated in cash on or before October 1 of each year to the cities and towns of the State in accordance with this section. The second one-half of the amount appropriated shall be allocated in cash on or before January 1 of each year to the cities and towns of the State in accordance with this section.

Seventy-five percent (75%) of the funds appropriated for cities and towns shall be distributed among the several eligible municipalities of the State in the percentage proportion that the population of each eligible municipality bears to the total population of all eligible municipalities according to the most recent annual estimates of population as certified to the Secretary of Revenue by the

State Budget Officer. This annual estimation of population shall include increases in the population within the municipalities caused by annexations accomplished through July 1 of the calendar year in which these funds are distributed. Twenty-five percent (25%) of said fund shall be distributed among the several eligible municipalities of the State in the percentage proportion that the mileage of public streets in each eligible municipality which does not form a part of the State highway system bears to the total mileage of the public streets in all eligible municipalities which do not constitute a part of the State highway system.

It shall be the duty of the mayor of each municipality to report to the Department of Transportation such information as it may request for its guidance in determining the eligibility of each municipality to receive funds under this section and in determining the amount of allocation to which each is entitled. Upon failure of any municipality to make such report within the time prescribed by the Department of Transportation, the Department of Transportation may disregard such defaulting unit in making said allotment.

The funds to be allocated under this section shall be paid in cash to the various eligible municipalities on or before October 1 and January 1 of each year as provided in this section. Provided that eligible municipalities are authorized within the discretion of their governing bodies to enter into contracts for the purpose of maintenance, repair, construction, reconstruction, widening, or improving streets of such municipalities at any time after January 1 of any calendar year in total amounts not to exceed ninety percent (90%) of the amount received by such municipality during the preceding fiscal year, in anticipation of the receipt of funds under this section during the next fiscal year, to be paid for out of such funds when received.

The Department of Transportation may withhold each year an amount not to exceed one percent (1%) of the total amount appropriated for distribution under this section for the purpose of correcting errors in allocations: Provided, that the amount so withheld and not used for correcting errors will be carried over and added to the amount to be allocated for the following year.

The word "street" as used in this section is hereby defined as any public road maintained by a municipality and open to use by the general public, and having an average width of not less than 16 feet. In order to obtain the necessary information to distribute the funds herein allocated, the Department of Transportation may require that each municipality eligible to receive funds under this section submit to it a statement, certified by a registered engineer or surveyor of the total number of miles of streets in such municipality. The Department of Transportation may in its discretion require the certification of mileage on a biennial basis.

(b) For purposes of this section and of G.S. 136-41.2 and 136-41.3, urban service districts defined by the governing board of a consolidated city-county in which street services are provided by the consolidated city-county, as defined by G.S. 160B-2(1), shall be considered eligible municipalities, and the allocations to be made thereby shall be made to the government of the consolidated city-county.

(c) Any funds allocated to the unincorporated area known as the Butner Reservation shall be transferred to the Town of Butner.

(d) Nature. - The General Assembly finds that the revenue distributed under this section is local revenue, not a State expenditure, for the purpose of Section 5(3) of Article III of the North Carolina Constitution. Therefore, the Governor may not reduce or withhold the distribution. (1951, c. 260, s. 2; c. 948, ss. 2, 3; 1953, c. 1127; 1957, c. 65, s. 11; 1963, c. 854, ss. 1, 2; 1969, c. 665, ss. 1, 2; 1971, c. 182, ss. 1-3; 1973, c. 476, s. 193; c. 500, s. 1; c. 507, s. 5; c. 537, s. 6; 1975, c. 513; 1977, c. 464, s. 7.1; 1979, 2nd Sess., c. 1137, s. 50; 1981, c. 690, s. 4; c. 859, s. 9.2; c. 1127, s. 54; 1985 (Reg. Sess., 1986), c. 982, s. 1; 1989, c. 692, s. 1.6; 1995, c. 390, s. 26; c. 461, s. 18; 1997-443, s. 11A.118(a); 2000-165, s. 1; 2002-120, s. 5; 2007-269, s. 13; 2011-145, s. 28.10(a); 2013-183, s. 3.1.)

§ 136-41.2. Eligibility for funds; municipalities incorporated since January 1, 1945.

(a) No municipality shall be eligible to receive funds under G.S. 136-41.1 unless it has conducted the most recent election required by its charter or the general law, whichever is applicable, for the purpose of electing municipal officials. The literal requirement that the most recent required election shall have been held may be waived only:

(1) Where the members of the present governing body were appointed by the General Assembly in the act of incorporation and the date for the first election of officials under the terms of that act has not arrived; or,

(2) Where validly appointed or elected officials have advertised notice of election in accordance with law, but have not actually conducted an election for the reason that no candidates offered themselves for office.

(b) No municipality shall be eligible to receive funds under G.S. 136-41.1 unless it has levied an ad valorem tax for the current fiscal year of at least five cents (5¢) on the one hundred dollars ($100.00) valuation upon all taxable property within its corporate limits, and unless it has actually collected at least fifty percent (50%) of the total ad valorem tax levied for the preceding fiscal year; provided, however, that, for failure to have collected the required percentage of its ad valorem tax levy for the preceding fiscal year:

(1) No municipality making in any year application for its first annual allocation shall be declared ineligible to receive such allocation; and

(2) No municipality shall be declared ineligible to receive its share of the annual allocation to be made in the year 1964.

(c) No municipality shall be eligible to receive funds under G.S. 136-41.1 unless it has formally adopted a budget ordinance in substantial compliance with G.S. 160-410.3, showing revenue received from all sources, and showing that funds have been appropriated for at least two of the following municipal services if the municipality was incorporated with an effective date prior to January 1, 2000, water distribution; sewage collection or disposal; garbage and refuse collection or disposal; fire protection; police protection; street maintenance, construction, or right-of-way acquisition; or street lighting, or at least four of the following municipal services if the municipality was incorporated with an effective date of on or after January 1, 2000: (i) police protection; (ii) fire protection; (iii) solid waste collection or disposal; (iv) water distribution; (v) street maintenance; (vi) street construction or right-of-way acquisition; (vii) street lighting; and (viii) zoning.

(d) The provisions of this section shall not apply to any municipality incorporated prior to January 1, 1945. (1963, c. 854, ss. 3, 3 1/2; 1985 (Reg. Sess., 1986), c. 934, ss. 5, 6; 1999-458, s. 5.)

§ 136-41.2A. Eligibility for funds; municipalities incorporated before January 1, 1945.

(a) No municipality shall be eligible to receive funds under G.S. 136-41.1 unless it has been within the four-year period next preceding the annual allocation of funds conducted an election for the purpose of electing municipal officials and currently imposes an ad valorem tax or provides other funds for the general operating expenses of the municipality.

(b) The provisions of this section apply only to municipalities incorporated prior to January 1, 1945. (1985 (Reg. Sess., 1986), c. 934, s. 4.)

§ 136-41.2B. Eligibility for funds; municipalities with no road miles ineligible.

No municipality shall be eligible to receive funds under G.S. 136-41.1 unless the municipality maintains public streets that (i) are within its jurisdiction and (ii) do not form a part of the State highway system. (2011-145, s. 28.10(b).)

§ 136-41.3. Use of funds; records and annual statement; excess accumulation of funds; contracts for maintenance, etc., of streets.

(a) Uses of Funds. - The funds allocated to cities and towns under the provisions of G.S. 136-41.2 shall be expended by said cities and towns only for the purpose of maintaining, repairing, constructing, reconstructing or widening of any street or public thoroughfare including bridges, drainage, curb and gutter, and other necessary appurtenances within the corporate limits of the municipality or for meeting the municipality's proportionate share of assessments levied for such purposes, or for the planning, construction and maintenance of bikeways, greenways, or sidewalks.

(b) Records and Annual Statement. - Each municipality receiving funds by virtue of G.S. 136-41.1 and 136-41.2 shall maintain a separate record of accounts indicating in detail all receipts and expenditures of such funds. It shall be unlawful for any municipal employee or member of any governing body to authorize, direct, or permit the expenditure of any funds accruing to any municipality by virtue of G.S. 136-41.1 and 136-41.2 for any purpose not herein authorized. Any member of any governing body or municipal employee shall be personally liable for any unauthorized expenditures. On or before the first day of August each year, the treasurer, auditor, or other responsible official of each municipality receiving funds by virtue of G.S. 136-41.1 and 136-41.2 shall file a statement under oath with the Secretary of Transportation showing in detail the expenditure of funds received by virtue of G.S. 136-41.1 and 136-41.2 during the preceding year and the balance on hand.

(c) Excess Accumulation of Funds Prohibited. - No funds allocated to municipalities pursuant to G.S. 136-41.1 and 136-41.2 shall be permitted to accumulate for a period greater than permitted by this section. Interest on accumulated funds shall be used only for the purposes permitted by the provisions of G.S. 136-41.3. Except as otherwise provided in this section, any municipality having accumulated an amount greater than the sum of the past 10 allocations made, shall have an amount equal to such excess deducted from the next allocation after receipt of the report required by this section. Such deductions shall be carried over and added to the amount to be allocated to municipalities for the following year. Notwithstanding the other provisions of this section, the Department shall adopt a policy to allow small municipalities to apply to the Department to be allowed to accumulate up to the sum of the past 20 allocations if a municipality's allocations are so small that the sum of the past 10 allocations would not be sufficient to accomplish the purposes of this section.

(d) Contracts for Maintenance and Construction. - In the discretion of the local governing body of each municipality receiving funds by virtue of G.S. 136-41.1 and 136-41.2 it may contract with the Department of Transportation to do the work of maintenance, repair, construction, reconstruction, widening or improving the streets in such municipality; or it may let contracts in the usual manner as prescribed by the General Statutes to private contractors for the performance of said street work; or may undertake the work by force account. The Department of Transportation within its discretion is hereby authorized to enter into contracts with municipalities for the purpose of maintenance, repair, construction, reconstruction, widening or improving streets of municipalities. And the Department of Transportation in its discretion may contract with any city or town which it deems qualified and equipped so to do that the city or town shall do the work of maintaining, repairing, improving, constructing, reconstructing, or widening such of its streets as form a part of the State highway system.

In the case of each eligible municipality, as defined in G.S. 136-41.2, having a population of less than 5,000, the Department of Transportation shall upon the request of such municipality made by official action of its governing body, on or prior to June 1, 1953, or June 1 in any year thereafter, for the fiscal year beginning July 1, 1953, and for the years thereafter do such street construction, maintenance, or improvement on nonsystem streets as the municipality may request within the limits of the current or accrued payments made to the municipality under the provisions of G.S. 136-41.1.

In computing the costs, the Department of Transportation may use the same rates for equipment, rental, labor, materials, supervision, engineering and other items, which the Department of Transportation uses in making charges to one of its own department or against its own department, or the Department of Transportation may employ a contractor to do the work, in which case the charges will be the contract cost plus engineering and inspection. The municipality is to specify the location, extent, and type of the work to be done, and shall provide the necessary rights-of-way, authorization for the removal of such items as poles, trees, water and sewer lines as may be necessary, holding the Department of Transportation free from any claim by virtue of such items of cost and from such damage or claims as may arise therefrom except from negligence on the part of the Department of Transportation, its agents, or employees.

If a municipality elects to bring itself under the provisions of the two preceding paragraphs, it shall enter into a two-year contract with the Department of Transportation and if it desires to dissolve the contract at the end of any two-year period it shall notify the Department of Transportation of its desire to terminate said contract on or before April 1 of the year in which such contract shall expire; otherwise, said contract shall continue for an additional two-year period, and if the municipality elects to bring itself under the provisions of the two preceding paragraphs and thereafter fails to pay its account to the Department of Transportation for the fiscal year ending June 30, by August 1 following the fiscal year, then the Department of Transportation shall apply the said municipality's allocation under G.S. 136-41.1 to this account until said account is paid and the Department of Transportation shall not be obligated to do any further work provided for in the two preceding paragraphs until such account is paid.

Section 143-129 of the General Statutes relating to the procedure for letting of public contracts shall not be applicable to contracts undertaken by any municipality with the Department of Transportation in accordance with the provisions of the three preceding paragraphs.

(e) Permitted Offsets to Funding. - The Department of Transportation is authorized to apply a municipality's share of funds allocated to a municipality under the provisions of G.S. 136-41.1 to any of the following accounts of the municipality with the said Department of Transportation, which the municipality fails to pay:

(1) Cost sharing agreements for right-of-way entered into pursuant to G.S. 136-66.3, but not to exceed ten percent (10%) of any one year's allocation until the debt is repaid,

(2) The cost of relocating municipally owned waterlines and other municipally owned utilities on a State highway project which is the responsibility of the municipality,

(3) For any other work performed for the municipality by the Department of Transportation or its contractor by agreement between the Department of Transportation and the municipality, and

(4) For any other work performed that was made necessary by the construction, reconstruction or paving of a highway on the State highway system for which the municipality is legally responsible. (1951, c. 260, s. 3; c. 948, s. 4; 1953, c. 1044; 1957, c. 65, s. 11; 1969, c. 665, ss. 3, 4; 1971, c. 182, s. 4; 1973, c. 193; c. 507, s. 5; 1977, c. 464, ss. 7.1, 20; c. 808; 1993 (Reg. Sess., 1994), c. 690, s. 1.1; 2011-145, s. 28.10(d); 2013-183, s. 3.3.)

§ 136-41.4. Municipal use of allocated funds; election.

(a) A municipality that qualifies for an allocation of funds pursuant to G.S. 136-41.1 shall have the following options:

(1) Accept all or a portion of funds allocated to the municipality for use as authorized by G.S. 136-41.3(a).

(2) Use some or all of its allocation to match federal funds administered by the Department for independent bicycle and pedestrian improvement projects within the municipality's limits, or within the area of any metropolitan planning organization or rural transportation planning organization.

(3) Elect to have some or all of the allocation reprogrammed for any Transportation Improvement Project currently on the approved project list within the municipality's limits or within the area of any metropolitan planning organization or rural transportation planning organization.

(b) If a municipality chooses to have its allocation reprogrammed, the amount that may be reprogrammed is an amount equal to that amount necessary to complete one full phase of the project selected by the municipality or an amount that, when added to the amount already programmed for the Transportation Improvement Project selected, would permit the completion of at least one full phase of the project. The restriction set forth in this subsection shall not apply to any bicycle or pedestrian projects. (2007-428, s. 5; 2013-183, s. 3.4.)

§ 136-42. Transferred to G.S. 136-42.2 by Session Laws 1971, c. 345, s. 2.

§ 136-42.1. Archaeological objects on highway right-of-way.

The Department of Transportation is authorized to expend highway funds for reconnaissance surveys, preliminary site examinations and salvage work necessary to retrieve and record data and the preservation of archaeological and paleontological objects of value which are located within the right-of-way acquired for highway construction. The Department of Cultural Resources shall be consulted when objects of scientific or historical significance might be anticipated or encountered in highway right-of-way and a determination made by that Department as to the national, State, or local importance of preserving any or all fossil relics, artifacts, monuments or buildings. The Department of Cultural Resources shall request advice from other agencies or institutions having special knowledge or skills that may not be available in the said Department for the determination of the presence of or for the evaluation and salvage of prehistoric archaeological or paleontological remains within the highway right-of-way. The Department of Transportation is authorized to contract with the Department of Cultural Resources and to provide funds necessary to perform reconnaissance surveys, preliminary site examination and salvage operation at those sites determined by the Department of Cultural Resources to be of sufficient importance to be preserved for the inspiration and benefit of the people of North Carolina. The Department of Cultural Resources is authorized to enter into contracts and to make arrangements to perform the necessary work pursuant to this section. The Department of Cultural Resources shall assume possession and responsibility for any and all historical objects and is authorized to enter into agreements with governmental units and agencies thereof, institutions, and charitable organizations for the preservation of any or all fossil relics, artifacts, monuments, or buildings. (1971, c. 345, s. 1; 1973, c. 476, s. 48; c. 507, s. 5; 1977, c. 464, s. 7.1.)

§ 136-42.2. Markers on highway; cooperation of Department of Transportation.

The Department of Transportation is hereby authorized to cooperate with the Department of Cultural Resources in marking historic spots along the State highways. (1927, c. 226, s. 1; 1933, c. 172, s. 17; 1943, c. 237; 1957, c. 65, s. 11; 1971, c. 345, s. 2; 1973, c. 476, s. 48; c. 507, s. 5; 1977, c. 464, s. 7.1.)

§ 136-42.3. Historical marker program.

The Department of Transportation may spend up to forty thousand dollars ($40,000) a year to purchase historical markers prepared and delivered to it by the Department of Cultural Resources. The Department of Transportation shall erect the markers on sites selected by the Department of Cultural Resources. This expenditure is hereby declared to be a valid expenditure of State highway maintenance funds. No provision in this section shall be construed to prevent the expenditure of any federal highway funds that may be available for this purpose. (1935, c. 197; 1943, c. 237; 1951, c. 766; 1955, c. 543, s. 2; 1957, c. 65, s. 11; 1971, c. 345, s. 2; 1973, c. 476, s. 48; c. 507, s. 5; 1977, c. 464, s. 7.1; 1983 (Reg. Sess., 1984), c. 1034, s. 129.)

§ 136-43. Transferred to § 136-42.3 by Session Laws 1971, c. 345, s. 2.

§ 136-43.1. Procedure for correction and relocation of historical markers.

Any person, firm or corporation who has knowledge or information, supported by historical data, books, records, writings, or other evidence, that any historical marker has been erected at an erroneous or mistaken site, or that the inscription appearing on any historical marker contains erroneous or mistaken information, shall have the privilege of presenting such knowledge or information and supporting evidence to the advisory committee described in the preamble of Public Laws 1935, c. 197 for its consideration. Upon being informed that any person desires to present such information, the Secretary of Cultural Resources shall notify such person of the date, place and time of the next meeting of the advisory committee. Any person, firm or corporation desiring to present such information to the advisory committee shall be allowed to appear before the committee for that purpose.

If, after considering the information and evidence presented, the advisory committee should find that any historical marker has been erected on an erroneous or mistaken site, or that erroneous or mistaken information is contained in the inscription appearing on any historical marker, it shall so inform the Department of Cultural Resources and the Department of Cultural Resources shall cause such marker to be relocated at the correct site, or shall cause the erroneous or mistaken inscription to be corrected, or both as the case may be. (1961, c. 267; 1973, c. 476, s. 48.)

§ 136-44. Maintenance of grounds.

The Department of Transportation is hereby authorized and directed through the highway supervisor of the district that includes Warren County to clean off and keep clean the premises and grounds at the old home of Nathaniel Macon, known as "Buck Springs," which are owned by the County of Warren, and also to look after the care and keeping the grounds surrounding the grave of Miss Anne Carter Lee, daughter of General Robert E. Lee, in Warren County.

The Department of Transportation is authorized and directed through the highway supervisor of the district that includes Pender County to maintain the grounds surrounding the grave of Governor Samuel Ashe in Pender County. (1939, c. 38; 1957, c. 65, s. 11; 1973, c. 507, s. 5; 1977, c. 464, s. 7.1; 2001-487, s. 125.1.)

Article 2A.

State Transportation Generally.

§ 136-44.1. Statewide transportation system; policies.

The Department of Transportation shall develop and maintain a statewide system of roads, highways, and other transportation systems commensurate with the needs of the State as a whole and it shall not sacrifice the general statewide interest to the purely local desires of any particular area. The Board of Transportation shall formulate general policies and plans for a statewide transportation system. The Board shall formulate policies governing the construction, improvement and maintenance of roads, highways, and other transportation systems of the State with due regard to farm-to-market roads and school bus routes. (1973, c. 507, s. 3; 1975, c. 716, s. 7; 2009-266, s. 18.)

§ 136-44.2. (Effective until July 1, 2014) Budget and appropriations.

(a) The Director of the Budget shall include in the "Current Operations Appropriations Act" an enumeration of the purposes or objects of the proposed expenditures for each of the construction, maintenance, and improvement programs for that budget period for the State primary, secondary, State parks road systems, and other transportation systems. The State primary system shall include all portions of the State highway system located both inside and outside municipal corporate limits that are designated by N.C., U.S. or Interstate numbers. The State secondary system shall include all of the State highway system located both inside and outside municipal corporate limits that is not a part of the State primary system. The State parks system shall include all State parks roads and parking lots that are not also part of the State highway system. The transportation systems shall also include State-maintained, nonhighway modes of transportation.

(b) All construction, maintenance, and improvement programs for which appropriations are requested shall be enumerated separately in the budget. Programs that are entirely State funded shall be listed separately from those programs involving the use of federal-aid funds. Proposed appropriations of State matching funds for each of the federal-aid construction programs shall be enumerated separately as well as the federal-aid funds anticipated for each program in order that the total construction requirements for each program may be provided for in the budget. Also, proposed State matching funds for the highway planning and research program shall be included separately along with the anticipated federal-aid funds for that purpose.

(c) Other program categories for which appropriations are requested, such as, but not limited to, maintenance, channelization and traffic control, bridge maintenance, public service and access road construction, transportation projects and systems, and ferry operations shall be enumerated in the budget.

(d) The Department of Transportation shall have all powers necessary to comply fully with provisions of present and future federal-aid acts. For purposes of this section, "federally eligible construction project" means any construction project except secondary road projects developed pursuant to G.S. 136-44.7 and 136-44.8 eligible for federal funds under any federal-aid act, whether or not federal funds are actually available.

(e) The "Current Operations Appropriations Act" shall also contain the proposed appropriations of State funds for use in each county for construction, maintenance, and improvement of secondary roads, to be allocated in accordance with G.S. 136-44.5 and 136-44.6. State funds appropriated for secondary roads shall not be transferred nor used except for the construction, maintenance, and improvement of secondary roads in the county for which they are allocated pursuant to G.S. 136-44.5 and 136-44.6.

(f) If the unreserved credit balance in the Highway Fund on the last day of a fiscal year is greater than the amount estimated for that date in the Current Operations Appropriations Act for the following fiscal year, the excess shall be used in accordance with this subsection. The Director of the Budget shall allocate the excess to a reserve (i) for access and public roads or (ii) for other urgent needs. The use of this reserve shall be subject to the following:

(1) Restrictions on use. - No more than five million dollars ($5,000,000) from this reserve may be spent on a single project. Funds from this reserve being used for an "other urgent need" project cannot be used for administrative costs, information technology costs, or economic development.

(2) Approval. - The Department of Transportation shall submit for approval to the Director of the Budget all expenditures from the reserve established under this subsection.

(3) Reporting. - At least five days, not including State holidays or weekend days, prior to submitting an expenditure request to the Director of the Budget under subdivision (2) of this subsection, the Department of Transportation shall submit a report on the expenditure request to the Fiscal Research Division and to the members of the House Appropriations Subcommittee on Transportation and the Senate Appropriations Committee on Department of Transportation. Such report shall be certified by the chief financial officer of the Department of Transportation and shall include (i) a project description, (ii) whether the project is for access and public roads or for other urgent needs, (iii) a justification of the project, (iv) the total project cost, (v) the amount of funding for the project coming from the reserve, and (vi) other funding sources for the project.

(4) Carryforward. - If on the last day of the fiscal year the balance in the reserve established by this subsection is greater than five million dollars ($5,000,000), then the Director of the Budget shall transfer the amount in excess of that sum to the Reserve for General Maintenance in the Highway Fund.

(g) The Department of Transportation may provide for costs incurred or accrued for traffic control measures to be taken by the Department at major events which involve a high degree of traffic concentration on State highways, and which cannot be funded from regular budgeted items. This authorization applies only to events which are expected to generate 30,000 vehicles or more per day. The Department of Transportation shall provide for this funding by allocating and reserving up to one hundred thousand dollars ($100,000) before any other allocations from the appropriations for State maintenance for primary and secondary road systems are made, based upon the same proportion as is appropriated to each system. (1973, c. 507, s. 3; 1977, c. 464, s. 7.1; 1981, c. 859, s. 84; 1983, c. 717, ss. 46, 47; 1987, c. 830, s. 113(b); 1989, c. 799, s. 12(a); 1991 (Reg. Sess., 1992), c. 907, s. 2; c. 1044, s. 35; 1997-443, s. 32.5; 2005-276, s. 28.1; 2005-382, s. 1; 2009-266, s. 19; 2011-145, s. 28.35(b); 2012-142, s. 24.6; 2013-183, s. 2.2(a).)

§ 136-44.2. (Effective July 1, 2014) Budget and appropriations.

G.S. 136-44.2 is set out twice. See notes.

(a) The Director of the Budget shall include in the "Current Operations Appropriations Act" an enumeration of the purposes or objects of the proposed expenditures for each of the maintenance and improvement programs for that budget period for the State primary, secondary, State parks road systems, and other transportation systems. The State primary system shall include all portions of the State highway system located both inside and outside municipal corporate limits that are designated by N.C., U.S. or Interstate numbers. The State secondary system shall include all of the State highway system located both inside and outside municipal corporate limits that is not a part of the State primary system. The State parks system shall include all State parks roads and parking lots that are not also part of the State highway system. The transportation systems shall also include State-maintained, nonhighway modes of transportation.

(b) All maintenance and improvement programs for which appropriations are requested shall be enumerated separately in the budget. Programs that are entirely State funded shall be listed separately from those programs involving the use of federal-aid funds. Proposed State matching funds for the highway planning and research program shall be included separately along with the anticipated federal-aid funds for that purpose.

(c) Other program categories for which appropriations are requested, such as, but not limited to, maintenance, channelization and traffic control, bridge maintenance, public service and access road construction, transportation projects and systems, and ferry operations shall be enumerated in the budget.

(d) The Department of Transportation shall have all powers necessary to comply fully with provisions of present and future federal-aid acts. For purposes of this section, "federally eligible construction project" means any construction project except secondary road projects developed pursuant to G.S. 136-44.8 eligible for federal funds under any federal-aid act, whether or not federal funds are actually available.

(e) The "Current Operations Appropriations Act" shall also contain the proposed appropriations of State funds for use in each county for maintenance and improvement of secondary roads, to be allocated in accordance with G.S. 136-44.6. State funds appropriated for secondary roads shall not be transferred nor used except for the construction, maintenance, and improvement of secondary roads in the county for which they are allocated pursuant to G.S. 136-44.6.

(f) If the unreserved credit balance in the Highway Fund on the last day of a fiscal year is greater than the amount estimated for that date in the Current Operations Appropriations Act for the following fiscal year, the excess shall be used in accordance with this subsection. The Director of the Budget shall allocate the excess to a reserve (i) for access and public roads or (ii) for other urgent road construction or road maintenance needs. The use of this reserve shall be subject to the following:

(1) Restrictions on use. - No more than five million dollars ($5,000,000) from this reserve may be spent on a single project. Funds from this reserve being used for an "other urgent road construction or road maintenance need" project cannot be used for nontransportation administrative costs, nontransportation information technology costs, or any economic development purpose.

(2) Approval. - The Department of Transportation shall submit for approval to the Director of the Budget all expenditures from the reserve established under this subsection.

(3) Reporting. - At least five days, not including State holidays or weekend days, prior to submitting an expenditure request to the Director of the Budget under subdivision (2) of this subsection, the Department of Transportation shall submit a report on the expenditure request to the Fiscal Research Division and to the members of the House Appropriations Subcommittee on Transportation and the Senate Appropriations Committee on Department of Transportation. Such report shall be certified by the chief financial officer of the Department of Transportation and shall include (i) a project description, (ii) whether the project is for access and public roads or for other urgent needs, (iii) a justification of the project, (iv) the total project cost, (v) the amount of funding for the project coming from the reserve, and (vi) other funding sources for the project.

(4) Carryforward. - If on the last day of the fiscal year the balance in the reserve established by this subsection is greater than five million dollars ($5,000,000), then the Director of the Budget shall transfer the amount in excess of that sum to the Reserve for General Maintenance in the Highway Fund.

(g) The Department of Transportation may provide for costs incurred or accrued for traffic control measures to be taken by the Department at major events which involve a high degree of traffic concentration on State highways, and which cannot be funded from regular budgeted items. This authorization applies only to events which are expected to generate 30,000 vehicles or more per day. The Department of Transportation shall provide for this funding by allocating and reserving up to one hundred thousand dollars ($100,000) before any other allocations from the appropriations for State maintenance for primary and secondary road systems are made, based upon the same proportion as is appropriated to each system. (1973, c. 507, s. 3; 1977, c. 464, s. 7.1; 1981, c. 859, s. 84; 1983, c. 717, ss. 46, 47; 1987, c. 830, s. 113(b); 1989, c. 799, s. 12(a); 1991 (Reg. Sess., 1992), c. 907, s. 2; c. 1044, s. 35; 1997-443, s. 32.5; 2005-276, s. 28.1; 2005-382, s. 1; 2009-266, s. 19; 2011-145, s. 28.35(b); 2012-142, s. 24.6; 2013-125, s. 1; 2013-183, s. 2.2(a), (b).)

§ 136-44.2A. (Repealed effective July 1, 2014 - see note) Secondary road construction program.

There shall be annually allocated from the Highway Fund to the Department of Transportation for secondary road construction programs developed pursuant to G.S. 136-44.8, a sum provided by law. (1981, c. 690, s. 6; 1989, c. 692, s. 1.7; 2005-404, s. 1; 2006-258, s. 1; 2013-183, s. 2.3(a), (b).)

§ 136-44.2B. Reports to appropriations committees of General Assembly.

In each year that an appropriation bill is considered by the General Assembly, the Department of Transportation shall make a report to the appropriations committee of each House on all services provided by the Department to the public for which a fee is charged. The report shall include an analysis of the cost of each service and the fee charged for that service. (1975, c. 875, s. 8; 1981, c. 690, s. 5.)

§ 136-44.2C: Repealed by Session Laws 2013-183, s. 2.4, effective July 1, 2013.

§ 136-44.2D. Secondary unpaved road paving program.

The Department of Transportation shall expend funds allocated to the paving of unpaved secondary roads for the paving of unpaved secondary roads based on a statewide prioritization. The Department shall pave the eligible unpaved secondary roads that receive the highest priority ranking within this statewide prioritization. Nothing in this subsection shall be interpreted to require the Department to pave any unpaved secondary roads that do not meet secondary road system addition standards as set forth in G.S. 136-44.10 and G.S. 136-102.6. The Highway Trust Fund shall not be used to fund the paving of unpaved secondary roads. (2013-183, s. 2.5.)

§ 136-44.3. Maintenance program.

The Department shall establish performance standards for the maintenance and operation of the State highway system. In each even-numbered year, the

Department of Transportation shall survey the condition of the State highway system and shall prepare a report of the findings of the survey. The report shall provide both quantitative and qualitative descriptions of the condition of the system and shall provide estimates of the following:

(1)   The annual cost to meet and sustain the established performance standards for the primary and secondary highway system, to include: (i) routine maintenance and operations, (ii) system preservation, and (iii) pavement and bridge rehabilitation.

(2)   Projected system condition and corresponding optimal funding requirements for a seven-year plan to sustain established performance standards.

(3)   Any significant variations in system conditions among highway divisions.

(4)   An assessment of the level of congestion throughout the primary highway system based on traffic data, and a ranking of the most congested areas based on travel time reliability and the average number of congested hours, together with the Department's recommendations for congestion reduction and mobility improvement.

On the basis of the report and from funds available, the Department of Transportation shall develop a statewide annual maintenance program for the State highway system, which shall be subject to the approval of the Board of Transportation and is consistent with performance standards.

The report on the condition of the State highway system and maintenance funding needs shall be presented to the Joint Legislative Transportation Oversight Committee by December 31 of each even-numbered year, and copies shall be made available to any member of the General Assembly upon request. (1973, c. 507, s. 3; 1975, c. 716, s. 7; 1977, c. 464, s. 39; 1997-443, s. 32.19; 2007-164, s. 1; 2013-360, s. 34.8.)

§ 136-44.4. Annual construction program; State primary and urban systems.

The Department of Transportation shall develop an annual construction program for the state-funded improvements on the primary and urban system highways and for all other federal-aid construction programs which shall be approved by the Board of Transportation. It shall include a statement of the immediate and long-range goals. The Department shall develop criteria for determining priorities of projects to insure that the long-range goals and the statewide needs as a whole are met, which shall be approved by the Board of Transportation. The annual construction program shall list all projects according to priority. A brief description of each project shall be given, identifying the highway number, county, nature of the improvement and the estimated cost of the project shall be indicated. Other transportation systems shall be similarly identified. Copies of the most recent annual work program shall be made available to any member of the General Assembly upon request. The Department of Transportation shall make annual reports after the completion of the fiscal year to be made available to the legislative committees and subcommittees for highway matters, county commissioners, and other persons upon request. These reports shall indicate the expenditure on each of the projects and the status of all projects set out in the work program. (1973, c. 507, s. 3; 1975, c. 716, s. 7; 1977, c. 464, s. 40; 2009-266, s. 21.)

§ 136-44.5. (Repealed effective July 1, 2014 - see note) Secondary roads; mileage study; allocation of funds.

(a)   Before July 1, in each calendar year, the Department of Transportation shall make a study of all State-maintained unpaved and paved secondary roads in the State. The study shall determine:

(1)   The number of miles of unpaved State-maintained roads in each county eligible for paving and the total number of miles that are ineligible;

(2)   The total number of miles of unpaved State-maintained roads in the State eligible for paving and the total number of miles that are ineligible; and

(3)   The total number of paved State-maintained roads in each county, and the total number of miles of paved State-maintained roads in the State.

In this subsection, (i) ineligible unpaved mileage is defined as the number of miles of unpaved roads that have unavailable rights-of-way or for which environmental permits cannot be approved to allow for paving, and (ii) eligible unpaved mileage is defined as the number of miles of unpaved roads that have not been previously approved for paving by any funding source or has the potential to be programmed for paving when rights-of-way or environmental permits are secured. Except for federal-aid programs, the Department shall allocate all secondary road improvement funds on the basis of a formula using the study figures.

(b) The amounts appropriated by law for secondary road construction, excluding unpaved secondary road funds, shall be allocated among counties based on the total number of secondary miles in a county in proportion to the total State-maintained secondary road mileage.

(c), (d) Repealed by Session Laws 2013-183, s. 22.6(a), effective July 1, 2013. (1973, c. 507, s. 3; 1975, c. 716, s. 7; 1989, c. 692, s. 1.8; 2005-404, s. 2; 2006-258, ss. 1, 2; 2013-183, s. 2.6(a), (b).)

§ 136-44.6. Uniformly applicable formula for the allocation of secondary roads maintenance and improvement funds.

The Department of Transportation shall develop a uniformly applicable formula for the allocation of secondary roads maintenance and improvement funds for use in each county. The formula shall take into consideration the number of paved and unpaved miles of state-maintained secondary roads in each county and such other factors as experience may dictate. This section shall not apply to projects to pave unpaved roads under G.S. 136-44.2D. (1973, c. 507, s. 3; 1975, c. 716, s. 7; c. 753; 2013-183, s. 2.6(c).)

§ 136-44.7. Secondary roads; right-of-way acquisition.

(a), (b) Repealed by Session Laws 2013-183, s. 2.7, effective July 1, 2013.

(c) When it is necessary for the Department of Transportation to acquire a right-of-way in order to pave a secondary road or undertake a maintenance project, the Department shall negotiate the acquisition of the right-of-way for a period of up to six months. At the end of that period, if one or more property owners have not dedicated the necessary right-of-way and at least seventy-five percent (75%) of the property owners adjacent to the project and the owners of the majority of the road frontage adjacent to the project have dedicated the necessary property for the right-of-way and have provided funds required by Department rule to the Department to cover the costs of condemning the remaining property, the Department shall initiate condemnation proceedings pursuant to Article 9 of this Chapter to acquire the remaining property necessary for the project.

(d)   The Division Engineer is authorized to reduce the width of a right-of-way to less than 60 feet to pave an unpaved secondary road with the allocated funds, provided that in all circumstances the safety of the public is not compromised and the minimum accepted design practice is satisfied. (1973, c. 507, s. 3; 1975, c. 716, s. 7; 1977, c. 464, s. 8; 1989, c. 692, s. 1.9; 1991 (Reg. Sess., 1992), c. 900, s. 99; 2001-501, s. 2; 2002-86, s. 1; 2013-183, s. 2.7.)

§ 136-44.7A. Submission of secondary roads construction programs to State agencies.

When the Department of Transportation proposes to pave an unpaved secondary road that crosses land controlled by a State agency, the Department of Transportation shall obtain the approval of that State agency before paving that secondary road. (1996, 2nd Ex. Sess., c. 18, s. 19.7.)

§ 136-44.7B. Permit issuance by Department of Environment and Natural Resources transportation construction projects.

Once the Department of Environment and Natural Resources or any agency within the Department of Environment and Natural Resources has issued a permit that is required for a transportation construction project to be undertaken by or on behalf of the Department of Transportation pursuant to the Transportation Improvement Program, that permit shall remain in effect until the project is completed. The permit shall not expire and shall not be modified or canceled for any reason, including a subsequent change in federal law or regulations or in State law or rules, unless at least one of the following occurs:

(1)   The modification or cancellation is requested by the Department of Transportation.

(2)   The modification or cancellation is clearly required by a change in federal law or regulations and a failure to modify or cancel the permit by the Department of Environment and Natural Resources will or may result in a loss of

federal program delegation or a significant reduction in the availability of federal funds to the Department of Environment and Natural Resources or to the Department of Transportation.

(3) The modification or cancellation is clearly required by a change in State law as a result of an act of the General Assembly that includes a statement that the General Assembly specifically intends the change in State law to apply to ongoing transportation construction projects.

(4) The modification or cancellation is ordered by a court of competent jurisdiction.

(5) The nature or scope of the transportation construction project is significantly expanded or otherwise altered.

(6) Federal law or regulation requires that the permit expire at the end of a specific term of years. (2003-284, s. 29.6.)

§ 136-44.7C. Analysis and approval of Department of Transportation environmental policies or guidelines affecting transportation projects.

(a) Analysis Required. - The Department of Transportation shall conduct an analysis of any proposed environmental policy or guideline adopted by the Department that affects Department of Transportation projects to determine if the policy or guideline will result in an increased cost to Department of Transportation projects.

(b) Report of Analysis; Approval of Policy or Guideline Required. - The analysis of a proposed policy or guideline required by subsection (a) of this section shall be reported to the Board of Transportation at least 30 days prior to the proposed effective date of the policy or guideline, and shall not go into effect until approved by the Board of Transportation. (2005-276, s. 28.8(b).)

§ 136-44.7D. Bridge construction guidelines.

A bridge crossing rivers and streams in watersheds shall be constructed to accommodate the hydraulics of a flood water level equal to the water level projected for a 100-year flood for the region in which the bridge is built. The bridge shall be built without regard for the riparian buffer zones as designated by the Department of Environment and Natural Resources, Division of Water Resources. No Memorandums of Agreement may be made between Departments to bypass this construction mandate. No agency rules shall be enacted contrary to this section. (2007-551, s. 4; 2013-413, s. 57(g).)

§ 136-44.7E. Compliance with federal guidelines for transportation projects.

The Department may continue to use the Merger '01 process provided the relevant portions of P.L. 109-59, Section 6002, (SAFETEA-LU) are incorporated to ensure the Department as the recipient agency is the co-lead agency with the United States Department of Transportation, delegating all other federal, state, or local agencies as participating or cooperating agencies. The Department's designation as a co-lead agency shall inure to the Department the authority to determine the purpose and need of a project and to determine viable alternatives. Any conflict between cooperating or participating agencies and the Department shall be resolved by the Department in favor of the completion of the project in conflict. (2007-551, s. 5.)

§ 136-44.8. (Effective until July 1, 2014) Submission of secondary roads construction and unpaved roads paving programs to the Boards of County Commissioners.

(a)   Repealed by Session Laws 2013-183, s. 2.8(a), effective July 1, 2013.

(a1)   Representatives of the Department of Transportation shall provide to the board of county commissioners in each county the proposed secondary road construction program and, if applicable to that county, a list of roads proposed for the annual paving program approved by the Board of Transportation. If a paving priority list is presented, it shall include the priority rating of each secondary road paving project included in the proposed paving program according to the criteria and standards adopted by the Board of Transportation.

(b)   through (d) Repealed by Session Laws 2013-183, s. 2.8(a), effective July 1, 2013.

(e)   The Board of Transportation shall adopt the annual secondary construction program for each county after having given the board of county commissioners of each county an opportunity to review the proposed construction program and to make recommendations as provided in this section. The Board of Transportation shall consider such recommendations insofar as they are compatible with its general plans, standards, criteria and available funds, but having due regard to development plans of the county and to the maintenance and improvement needs of all existing roads in the county.

(f)   The secondary road construction and unpaved roads paving programs adopted by the Board of Transportation shall be followed by the Department of Transportation unless changes are approved by the Board of Transportation and notice of any changes is given to the board of county commissioners. Upon request, the most recent secondary road construction and unpaved roads paving programs adopted shall be submitted to any member of the General Assembly. The Department of Transportation shall make the annual construction program for each county available to the newspapers having a general circulation in the county. (1973, c. 507, s. 3; 1975, c. 716, s. 7; 1977, c. 464, s. 9; 1981, c. 536; 2013-183, s. 2.8(a).)

§ 136-44.8. (Effective July 1, 2014) Submission of unpaved secondary roads paving programs to the Boards of County Commissioners.

G.S. 136-44.8 is set out twice. See notes.

(a)   Repealed by Session Laws 2013-183, s. 2.8(a), effective July 1, 2013.

(a1)   In each county having unpaved roads programmed for paving, representatives of the Department of Transportation shall annually provide to the board of county commissioners in those counties a list of roads proposed for the annual paving program approved by the Board of Transportation. The paving priority list shall include the priority rating of each secondary road paving project included in the proposed paving program according to the criteria and standards adopted by the Board of Transportation.

(b)   through (d) Repealed by Session Laws 2013-183, s. 2.8(a), effective July 1, 2013.

(e) Repealed by Session Laws 2013-183, s. 2.8(b), effective July 1, 2014.

(f) The unpaved secondary roads paving programs adopted by the Board of Transportation shall be followed by the Department of Transportation unless changes are approved by the Board of Transportation and notice of any changes is given to the board of county commissioners. Upon request, the most recent unpaved secondary roads paving programs adopted shall be submitted to any member of the General Assembly. The Department of Transportation shall make the annual construction program for each affected county available to the newspapers having a general circulation in the county. (1973, c. 507, s. 3; 1975, c. 716, s. 7; 1977, c. 464, s. 9; 1981, c. 536; 2013-183, s. 2.8(a), (b).)

§ 136-44.9. Secondary roads; annual statements.

The Department of Transportation shall, before the end of the calendar year, prepare and file with the board of county commissioners a statement setting forth (i) each secondary highway designated by number, located in the county upon which the paving or improvement was made during the calendar year; (ii) the amount expended for improvements of each such secondary highway during the calendar year; and (iii) the nature of such improvements. The Department of Transportation, in its annual report, shall report on each secondary road construction project including the stage of completion and funds expended. The pertinent portion of these reports for each county shall be made available to the board of county commissioners. (1973, c. 507, s. 3; 1975, c. 615; c. 716, s. 7.)

§ 136-44.10. Additions to secondary road system.

The Board of Transportation shall adopt uniform statewide or regional standards and criteria which the Department of Transportation shall follow for additions to the secondary road system. These standards and criteria shall be promulgated and copies made available for free distribution. (1973, c. 507, s. 3; 1975, c. 716, s. 7; 1977, c. 464, ss. 8, 21.)

§ 136-44.11. Right-of-way acquisitions; preliminary engineering annual report.

(a)   The Department of Transportation shall include in its annual report projects for which preliminary engineering has been performed more than two years but where there has been no right-of-way acquisition, projects where right-of-way has been acquired more than two years but construction contracts have not been let. The report shall include the year or years in which the preliminary engineering was performed and the cost incurred, the number of right-of-way acquisitions for each project, the dates of the first and last acquisition and the total expenditure for right-of-way acquisition. The report shall include the status of the construction project for which the preliminary engineering was performed or the right-of-way acquired and the reasons for delay, if any.

(b)   Requests to the Board of Transportation for allocation of funds for the purchase of right-of-way shall include an estimated time schedule to complete all necessary right-of-way purchases related to a specific project, and a proposed date to award construction contracts for that project. If the anticipated construction contract date is more than two years beyond the estimated completion of the related right-of-way purchases, the approval of both the Board of Transportation and the Director of the Budget is required. (1973, c. 507, s. 3; 1975, c. 716, s. 7; 1981, c. 859, s. 69.)

§ 136-44.12. Maintenance of roads and parking lots in areas administered by the Division of Parks and Recreation.

The Department of Transportation shall maintain all roads and parking lots which are not part of the State Highway System, leading into and located within the boundaries of all areas administered by the Division of Parks and Recreation of the Department of Environment and Natural Resources.

All such roads and parking lots shall be planned, designed, and engineered through joint action between the Department of Transportation and the Division of Parks and Recreation of the Department of Environment and Natural Resources. This joint action shall encompass all accepted park planning and design principles. Particular concern shall be given to traffic counts and vehicle weight, minimal cutting into or through any natural and scenic areas, width of shoulders, the cutting of natural growth along roadways, and the reduction of any potential use of roads or parking lots for any purpose other than by park users. All State park roads and parking lots shall conform to the standards regarding width and other roadway specifications as agreed upon by the

Division of Parks and Recreation of the Department of Environment and Natural Resources and the Department of Transportation.

The State park road systems may be closed to the public in accordance with approved park practices that control the use of State areas so as to protect these areas from overuse and abuse and provide for functional use of the park areas, or for any other purpose considered in the best interest of the public by the Division of Parks and Recreation of the Department of Environment and Natural Resources.

Nothing herein shall be construed to include the transfer to the Department of Transportation the powers now vested in the Division of Parks and Recreation of the Department of Environment and Natural Resources relating to the patrol and safeguarding of State park roads or State park parking lots. (1973, c. 123, ss. 1-3; 1977, c. 771, s. 4; 1989, c. 727, s. 218(89); c. 799, s. 12(b); 1991 (Reg. Sess., 1992), c. 907, s. 3; 1997-443, s. 11A.119(a).)

§ 136-44.13. Reserved for future codification purposes.

§ 136-44.14. Curb ramps or curb cuts for handicapped persons.

(a) Curbs constructed on each side of any street or road, where curbs and sidewalks are provided and at other major points of pedestrian flow, shall meet the following minimum requirements:

(1) No less than two curb ramps or curb cuts shall be provided per lineal block, located at intersections.

(2) In no case, shall the width of a curb ramp or curb cut be less than 40 inches.

(3) The maximum gradient of such curb ramps or curb cuts shall be eight and thirty-three one-hundredths percent (8.33%) (12 inches slope for every one-inch rise) in relationship to the grade of the street or road.

(4) One curb ramp or curb cut may be provided under special conditions between each radius point of a street turnout of an intersection, if adequate provisions are made to prevent vehicular traffic from encroaching on the ramp.

(b) Minimum requirements for curb ramps or curb cuts under subsection (a) shall be met (i) in the initial construction of such curbs, and (ii) whenever such curbs are reconstructed, including, but not limited to, reconstruction for maintenance procedures and traffic operations, repair, or correction of utilities.

(c) The Department of Transportation, Division of Highways, Highway Design Section, is authorized and directed to develop guidelines to implement this Article in consultation with the Governor's Study Committee on Architectural Barriers (or the Committee on Barrier-Free Design of the Governor's Committee on Employment of the Handicapped if the Governor's Study Committee on Architectural Barriers ceases to exist). All curb ramps or curb cuts constructed or reconstructed in North Carolina shall conform to the guidelines of the Highway Design Section.

(d) The Department of Transportation, Division of Highways, Highway Design Section, is authorized and directed to provide free copies of this Article together with implementary guidelines and standards, to municipal and county governments and public utilities operating within the State. (1973, c. 718, ss. 1-4.)

§ 136-44.15: Expired.

§ 136-44.16. Authorized use of contract maintenance resurfacing program funds.

Of the contract maintenance resurfacing program funds appropriated by the General Assembly to the Department of Transportation, an amount not to exceed fifteen percent (15%) of the Board of Transportation's allocation of these funds may be used for widening existing narrow pavements. (1997-443, s. 32.12; 2003-112, s. 1.)

§ 136-44.17. Reserved for future codification purposes.

§ 136-44.18. Reserved for future codification purposes.

§ 136-44.19. Reserved for future codification purposes.

Article 2B.

Public Transportation.

§ 136-44.20. Department of Transportation designated agency to administer and fund public transportation programs; authority of political subdivisions.

(a)   The Department of Transportation is hereby designated as the agency of the State of North Carolina responsible for administering all federal and/or State programs relating to public transportation; and the Department is hereby granted authority to do all things required under applicable federal and/or State legislation to administer properly public transportation programs within North Carolina. Such authority shall include, but shall not be limited to, the power to receive federal funds and distribute federal and State financial assistance for inter-city rail or bus passenger service crossing one or more county lines.

(b)   The Department of Transportation, upon approval by the Board of Transportation, is authorized to provide the matching share of federal public transportation assistance programs through private resources, local government funds, or State appropriations provided by the General Assembly.

(b1)   The Secretary may, subject to the appropriations made by the General Assembly for any fiscal year, enter into State Full Funding Grant Agreements with a Regional Public Transportation Authority (RPTA) duly created and existing pursuant to Article 26 of Chapter 160A, a Regional Transportation Authority (RTA) duly created and existing pursuant to Article 27 of Chapter 160A, or a city organized under the laws of this State as defined in G.S. 160A-1(2), to provide State matching funds for "new start" fixed guideway projects in development by any entity pursuant to 49 U.S.C. § 5309. These grant agreements shall be executable only upon an Authority's or city's completion of and the Federal Transit Administration (FTA) approval of Preliminary Engineering and Environmental Impact Studies in anticipation of federal funding pursuant to 49 U.S.C. § 5309.

Prior to executing State Full Funding Grant Agreements, the Secretary shall submit proposed grant agreements or amendments to the Joint Legislative Transportation Oversight Committee for review. The agreements, consistent with federal guidance, shall define the limits of the "new starts" projects within the State, commit maximum levels of State financial participation, and establish terms and conditions of State financial participation.

State Full Funding Grant Agreements may provide for contribution of State funds in multiyear allotments. The multiyear allotments shall be based upon the Department's estimates, made in conjunction with an Authority or city, of the grant amount required for "new start" project work to be performed in the appropriation fiscal year.

State funds may be used to fund fixed guideway projects developed without federal funding by the Department, a Regional Public Transportation Authority (RPTA) duly created and existing pursuant to Article 26 of Chapter 160A of the General Statutes, a Regional Transportation Authority (RTA) duly created and existing pursuant to Article 27 of Chapter 160A of the General Statutes, or a unit of local government. In addition, State funds may be used to pay administrative costs incurred by the Department while participating in such fixed guideway projects.

(c) Nothing herein shall be construed to prevent a political subdivision of the State of North Carolina from applying for and receiving direct assistance from the United States government under the provisions of any applicable legislation.

(d) Repealed by Session Laws 2011-145, s. 28.12, effective July 1, 2011. (1975, c. 451; 1977, c. 341, s. 2; 1983, c. 616; 1989, c. 692, s. 2.3; c. 700, s. 1; 1993, c. 488, s. 2; 2000-67, s. 25.7; 2009-409, s. 1; 2011-145, s. 28.12.)

§ 136-44.21. Ridesharing arrangement defined.

Ridesharing arrangement means the transportation of persons in a motor vehicle where such transportation is incidental to another purpose of the driver and is not operated or provided for profit. The term shall include ridesharing arrangements such as carpools, vanpools and buspools. (1981, c. 606, s. 1.)

§ 136-44.22. Workers' Compensation Act does not apply to ridesharing arrangements.

Chapter 97 of the General Statutes shall not apply to a person injured while participating in a ridesharing arrangement between his or her place of residence and a place of employment or termini near such place, provided that if the employer owns, leases or contracts for the motor vehicle used in such an arrangement, Chapter 97 of the General Statutes shall apply. (1981, c. 606, s. 1.)

§ 136-44.23. Ridesharing arrangement benefits are not income.

Any benefits, other than salary or wages, received by a driver or a passenger while in a ridesharing arrangement shall not constitute income for the purposes of Article 4 of Chapter 105 of the General Statutes. (1981, c. 606, s. 1.)

§ 136-44.24. Ridesharing arrangements exempt from municipal licenses and taxes.

No county, city, town or other municipal corporation may require a business license for a ridesharing arrangement, nor may they require any additional tax, fee, or registration on a vehicle used in a ridesharing arrangement. (1981, c. 606, s. 1.)

§ 136-44.25. Wage and Hour Act inapplicable to ridesharing arrangements.

The provisions of Article 2A of Chapter 95 of the General Statutes of North Carolina shall not apply to an employee while participating in any ridesharing arrangement as defined in G.S. 136-44.21, as provided in G.S. 95-25.14(b)(6). (1981, c. 606, s. 1; c. 663, s. 14.)

§ 136-44.26. Use of public motor vehicles for ridesharing.

Motor vehicles owned or operated by any State or local agency may be used in ridesharing arrangements for public employees, provided the public employees benefiting from said ridesharing arrangements shall pay fees which shall cover all capital operating costs of the ridesharing arrangements. (1981, c. 606, s. 1.)

§ 136-44.27. North Carolina Elderly and Disabled Transportation Assistance Program.

(a)   There is established the Elderly and Disabled Transportation Assistance Program that shall provide State financed elderly and disabled transportation services for counties within the State. The Department of Transportation is designated as the agency of the State responsible for administering State funds appropriated to purchase elderly and disabled transportation services for counties within the State. The Department shall develop appropriate procedures regarding the distribution and use of these funds and shall adopt rules to implement these procedures. No funds appropriated pursuant to this act may be used to cover State administration costs.

(b)   For the purposes of this section, an elderly person is defined as one who has reached the age of 60 or more years, and a disabled person is defined as one who has a physical or mental impairment that substantially limits one or more major life activities, an individual who has a record of such impairment, or an individual who is regarded as having such an impairment. Certification of eligibility shall be the responsibility of the county.

(c)   All funds distributed by the Department under this section are intended to purchase additional transportation services, not to replace funds now being used by local governments for that purpose. These funds are not to be used towards the purchase of transportation vehicles or equipment. To this end, only those counties maintaining elderly and disabled transportation services at a level consistent with those in place on January 1, 1987, shall be eligible for additional transportation assistance funds.

(d)   The Public Transportation Division of the Department of Transportation shall distribute these funds to the counties according to the following formula: fifty percent (50%) divided equally among all counties; twenty-two and one-half percent (22 1/2%) based upon the number of elderly residents per county as a percentage of the State's elderly population; twenty-two and one-half percent (22 1/2%) based upon the number of disabled residents per county as a percentage of the State's disabled population; and, the remaining five percent (5%) based upon a population density factor that recognizes the higher transportation costs in sparsely populated counties.

(e) Funds distributed by the Department under this section shall be used by counties, public transportation authorities, or regional public transportation authorities in a manner consistent with transportation development plans which have been approved by the Department and the Board of County Commissioners. To receive funds apportioned for a given fiscal year, a county shall have an approved transportation development plan. Funds that are not obligated in a given fiscal year due to the lack of such a plan will be distributed to the eligible counties based upon the distribution formula prescribed by subsection (d) of this section.

(f) A regional public transportation authority created pursuant to Article 25 or Article 26 of Chapter 160A of the General Statutes may, upon written agreement with the municipalities served by a public transportation authority or counties served by the regional public transportation authority, apply for and receive any funds to which the member municipality or counties are entitled to receive based on the distribution formula set out in subsection (d) of this section. (1987 (Reg. Sess., 1988), c. 1095, ss. 1(a), 1(b); c. 1101, s. 8.2; 1989, c. 752, s. 105(b); 1993, c. 321, s. 147; 2011-207, s. 1.)

§ 136-44.28. Reserved for future codification purposes.

§ 136-44.29. Reserved for future codification purposes.

Article 2C.

House Movers Licensing Board.

§§ 136-44.30 through 136-44.34: Repealed by Session Laws 1977, c. 579.

Article 2D.

Railroad Revitalization.

§ 136-44.35. Railroad revitalization and corridor preservation a public purpose.

The General Assembly hereby finds that programs for railroad revitalization which assure the maintenance of safe, adequate, and efficient rail transportation services and that programs for railway corridor preservation which assure the availability of such corridors in the future are vital to the continued growth and prosperity of the State and serve the public purpose. (1979, c. 658, s. 1; 1989, c. 600, s. 1.)

§ 136-44.36. Department of Transportation designated as agency to administer federal and State railroad revitalization programs.

(a) The General Assembly hereby designates the Department of Transportation as the agency of the State of North Carolina responsible for administering all State and federal railroad revitalization programs. The Department of Transportation is authorized to develop, and the Board of Transportation is authorized to adopt, a State railroad plan, and the Department of Transportation is authorized to do all things necessary under applicable State and federal legislation to properly administer State and federal railroad revitalization programs within the State. Such authority shall include, but shall not be limited to, the power to receive federal funds and distribute and expend federal and State funds for rail programs designed to cover the costs of acquiring, by purchase, lease or other manner as the department considers appropriate, a railroad line or other rail property to maintain existing or to provide future rail service; the costs of rehabilitating and improving rail property on railroad lines to the extent necessary to permit safe, adequate and efficient rail service on such lines; and the costs of constructing rail or rail related facilities for the purpose of improving the quality, efficiency and safety of rail service. The Department shall also have the authority to preserve railroad corridors for future railroad use and interim compatible uses and may lease such corridors for interim compatible uses. Such authority shall also include the power to receive and administer federal financial assistance without State financial participation to railroad companies to cover the costs of local rail service continuation payments, of rail line rehabilitation, and of rail line construction as listed above. This Article shall not be construed to grant to the department the power or authority to operate directly any rail line or rail facilities.

(b) Notwithstanding subsection (a) of this section, the acceptance of federal funds by the Department of Transportation for rail programs shall be subject to the following:

(1) Report. - For any project under subsection (a) of this section, the Department of Transportation shall report the project details, including the amounts of federal funds and any State matching funds, as well as the expected annual maintenance and operational costs to the State of the project for the next 25 years, to the Joint Legislative Transportation Oversight Committee if the General Assembly is not in session, or to the House Appropriations Subcommittee on Transportation and the Senate Committee on Appropriations on Department of Transportation if the General Assembly is in session.

(2) Consultation. - If either the amount of State matching funds required by the federal grant or the amount of future annual maintenance and operational costs of the project are reasonably expected to exceed three million dollars ($3,000,000), then the Department shall not accept the federal funds prior to consultation with the Joint Legislative Transportation Oversight Committee if the General Assembly is not in session, or with the House Appropriations Subcommittee on Transportation and the Senate Committee on Appropriations on Department of Transportation if the General Assembly is in session. Failure of the Joint Legislative Transportation Oversight Committee, the House Appropriations Subcommittee on Transportation, or the Senate Committee on Appropriations on Department of Transportation to hold a meeting with the Department of Transportation within 60 days of a written request for a meeting from the Department of Transportation shall be deemed a waiver of consultation by the committee.

(3) Approval. - If either the amount of State matching funds required by the federal grant or the amount of future annual maintenance and operational costs of the project are reasonably expected to exceed five million dollars ($5,000,000), then the Department's acceptance of funds shall be subject to approval of the project by an act of the General Assembly. If 30 days have passed since consultation or the expiration of the consultation period under subdivision (2) of this subsection, then the inaction of the General Assembly, including the lack of an extra session to address the project, shall be deemed an approval of the project, and the Department may accept the funds without an act of the General Assembly.

For purposes of this subsection, the terms "State matching funds" and "annual maintenance and operational costs to the State" shall not include funds that may pass through the Department of Transportation but that originally came from a non-State source. (1979, c. 658, s. 2; 1987 (Reg. Sess., 1988), c. 1071, s. 1; 1989, c. 600, s. 2; 2011-145, s. 28.15.)

§ 136-44.36A. Railway corridor preservation.

The North Carolina Department of Transportation is authorized, pursuant to 16 U.S.C.A. § 1247(d), to preserve rail transportation corridors and permit compatible interim uses of such corridors. (1987 (Reg. Sess., 1988), c. 1071, s. 2.)

§ 136-44.36B. Power of Department to preserve and acquire railroad corridors.

In exercising its power to preserve railroad corridors, the Department of Transportation may acquire property for new railroad corridors and may acquire property that is or has been part of a railroad corridor by purchase, gift, condemnation, or other method, provided that the Department may not condemn part of an existing, active railroad line. The procedures in Article 9 of this Chapter apply when the Department condemns property to preserve or acquire a railroad corridor. (1989, c. 600, s. 3; 1991, c. 673, s. 1.)

§ 136-44.36C. Installment contracts authorized.

The Department of Transportation may purchase active or inactive railroad lines, corridors, rights-of-way, locomotives, rolling stock, and other rail property, both real and personal, by installment contracts which create in the property purchased a security interest to secure payment of the purchase money. No deficiency judgment may be rendered against the Department of Transportation in any action for breach of a contractual obligation authorized by this section, and the taxing power of the State is not and may not be pledged directly or indirectly to secure any money due the seller. (1991, c. 673, s. 2.)

§ 136-44.36D. Recreational leasing requirements.

Portions of rail corridors held by the North Carolina Department of Transportation in fee simple absolute may be leased by the Department for interim public recreation use provided the following conditions are met:

(1) Before requesting trail use, a sponsoring unit of local government has held a public hearing in accordance with G.S. 143-318.12 and notified the owners of all parcels of land abutting the corridor as shown on the county tax listing of the hearing date, place, and time by first-class mail at the last addresses listed for such owners on the county tax abstracts. A transcript of all public comments presented at the hearing has been sent to the North Carolina Department of Transportation at the time of requesting use of the corridor.

(2) A unit of local government has requested use of the rail corridor or a portion thereof for interim public recreational trail use, and agrees in writing to assume all development costs as well as management, security, and liability responsibilities as defined by the North Carolina Department of Environment and Natural Resources and the North Carolina Department of Transportation.

(3) Adjacent property owners are offered broad voting representation by membership in the organization, if any, that is delegated most immediate responsibility for development and management of the rail-trail by the sponsoring local government.

(4) The North Carolina Department of Transportation has determined that there will not likely be a need to resume active rail service in the leased portion of the rail corridor for at least 10 years.

(5) Any lease or other agreement allowing trail use includes terms for resumption of active rail use which will assure unbroken continuation of the corridor's perpetual use for railroad purposes and interim compatible uses.

(6) Use of the rail corridor or portions thereof as a recreational trail does not interfere with the ultimate transportation purposes of the corridor as determined by the North Carolina Department of Transportation. (1991, c. 751, s. 1; 1997-443, s. 11A.119(a).)

§ 136-44.37. Department to provide nonfederal matching share.

The Department of Transportation upon approval by the Board of Transportation and the Director of the Budget may provide for the matching share of federal rail revitalization assistance programs through private resources, county funds or State appropriations as may be provided by the General Assembly. (1979, c. 658, s. 3; 1983, c. 717, s. 48; 1985 (Reg. Sess., 1986), c. 955, ss. 47, 48; 2006-203, s. 76.)

§ 136-44.38. Department to provide State and federal financial assistance to cities and counties for rail revitalization.

(a) The Department of Transportation is authorized to distribute to cities and counties State financial assistance for local rail revitalization programs provided that every rail revitalization project for which State financial assistance would be utilized must be approved by the Board of Transportation and by the Director of the Budget.

(b) Repealed by Session Laws 1989, c. 600, s. 4. (1979, c. 658, s. 3; 1983, c. 717, s. 48; 1985 (Reg. Sess., 1986), c. 955, ss. 49, 50; 1989, c. 600, s. 4; 2006-203, s. 77.)

§ 136-44.39. Department to provide State and federal financial assistance to short-line railroads.

The Department of Transportation is authorized to provide assistance to short-line railroads to continue and enhance rail service in the State so as to assist in economic development and access to ports and military installations. Assistance under this section may involve both the Rail Industrial Access Program and the Short Line Infrastructure Access Program, as well as other innovative programs. Grants under this section shall not exceed fifty percent (50%) of the nonfederal share and must be matched by equal or greater funding from the applicant. (2011-145, s. 28.13.)

§§ 136-44.40 through 136-44.49. Reserved for future codification purposes.

Article 2E.

Transportation Corridor Official Map Act.

§ 136-44.50. Transportation corridor official map act.

(a) A transportation corridor official map may be adopted or amended by any of the following:

(1) The governing board of any local government for any thoroughfare included as part of a comprehensive plan for streets and highways adopted pursuant to G.S. 136-66.2 or for any proposed public transportation corridor included in the adopted long-range transportation plan.

(2) The Board of Transportation, or the governing board of any county, for any portion of the existing or proposed State highway system or for any public transportation corridor, to include rail, that is in the Transportation Improvement Program.

(3) Regional public transportation authorities created pursuant to Article 26 of Chapter 160A of the General Statutes or regional transportation authorities created pursuant to Article 27 of Chapter 160A of the General Statutes for any portion of the existing or proposed State highway system, or for any proposed public transportation corridor, or adjacent station or parking lot, included in the adopted long-range transportation plan.

(4) The North Carolina Turnpike Authority for any project being studied pursuant to G.S. 136-89.183.

(5) The Wilmington Urban Area Metropolitan Planning Organization for Department projects R-3300 and U-4751.

Before a city adopts a transportation corridor official map that extends beyond the extraterritorial jurisdiction of its building permit issuance and subdivision control ordinances, or adopts an amendment to a transportation corridor official map outside the extraterritorial jurisdiction of its building permit issuance and subdivision control ordinances, the city shall obtain approval from the Board of County Commissioners.

(a1) No property may be regulated under this Article until:

(1) The governing board of the city, the county, the regional transportation authority, the North Carolina Turnpike Authority, or the Department of Transportation has held a public hearing in each county affected by the map on the proposed map or amendment. Notice of the hearing shall be provided:

a. By publication at least once a week for four successive weeks prior to the hearing in a newspaper having general circulation in the county in which the transportation corridor to be designated is located.

b. By two week written notice to the Secretary of Transportation, the Chairman of the Board of County Commissioners, and the Mayor of any city or town through whose corporate or extraterritorial jurisdiction the transportation corridor passes.

c. By posting copies of the proposed transportation corridor map or amendment at the courthouse door for at least 21 days prior to the hearing date. The notice required in sub-subdivision a. above shall make reference to this posting.

d. By first-class mail sent to each property owner affected by the corridor. The notice shall be sent to the address listed for the owner in the county tax records.

(1a) The transportation corridor official map has been adopted or amended by the governing board of the city, the county, the regional transportation authority, the North Carolina Turnpike Authority, or the Department.

(2) A permanent certified copy of the transportation corridor official map or amendment has been filed with the register of deeds. The boundaries may be defined by map or by written description, or a combination thereof. The copy shall measure approximately 20 inches by 12 inches, including no less than one and one-half inches binding space on the left-hand side.

(3) The names of all property owners affected by the corridor have been submitted to the Register of Deeds.

(b) Transportation corridor official maps and amendments shall be distributed and maintained in the following manner:

(1) A copy of the official map and each amendment thereto shall be filed in the office of the city clerk and in the office of the district engineer.

(2) A copy of the official map, each amendment thereto and any variance therefrom granted pursuant to G.S. 136-44.52 shall be furnished to the tax supervisor of any county and tax collector of any city affected thereby. The portion of properties embraced within a transportation corridor and any variance granted shall be clearly indicated on all tax maps maintained by the county or city for such period as the designation remains in effect.

(3) Notwithstanding any other provision of law, the certified copy filed with the register of deeds shall be placed in a book maintained for that purpose and cross-indexed by number of road, street name, or other appropriate description. The register of deeds shall collect a fee of five dollars ($5.00) for each map sheet or page recorded.

(4) The names submitted as required under subdivision (a1)(3) of this section shall be indexed in the "grantor" index by the Register of Deeds.

(c) Repealed by Session Laws 1989, c. 595, s. 1.

(d) Within one year following the establishment of a transportation corridor official map or amendment, work shall begin on an environmental impact statement or preliminary engineering. The failure to begin work on the environmental impact statement or preliminary engineering within the one-year period shall constitute an abandonment of the corridor, and the provisions of this Article shall no longer apply to properties or portions of properties embraced within the transportation corridor. A local government may prepare environmental impact studies and preliminary engineering work in connection with the establishment of a transportation corridor official map or amendments to a transportation corridor official map. When a city or county prepares a transportation corridor official map for a street or highway that has been designated a State responsibility pursuant to G.S. 136-66.2, the environmental impact study and preliminary engineering work shall be reviewed and approved by the Department of Transportation. An amendment to a corridor shall not extend the one-year period provided by this section unless it establishes a substantially different corridor in a primarily new location.

(e) The term "amendment" for purposes of this section includes any change to a transportation corridor official map, including:

(1) Failure of the Department of Transportation, the North Carolina Turnpike Authority, a city, a county, or a regional transportation authority to begin work on

an environmental impact statement or preliminary engineering as required by this section; or

(2)   Deletion of the corridor from the transportation corridor official map by action of the Board of Transportation, the North Carolina Turnpike Authority, or deletion of the corridor from the long-range transportation plan of a city, county, or regional transportation authority by action of the city, county, or regional transportation authority governing Board.

(f)   The term "transportation corridor" as used in this Article does not include bikeways or greenways. (1987, c. 747, s. 19; 1989, c. 595, s. 1; 1998-184, s. 1; 2005-275, s. 1; 2005-418, s. 9; 2006-237, s. 1; 2008-180, s. 3; 2009-332, ss. 1, 2; 2009-570, s. 44; 2013-183, s. 4.4.)

§ 136-44.51. Effect of transportation corridor official map.

(a)   After a transportation corridor official map is filed with the register of deeds, no building permit shall be issued for any building or structure or part thereof located within the transportation corridor, nor shall approval of a subdivision, as defined in G.S. 153A-335 and G.S. 160A-376, be granted with respect to property within the transportation corridor. The Secretary of Transportation or his designee, the director of a regional public transportation authority, or the director of a regional transportation authority, as appropriate, shall be notified within 10 days of all submittals for corridor map determination, as provided in subsections (b) and (c) of this section.

(b)   In any event, no application for building permit issuance or subdivision plat approval for a tract subject to a valid transportation corridor official map shall be delayed by the provisions of this section for more than three years from the date of its original submittal to the appropriate local jurisdiction. A submittal to the local jurisdiction for corridor map determination shall require only the name of the property owner, the street address of the property parcel, the parcel number or tax identification number, a vicinity map showing the location of the parcel with respect to nearby roads and other landmarks, a sketch of the parcel showing all existing and proposed structures or other uses of the property, and a description of the proposed improvements. If the impact of an adopted corridor on a property submittal for corridor map determination is still being reviewed after the three-year period established pursuant to this subsection, the entity that adopted the transportation corridor official map affecting the issuance of building permits or subdivision plat approval shall issue approval for an otherwise eligible request or initiate acquisition proceedings on the affected properties. If the entity that adopted the transportation corridor official map has not initiated acquisition proceedings or issued approval within the time limit established pursuant to this subsection, an applicant within the corridor may treat the real property as unencumbered and free of any restriction on sale, transfer, or use established by this Article.

(c) No submittal to a local jurisdiction for corridor map determination shall be construed to be an application for building permit issuance or subdivision plat approval. The provisions of this section shall not apply to valid building permits issued prior to August 7, 1987, or to building permits for buildings and structures which existed prior to the filing of the transportation corridor, provided the size of the building or structure is not increased and the type of building code occupancy as set forth in the North Carolina Building Code is not changed. (1987, c. 747, s. 19; 1998-184, s. 1; 2011-242, s. 1.)

§ 136-44.52. Variance from transportation corridor official map.

(a) The Department of Transportation, the regional public transportation authority, the regional transportation authority, or the local government which initiated the transportation corridor official map shall establish procedures for considering petitions for variance from the requirements of G.S. 136-44.51.

(b) The procedure established by the State shall provide for written notice to the Mayor and Chairman of the Board of County Commissioners of any affected city or county, and for the hearing to be held in the county where the affected property is located.

(c) Local governments may provide for petitions for variances to be heard by the board of adjustment or other boards or commissions which can hear variances authorized by G.S. 160A-388. The procedures for boards of adjustment shall be followed except that no vote greater than a majority shall be required to grant a variance.

(c1) The procedure established by a regional public transportation authority or a regional transportation authority pursuant to subsection (a) of this section shall provide for a hearing de novo by the Department of Transportation for any petition for variance which is denied by the regional public transportation authority or the regional transportation authority. All hearings held by the Department of Transportation under this subsection shall be conducted in accordance with procedures established by the Department of Transportation pursuant to subsection (a) of this section.

(d) A variance may be granted upon a showing that:

(1) Even with the tax benefits authorized by this Article, no reasonable return may be earned from the land; and

(2) The requirements of G.S. 136-44.51 result in practical difficulties or unnecessary hardships. (1987, c. 747, s. 19; 1998-184, s. 1; 2008-180, s. 4.)

§ 136-44.53. Advance acquisition of right-of-way within the transportation corridor.

(a) After a transportation corridor official map is filed with the register of deeds, a property owner has the right of petition to the filer of the map for acquisition of the property due to an imposed hardship. The Department of Transportation, the regional public transportation authority, the regional transportation authority, or the local government that initiated the transportation corridor official map may make advanced acquisition of specific parcels of property when that acquisition is determined by the respective governing board to be in the best public interest to protect the transportation corridor from development or when the transportation corridor official map creates an undue hardship on the affected property owner. The procedure established by a regional public transportation authority or a regional transportation authority pursuant to subsection (b) of this section shall provide for a hearing de novo by the Department of Transportation for any request for advance acquisition due to hardship that is denied by an authority. All hearings held by the Department under this subsection shall be conducted in accordance with procedures established by the Department pursuant to subsection (b) of this section. Any decision of the Department pursuant to this subsection shall be final and binding. Any property determined eligible for hardship acquisition shall be acquired within three years of the finding or the restrictions of the map shall be removed from the property.

(b) Prior to making any advanced acquisition of right-of-way under the authority of this Article, the Board of Transportation or the respective governing board which initiated the transportation corridor official map shall develop and adopt appropriate policies and procedures to govern the advanced acquisition of right-of-way and to assure that the advanced acquisition is in the best overall public interest.

(c) When a local government makes an advanced right-of-way acquisition of property within a transportation corridor official map for a street or highway that has been determined to be a State responsibility pursuant to the provisions of G.S. 136-66.2, the Department of Transportation shall reimburse the local government for the cost of any advanced right-of-way acquisition at the time the street or highway is constructed. The Department of Transportation shall have no responsibility to reimburse a municipality for any advanced right-of-way acquisition for a street or highway that has not been designated a State responsibility pursuant to the provisions of G.S. 136-66.2 prior to the initiation of the advanced acquisition by the city. The local government shall obtain the concurrence of the Department of Transportation in all instances of advanced acquisition.

(d) In exercising the authority granted by this section, a local government is authorized to expend its funds for the protection of rights-of-way shown on a duly adopted transportation corridor official map whether the right-of-way to be acquired is located inside or outside the municipal corporate limits. (1987, c. 747, s. 19; 1998-184, s. 1; 2008-180, s. 5; 2008-187, s. 47.7.)

§ 136-44.54. Standard for appraisal of right-of-way within corridor.

The Department shall utilize the criteria contained in 49 C.F.R. § 24.103 (1997) when appraising right-of-way in a transportation corridor designated under this Article. (1998-184, s. 1.)

Article 3.

State Highway System.

Part 1. Highway System.

§ 136-45. General purpose of law; control, repair and maintenance of highways.

The general purpose of the laws creating the Department of Transportation is that said Department of Transportation shall take over, establish, construct, and maintain a statewide system of hard-surfaced and other dependable highways running to all county seats, and to all principal towns, State parks, and principal State institutions, and linking up with state highways of adjoining states and with national highways into national forest reserves by the most practical routes, with special view of development of agriculture, commercial and natural resources of the State, and, except as otherwise provided by law, for the further purpose of permitting the State to assume control of the State highways, repair, construct, and reconstruct and maintain said highways at the expense of the entire State, and to relieve the counties and cities and towns of the State of this burden. (1921, c. 2, s. 2; C.S., s. 3846(a); 1943, c. 410; 1957, c. 65, s. 11; 1973, c. 507, s. 5; 1977, c. 464, s. 7.1; 2007-428, s. 2.)

§§ 136-46 through 136-47. Repealed by Session Laws 1977, c. 464, s. 22.

§§ 136-48 through 136-50. Repealed by Session Laws 1943, c. 410.

Part 2. County Public Roads Incorporated into State Highway System.

§ 136-51. Maintenance of county public roads vested in Department of Transportation.

From and after July 1, 1931, the exclusive control and management and responsibility for all public roads in the several counties shall be vested in the Department of Transportation as hereinafter provided, and all county, district, and township highway or road commissioners, by whatever name designated, and whether created under public, public-local, or private acts, shall be abolished:

Provided, that for the purpose of providing for the payment of any bonded or other indebtedness, and for the interest thereon, that may be outstanding as an obligation of any county, district, or township commission herein abolished, the boards of county commissioners of the respective counties are hereby constituted fiscal agents, and are vested with authority and it shall be their duty to levy such taxes on the taxable property or persons within the respective county, district, or township by or for which said bonds or other indebtedness were issued or incurred and as are now authorized by law to the extent that the same may be necessary to provide for the payment of such obligations; and the respective commissions herein abolished shall on or before July 1, 1931, turn over to said boards of county commissioners any moneys on hand or evidences of indebtedness properly applicable to the discharge of any such indebtedness (except such moneys as are mentioned in paragraph (a) above); and all uncollected special road taxes shall be payable to said boards of county commissioners, and the portion of said taxes applicable to indebtedness shall be applied by said commissioners to said indebtedness, or invested in a sinking fund according to law. All that portion of said taxes or other funds coming into the hands of said county commissioners and properly applicable to the maintenance or improvement of the public roads of the county shall be held by them as a special road fund and disbursed upon proper orders of the Department of Transportation.

Provided, further, that in order to fully carry out the provisions of this section the respective boards of county commissioners are vested with full authority to prosecute all suitable legal actions.

Nothing in this section shall prevent a county from participating in the cost of rights-of-way, construction, reconstruction, improvement, or maintenance of a road on the State highway system under agreement with the Department of Transportation. A county is authorized and empowered to acquire land by dedication and acceptance, purchase, or eminent domain and make improvements to portions of the State highway system lying within or outside the county limits utilizing local funds that have been authorized for that purpose. The provisions of G.S. 153A-15 apply to any county attempting to acquire property outside its limits. All improvements to the State highway system shall be done in accordance with the specifications and requirements of the Department of Transportation. (1931, c. 145, s. 7; 1933, c. 172, s. 17; 1957, c. 65, s. 11; 1973, c. 507, s. 5; 1977, c. 464, s. 7.1; 2007-428, s. 3.)

§§ 136-52 through 136-53. Repealed by Session Laws 1977, c. 464, s. 22.

Part 3. Power to Make Changes in Highway System.

§ 136-54. Power to make changes.

The Board of Transportation shall be authorized, when in its judgment the public good requires it, to change, alter, add to, or abandon and substitute new sections for, any portion of the State highway system. (1927, c. 46, s. 1; 1933, c. 172, s. 17; 1957, c. 65, s. 11; 1965, c. 538, s. 2; 1967, c. 1128, s. 1; 1973, c. 507, s. 5; 1977, c. 464, s. 23.)

§ 136-55. Repealed by Session Laws 1979, c. 143, s. 1.

§ 136-55.1. Notice of abandonment.

(a)   At least 60 days prior to any action by the Department of Transportation abandoning a segment of road and removing the same from the State highway system for maintenance, except roads abandoned on request of the county commissioners under G.S. 136-63, the Department of Transportation shall notify by registered mail or personal delivery all owners of property adjoining the section of road to be abandoned whose whereabouts can be ascertained by due diligence. Said notice shall describe the section of road which is proposed to be abandoned and shall give the date, place and time of the Department of Transportation meeting at which the action abandoning said section of road is to be taken.

(b)   In keeping with its overall zoning scheme and long-range plans regarding the extraterritorial jurisdiction area, a municipality may keep open and assume responsibility for maintenance of a road within one mile of its corporate limits once it is abandoned from the State highway system. (1957, c. 1063; 1967, c. 1128, s. 3; 1973, c. 507, s. 5; 1977, c. 464, s. 7.1; 1993, c. 533, s. 13.)

§ 136-56. Repealed by Session Laws 1967, c. 1128, s. 4.

§ 136-57. Repealed by Session Laws 1965, c. 538, s. 1.

§ 136-58. Repealed by Session Laws 1977, c. 464, s. 22.

§ 136-59. No court action against Board of Transportation.

No action shall be maintained in any of the courts of this State against the Board of Transportation to determine the location of any State highways or portion thereof, by any person, corporation, or municipal corporation. (1927, c. 46, s. 7; 1933, c. 172, s. 17; 1957, c. 65, s. 11; 1967, c. 1128, s. 5; 1973, c. 507, s. 5.)

§§ 136-60 through 136-61. Repealed by Session Laws 1973, c. 507, s. 23.

§ 136-62. Right of petition.

The citizens of the State shall have the right to present petitions to the board of county commissioners, and through the board to the Department of Transportation, concerning additions to the system and improvement of roads. The board of county commissioners shall receive such petitions, forwarding them on to the Board of Transportation with their recommendations. Petitions on hand at the time of the periodic preparation of the secondary road plan shall be considered by the representatives of the Department of Transportation in preparation of that plan, with report on action taken by these representatives on such petitions to the board of commissioners at the time of consultation. The citizens of the State shall at all times have opportunities to discuss any aspect of secondary road additions, maintenance, and construction, with representatives of the Department of Transportation in charge of the preparation of the secondary road plan, and if not then satisfied opportunity to discuss any such aspect with the division engineer, the Secretary of Transportation, and the Board of Transportation in turn. (1931, c. 145, s. 14; 1933, c. 172, s. 17; 1957, c. 65, s. 7; 1965, c. 55, s. 12; 1973, c. 507, s. 5; 1977, c. 464, ss. 7.1, 24, 24.1.)

§ 136-63. Change or abandonment of roads.

(a)   The board of county commissioners of any county may, on its own motion or on petition of a group of citizens, request the Board of Transportation to change or abandon any road in the secondary system when the best interest of the people of the county will be served thereby. The Board of Transportation shall thereupon make inquiry into the proposed change or abandonment, and if in its opinion the public interest demands it, shall make such change or abandonment. If the change or abandonment shall affect a road connecting with any street of a city or town, the change or abandonment shall not be made until the street-governing body of the city or town shall have been duly notified and given opportunity to be heard on the question. Any request by a board of county commissioners or street-governing body of a city refused by the Board of Transportation may be presented again upon the expiration of 12 months.

(b) In keeping with its overall zoning scheme and long-range plans regarding the extraterritorial jurisdiction area, a municipality may keep open and assume responsibility for maintenance of a road within one mile of its corporate limits once it is abandoned from the State highway system. (1931, c. 145, s. 15; 1957, c. 65, s. 8; 1965, c. 55, s. 13; 1973, c. 507, s. 22 1/2; 1975, c. 19, s. 45; 1977, c. 464, s. 25; 1993, c. 533, s. 14.)

§ 136-64. Filing of complaints with Department of Transportation; hearing and appeal.

In the event of failure to maintain the roads of the State highway system or any county road system in good condition, the board of county commissioners of such county may file complaint with the Department of Transportation. When any such complaint is filed, the Department of Transportation shall at once investigate the same, and if the same be well founded, the said Department of Transportation shall at once order the repair and maintenance of the roads complained of and investigate the negligence of the persons in charge of the roads so complained of, and if upon investigation the person in charge of the road complained of be at fault, he may be discharged from the service of the Department of Transportation. The board of commissioners of any county, who shall feel aggrieved at the action of the Department of Transportation upon complaint filed, may appeal from the decision of the Department of Transportation to the Governor, and it shall be the duty of the Governor to adjust the differences between the board of county commissioners and the Department of Transportation. (1921, c. 2, s. 20; C.S., s. 3846(11); 1931, c. 145, s. 17; 1933, c. 172, s. 17; 1957, c. 65, s. 11; 1973, c. 507, s. 5; 1977, c. 464, s. 7.1.)

§ 136-64.1. Applications for intermittent closing of roads within watershed improvement project by Department of Transportation; notice; regulation by Department; delegation of authority; markers.

(a) Upon proper application by the board of commissioners of a drainage district established under the provisions of Chapter 156 of the General Statutes of North Carolina, by the board of trustees of a watershed improvement district established under the provisions of Article 2 of Chapter 139 of the General Statutes, by the board of county commissioners of any county operating a county watershed improvement program under the provisions of Article 3 of Chapter 139 of the General Statutes, by the board of commissioners of any watershed improvement commission appointed by a board of county commissioners or by the board of supervisors of any soil and water conservation district designated by a board of county commissioners to exercise authority in carrying out a county watershed improvement program, the Department of Transportation, for roads coming under its jurisdictional control, is hereby authorized to permit the intermittent closing of any secondary road within the boundaries of any watershed improvement project operated by the applicants, whenever in the judgment of the Department of Transportation it is necessary to do so, and when the secondary road will be intermittently subject to inundation by floodwaters retained by an approved watershed improvement project.

(b) Before any permit may be issued for the temporary inundation and closing of such a road, an application for such permit shall be made to the Department of Transportation by the public body having jurisdiction over the watershed improvement project. The application shall specify the secondary road involved, the anticipated frequency and duration of intermittent flooding of the secondary road involved, and shall request that a permit be granted to the applicant public body to allow the intermittent closing of the road.

(c) Upon receipt of such an application the Department of Transportation shall give public notice of the proposed action by publication once each week for two consecutive weeks in a newspaper of general circulation in the county or counties within which the proposed intermittent closing of road or roads would occur; and such notices shall contain a description of the places of beginning and the places of ending of such intermittent closing. In addition, the Department of Transportation shall give notice to all public utilities or common carriers having facilities located within the rights-of-way of any roads being closed by mailing copies of such notices to the appropriate offices of the public utility or common carrier having jurisdiction over the affected facilities of the public utility or common carrier. Not sooner than 14 days after publication and mailing of notices, the Department of Transportation or the municipality may issue its permit with respect to such road.

(d) The Department of Transportation shall have the discretion to deny any application submitted pursuant to this section, or it may grant a permit on any condition it deems warranted. The Department, however, shall consider the use of alternate routes available during flooding of the roads, and any inconvenience to the public or temporary loss of access to business, homes and property. The Department shall have the authority to promulgate regulations for the issuance of permits under this section and it may delegate the authority for the consideration, issuance or denial of such permits to the Chief Engineer. Any applicant granted a permit pursuant to this section shall cause suitable markers to be installed on the secondary road to advise the general public of the intermittent closing of the road or roads involved. Such markers shall be located and approved by the Chief Engineer. (1975, c. 639, s. 1; 1977, c. 464, s. 7.1; 2012-85, s. 6.)

§§ 136-65 through 136-66: Repealed by Session Laws 1943, c. 410.

Article 3A.

Transportation Systems in and around Municipalities.

§ 136-66.1. Responsibility for streets inside municipalities.

Responsibility for streets and highways inside the corporate limits of municipalities is hereby defined as follows:

(1) The State Highway System. - The State highway system inside the corporate limits of municipalities shall consist of a system of major streets and highways necessary to move volumes of traffic efficiently and effectively from points beyond the corporate limits of the municipalities through the municipalities and to major business, industrial, governmental and institutional destinations located inside the municipalities. The Department of Transportation shall be responsible for the maintenance, repair, improvement, widening, construction and reconstruction of this system. These streets and highways within corporate limits are of primary benefit to the State in developing a statewide coordinated system of primary and secondary streets and highways. Each highway division shall develop an annual work plan for maintenance and contract resurfacing, within their respective divisions, consistent with the needs, inasmuch as possible, as identified in the report developed in accordance with G.S. 136-44.3. In developing the annual work plan, the highway division shall

give consideration to any special needs or information provided by the municipalities within their respective divisions. The plan shall be made available to the municipalities within the respective divisions upon request.

(2) The Municipal Street System. - In each municipality the municipal street system shall consist of those streets and highways accepted by the municipality which are not a part of the State highway system. The municipality shall be responsible for the maintenance, construction, reconstruction, and right-of-way acquisition for this system.

(3) Maintenance of State Highway System by Municipalities. - Any city or town, by written contract with the Department of Transportation, may undertake to maintain, repair, improve, construct, reconstruct or widen those streets within municipal limits which form a part of the State highway system, and may also, by written contract with the Department of Transportation, undertake to install, repair and maintain highway signs and markings, electric traffic signals and other traffic-control devices on such streets. All work to be performed by the city or town under such contract or contracts shall be in accordance with Department of Transportation standards, and the consideration to be paid by the Department of Transportation to the city or town for such work, whether in money or in services, shall be adequate to reimburse the city or town for all costs and expenses, direct or indirect, incurred by it in the performance of such work. The city or town under contract with the Department shall develop an annual work plan for maintenance of the State highway system consistent with the needs, inasmuch as possible, as identified in the report developed in accordance with G.S. 136-44.3. The annual work plan shall be submitted to the respective division engineers and shall be mutually agreeable to both parties.

(4) If the governing body of any municipality determines that it is in the best interest of its citizens to do so, it may expend its funds for the purpose of making any of the following improvements on streets that are within its corporate limits and form a part of the State highway system:

a. Construction of curbing and guttering.

b. Adding of lanes for automobile parking.

c. Constructing street drainage facilities which may by reasonable engineering estimates be attributable to that amount of surface water collected upon and flowing from municipal streets which do not form a part of the State highway system.

d. Constructing sidewalks.

e. Intersection improvements, if the governing body determines that such improvements will decrease traffic congestion, improve safety conditions, and improve air quality.

In exercising the authority granted herein, the municipality may, with the consent of the Department of Transportation, perform the work itself, or it may enter into a contract with the Department of Transportation to perform such work. Any work authorized by this subdivision shall be financed entirely by the municipality and be approved by the Department of Transportation.

The cost of any work financed by a municipality under this subdivision may be assessed against the properties abutting the street or highway upon which such work was performed in accordance with the procedures of either Article 10 of Chapter 160A of the General Statutes or any charter provisions or local acts applicable to the particular municipality. (1959, c. 687, s. 1; 1969, cc. 798, 978; 1973, c. 507, s. 5; 1975, c. 664, s. 3; 1977, c. 464, s. 7.1; 1987, c. 747, s. 2; 1993 (Reg. Sess., 1994), c. 690, s. 1; 1995, c. 163, s. 14; 2005-382, s. 2.)

§ 136-66.2. Development of a coordinated transportation system and provisions for streets and highways in and around municipalities.

(a) Each municipality, not located within a metropolitan planning organization (MPO) as recognized in G.S. 136-200.1, with the cooperation of the Department of Transportation, shall develop a comprehensive transportation plan that will serve present and anticipated travel demand in and around the municipality. The plan shall be based on the best information available including, but not limited to, population growth, economic conditions and prospects, and patterns of land development in and around the municipality, and shall provide for the safe and effective use of the transportation system. In the development of the plan, consideration shall be given to all transportation modes including, but not limited to, the street system, transit alternatives, bicycle, pedestrian, and operating strategies. The Department of Transportation may provide financial and technical assistance in the preparation of such plans. Each MPO, with cooperation of the Department of Transportation, shall develop a comprehensive transportation plan in accordance with 23 U.S.C. § 134. In addition, an MPO may include projects in its transportation plan that are not included in a financially constrained plan or are anticipated to be needed beyond the horizon year as required by 23 U.S.C. § 134. For municipalities located within an MPO, the development of a comprehensive transportation plan will take place through the metropolitan planning organization. For purposes of transportation planning and programming, the MPO shall represent the municipality's interests to the Department of Transportation.

(b) After completion and analysis of the plan, the plan shall be adopted by both the governing body of the municipality or MPO and the Department of Transportation as the basis for future transportation improvements in and around the municipality or within the MPO. The governing body of the municipality and the Department of Transportation shall reach agreement as to which of the existing and proposed streets and highways included in the adopted plan will be a part of the State highway system and which streets will be a part of the municipal street system. As used in this Article, the State highway system shall mean both the primary highway system of the State and the secondary road system of the State within municipalities.

(b1) The Department of Transportation may participate in the development and adoption of a transportation plan or updated transportation plan when all local governments within the area covered by the transportation plan have adopted land development plans within the previous five years. The Department of Transportation may participate in the development of a transportation plan if all the municipalities and counties within the area covered by the transportation plan are in the process of developing a land development plan. The Department of Transportation may not adopt or update a transportation plan until a local land development plan has been adopted. A qualifying land development plan may be a comprehensive plan, land use plan, master plan, strategic plan, or any type of plan or policy document that expresses a jurisdiction's goals and objectives for the development of land within that jurisdiction. At the request of the local jurisdiction, the Department may review and provide comments on the plan but shall not provide approval of the land development plan.

(b2) The municipality or the MPO shall provide opportunity for public comments prior to adoption of the transportation plan.

(b3) Each county, with the cooperation of the Department of Transportation, may develop a comprehensive transportation plan utilizing the procedures specified for municipalities in subsection (a) of this section. This plan may be adopted by both the governing body of the county and the Department of Transportation. For portions of a county located within an MPO, the development of a comprehensive transportation plan shall take place through the metropolitan planning organization.

(b4)   To complement the roadway element of the transportation plan, municipalities and MPOs may develop a collector street plan to assist in developing the roadway network. The Department of Transportation may review and provide comments but is not required to provide approval of the collector street plan.

(c)   From and after the date that the plan is adopted, the streets and highways designated in the plan as the responsibility of the Department of Transportation shall become a part of the State highway system and all such system streets shall be subject to the provisions of G.S. 136-93, and all streets designated in the plan as the responsibility of the municipality shall become a part of the municipal street system.

(d)   For municipalities not located within an MPO, either the municipality or the Department of Transportation may propose changes in the plan at any time by giving notice to the other party, but no change shall be effective until it is adopted by both the Department of Transportation and the municipal governing board. For MPOs, either the MPO or the Department of Transportation may propose changes in the plan at any time by giving notice to the other party, but no change shall be effective until it is adopted by both the Department of Transportation and the MPO.

(e)   Until the adoption of a comprehensive transportation plan that includes future development of the street system in and around municipalities, the Department of Transportation and any municipality may reach an agreement as to which existing or proposed streets and highways within the municipal boundaries shall be added to or removed from the State highway system.

(f)   Streets within municipalities which are on the State highway system as of July 1, 1959, shall continue to be on that system until changes are made as provided in this section.

(g)   The street and highway elements of the plans developed pursuant to G.S. 136-66.2 shall serve as the plan referenced in G.S. 136-66.10(a). (1959, c. 687, s. 2; 1969, c. 794, s. 3; 1973, c. 507, s. 5; 1977, c. 464, s. 7.1; 2001-168, s. 1.)

§ 136-66.3. Local government participation in improvements to the State transportation system.

(a)   Municipal Participation Authorized. - A municipality may, but is not required to, participate in the right-of-way and construction cost of a State transportation improvement approved by the Board of Transportation under G.S. 143B-350(f)(4) that is located in the municipality or its extraterritorial jurisdiction.

(b)   Process for Initiating Participation. - A municipality interested in participating in the funding of a State highway improvement project may submit a proposal to the Department of Transportation. The Department and the municipality shall include their respective responsibilities for a proposed municipal participation project in any agreement reached concerning participation.

(c)   Type of Participation Authorized. - A municipality is authorized and empowered to acquire land by dedication and acceptance, purchase, or eminent domain, and make improvements to portions of the State transportation system lying within or outside the municipal corporate limits utilizing local funds that have been authorized for that purpose. All improvements to State transportation systems shall be done in accordance with the specifications and requirements of the Department of Transportation.

(c1)   Repealed by Session Laws 2013-183, s. 4.5, effective July 1, 2013.

(c2)   Distribution of State Funds Made Available by County or Municipal Participation. - Any State or federal funds allocated to a project that are made available by county or municipal participation in a project contained in the Transportation Improvement Program under G.S. 143B-350(f)(4) shall be subject to G.S. 136-189.11.

(c3)   Repealed by Session Laws 2013-183, s. 4.5, effective July 1, 2013.

(c4)   Pedestrian Safety Improvements. - The Department of Transportation shall accept and use any funding provided by a municipal government for a pedestrian safety improvement project on a State road within the municipality's limits, provided the municipality funds one hundred percent (100%) of the project and the Department of Transportation retains the right to approve the design and oversee the construction, erection, or installation of the pedestrian safety improvement.

(d)   Authorization to Participate in Development-Related Improvements. - When in the review and approval by a local government of plans for the development of property abutting a State transportation system it is determined by the municipality that improvements to the State highway system are necessary to provide for the safe and orderly movement of traffic, the local government is authorized to construct, or have constructed, said improvements to the State transportation system in vicinity of the development. For purposes of this section, improvements include but are not limited to additional travel lanes, turn lanes, curb and gutter, drainage facilities, and other transportation system improvements. All improvements to a State transportation system shall be constructed in accordance with the specifications and requirements of the Department of Transportation and be approved by the Department of Transportation.

(e) Authorization to Participate in Project Additions. - Pursuant to an agreement with the Department of Transportation, a county or municipality may reimburse the Department of Transportation for the cost of all improvements, including additional right-of-way, for a street, highway improvement projects, or other transportation system improvements approved by the Board of Transportation under G.S. 143B-350(f)(4), that are in addition to those improvements that the Department of Transportation would normally include in the project.

(e1) Reimbursement Procedure. - Upon request of the county or municipality, the Department of Transportation shall allow the local government a period of not less than three years from the date construction of a project undertaken under subsection (e) of this section is initiated to reimburse the Department their agreed upon share of the costs necessary for the project. The Department of Transportation shall not charge a local government any interest during the initial three years.

(f) Report to General Assembly. - The Department shall report in writing, on a monthly basis, to the Joint Legislative Commission on Governmental Operations on all agreements entered into between counties, municipalities and the Department of Transportation. The report shall state in summary form the contents of such agreements.

(g) Local Government Acquisition of Rights-of-Way. - In the acquisition of rights-of-way for any State street, highway, or other transportation project, the county or municipality shall be vested with the same authority to acquire such rights-of-way as is granted to the Department of Transportation in this Chapter. In the acquisition of such rights-of-way, counties and municipalities may use the procedures provided in Article 9 of this Chapter, and wherever the words "Department of Transportation" appear in Article 9 they shall be deemed to include "county," "municipality" or local governing body, and wherever the words "Administrator," "Administrator of Highways," "Administrator of the Department of Transportation," or "Chairman of the Department of Transportation" appear in Article 9 they shall be deemed to include "county or municipal clerk". It is the intention of this subsection that the powers herein granted to municipalities for the purpose of acquiring rights-of-way shall be in addition to and supplementary to those powers granted in any local act or in any other general statute, and in any case in which the provisions of this subsection or Article 9 of this Chapter are in conflict with the provisions of any local act or any other provision of any general statute, then the governing body of the county or municipality may in its discretion proceed in accordance with the provisions of such local act or other general statute, or, as an alternative method of procedure, in accordance with the provisions of this subsection and Article 9 of this Chapter.

(h) Department Authority Concerning Rights-of-Way. - In the absence of an agreement, the Department of Transportation shall retain authority to pay the full cost of acquiring rights-of-way where the proposed project is deemed important to a coordinated State transportation system.

(i) Changes to Local Government Participation Agreement. - Either the local government or the Department of Transportation may at any time propose changes in the agreement setting forth their respective responsibilities by giving notice to the other party, but no change shall be effective until it is adopted by both the municipal governing body and the Department of Transportation.

(j) Local Governments Party to Rights-of-Way Proceeding. - Any municipality that agrees to contribute any part of the cost of acquiring rights-of-way for any State transportation system shall be a proper party in any proceeding in court relating to the acquisition of such rights-of-way.

(k) Repealed by Session Laws 2008-180, s. 6, effective August 4, 2008. (1959, c. 687, s. 3; 1965, c. 867; 1967, c. 1127; 1973, c. 507, s. 5; 1977, c. 464, s. 7.1; 1987, c. 747, s. 3; 1989, c. 595, ss. 2, 3; 1991, c. 21, s. 1; 2000-188, s. 1; 2001-245, s. 2; 2008-180, s. 6; 2009-266, s. 23; 2010-37, s. 1; 2013-183, s. 4.5.)

§ 136-66.4. Rules and regulations; authority of municipalities.

The Department of Transportation shall have authority to adopt such rules and regulations as are necessary to carry out the responsibilities of the Department of Transportation under this Article, and municipalities shall have and may exercise such authority as is necessary to carry out their responsibilities under this Article. (1959, c. 687, s. 4; 1973, c. 507, s. 5; 1977, c. 464, s. 7.1.)

§ 136-66.5. Improvements in urban areas to reduce traffic congestion.

(a)   The Department of Transportation is authorized to enter into contracts with municipalities for improvement projects which are a part of an overall plan authorized under the provisions of section 135 of Title 23 of the United States Code, the purpose of which is to facilitate the flow of people and goods in urban areas. In connection with these contracts, the Department of Transportation and the municipalities are authorized to enter into contracts for improvement projects on the municipal system of streets, and pursuant to contract with the municipalities, the Department of Transportation is authorized to construct or to let to contract the said improvement projects on streets on the municipal street system or other transportation system; provided that no portion of the cost of the improvements made on the municipal system shall be paid from Department of Transportation funds except the proportionate share of funds received from the United States Department of Transportation and allocated for the purposes set out in section 135 of Title 23 of the United States Code. Pursuant to contract with the Department of Transportation, the municipalities may construct or let to contract the said improvement projects on the municipal system and the Department of Transportation is authorized to pay over to the municipalities the proportionate share of funds received pursuant to section 135 of Title 23 of the United States Code; provided that no portion of the costs of the improvements made on the municipal system shall be paid for from the State Highway Fund except those received from the United States Department of Transportation and allocated for the purpose set out in section 135 of Title 23 of the United States Code.

(b)   The municipalities are authorized to enter into contracts with the Department of Transportation for improvement projects which are a part of an overall plan authorized under the provisions of section 135 of Title 23 of the United States Code, the purpose of which is to facilitate the flow of traffic in urban areas, on the State highway system streets within the municipalities with the approval of the United States Department of Transportation. Pursuant to contract for the foregoing improvement projects, the municipalities are authorized to construct or let to contract the said improvement projects and the Department of Transportation is authorized to reimburse the municipalities for the cost of the construction of the said improvement projects.

(c) The municipalities in which improvements are made pursuant to section 135 of Title 23 of the United States Code shall provide proper maintenance and operation of such completed projects and improvements on the municipal system streets and other transportation infrastructure or will provide other means for assuring proper maintenance and operation as is required by the Department of Transportation. In the event the municipality fails to maintain such project or provide for their proper maintenance, the Department of Transportation is authorized to maintain the said projects and improvements and deduct the cost from allocations to the municipalities made under the provisions of G.S. 136-41.1. (1969, c. 794, s. 1; 1973, c. 507, ss. 5, 19; 1977, c. 464, s. 7.1; 2009-266, s. 24.)

§ 136-66.6. Arrangements in a consolidated city-county.

The provisions of this Article applying to municipalities apply to each consolidated city-county with respect to each urban service district defined by its governing board that includes the total area of a previously existing municipality in the same manner as if the urban service district were a municipality. The provisions of this Article do not apply to any consolidated city-county with respect to an urban service district defined by its governing board within previously unincorporated areas of the county unless the governing board determines that street services are to be provided within such urban service district. (1973, c. 537, s. 7.)

§ 136-66.7. Authority to include a Municipal Street System street in right-of-way of State Highway System.

(a) Notwithstanding any other provisions of Article 3A of Chapter 136, the provisions of Article 15 of Chapter 160A, or of any other statute, the Department of Transportation may include all or part of a Municipal Street System street as part of the right-of-way of a State Highway System street, highway, or bridge whenever the Board of Transportation determines that inclusion of the Municipal

Street System street is necessary to improve, relocate, or construct a State Highway System street, highway, or bridge.

(b) Beginning January 1, 1985, the Department may not exercise such authority unless 90 days written notice to the governing body of the affected municipality is provided; and the Department shall hold a public hearing on the issue with 30 days published notice upon the written official request of the governing body received by the Department no less than 45 days after receipt of the notice to the governing body. (1983 (Reg. Sess., 1984), c. 1020.)

§ 136-66.8. Agreements with units of local government to expedite projects.

(a) Agreements Authorized. - The Department of Transportation may enter into agreements with units of local government for the purpose of expediting transportation projects currently programmed in the Transportation Improvement Plan.

(b) Form of Agreements. - The agreements affected by this section shall be between the Department of Transportation and units of local government. The agreements may authorize units of local government to construct projects scheduled in the Transportation Improvement Plan more than two years from the date of the agreement. The units of local government shall fund one hundred percent (100%) of the project at current prices. In a future year, when the project is funded from State and federal sources, the units of local government shall be reimbursed an appropriate share of the funds, at the future programmed project funding amount, as identified and scheduled in the Transportation Improvement Plan.

(c) Report. - The Department of Transportation shall report to the Joint Legislative Transportation Oversight Committee by December 1, 2006, on any agreements executed with units of local government pursuant to this section. (2006-135, s. 3.)

§ 136-66.9. Reserved for future codification purposes.

Article 3B.

Dedication of Right-of-Way with Density or Development Rights Transfer.

§ 136-66.10. Dedication of right-of-way under local ordinances.

(a) Whenever a tract of land located within the territorial jurisdiction of a city or county's zoning or subdivision control ordinance or any other land use control ordinance authorized by local act is proposed for subdivision or for use pursuant to a zoning or building permit, and a portion of it is embraced within a corridor for a street or highway on a plan established and adopted pursuant to G.S. 136-66.2, a city or county zoning or subdivision ordinance may provide for the dedication of right-of-way within that corridor pursuant to any applicable legal authority, or:

(1) A city or county may require an applicant for subdivision plat approval or for a special use permit, conditional use permit, or special exception, or for any other permission pursuant to a land use control ordinance authorized by local act to dedicate for street or highway purpose, the right-of-way within such corridor if the city or county allows the applicant to transfer density credits attributable to the dedicated right-of-way to contiguous land owned by the applicant. No dedication of right-of-way shall be required pursuant to this subdivision unless the board or agency granting final subdivision plat approval or the special use permit, conditional use permit, special exception, or permission shall find, prior to the grant, that the dedication does not result in the deprivation of a reasonable use of the original tract and that the dedication is either reasonably related to the traffic generated by the proposed subdivision or use of the remaining land or the impact of the dedication is mitigated by measures provided in the local ordinance.

(2) If a city or county does not require the dedication of right-of-way within the corridor pursuant to subdivision (1) of this subsection or other applicable legal authority, but an applicant for subdivision plat approval or a zoning or building permit, or any other permission pursuant to a land use control ordinance authorized by local act elects to dedicate the right-of-way, the city or county may allow the applicant to transfer density credits attributable to the dedicated right-of-way to contiguous land that is part of a common development plan or to transfer severable development rights attributable to the dedicated right-of-way to noncontiguous land in designated receiving districts pursuant to G.S. 136-66.11.

(b) When used in this section, the term "density credit" means the potential for the improvement or subdivision of part or all of a parcel of real property, as permitted under the terms of a zoning and/or subdivision ordinance, and/or other land use control ordinance authorized by local act, expressed in dwelling unit equivalents or other measures of development density or intensity or a fraction or multiple of that potential that may be transferred to other portions of the same parcel or to contiguous land in that is part of a common development plan. (1987, c. 747, s. 7; 1989, c. 595, s. 4.)

§ 136-66.11. Transfer of severable development rights.

(a) When used in this section and in G.S. 136-66.10, the term "severable development right" means the potential for the improvement or subdivision of part or all of a parcel of real property, as permitted under the terms of a zoning and/or subdivision ordinance, expressed in dwelling unit equivalents or other measures of development density or intensity or a fraction or multiple of that potential that may be severed or detached from the parcel from which they are derived and transferred to one or more other parcels located in receiving districts where they may be exercised in conjunction with the use or subdivision of property, in accordance with the provisions of this section.

(b) A city or county may provide in its zoning and subdivision control ordinances for the establishment, transfer, and exercise of severable development rights to implement the provisions of G.S. 136-66.10 and this section.

(c) City or county zoning or subdivision control provisions adopted pursuant to this authority shall provide that if right-of-way area is dedicated and severable development rights are provided pursuant to G.S. 136-66.10(a)(2) and this section, within 10 days after the approval of the final subdivision plat or issuance of the building permit, the city or county shall convey to the dedicator a deed for the severable development rights that are attributable to the right-of-way area dedicated under those subdivisions. If the deed for the severable development rights conveyed by the city or county to the dedicator is not recorded in the office of the register of deeds within 15 days of its receipt, the deed shall be null and void.

(d) In order to provide for the transfer of severable development rights pursuant to this section, the governing board shall amend the zoning ordinance to designate severable development rights receiving districts. These districts may be designated as separate use districts or as overlaying other zoning districts. No severable development rights shall be exercised in conjunction with the development of subdivision of any parcel of land that is not located in a receiving district. A city or county may, however, limit the maximum development density or intensity or the minimum size of lots allowed when severable development rights are exercised in conjunction with the development or subdivision of any eligible site in a receiving district. No plat for a subdivision in conjunction with which severable development rights are exercised shall be recorded by the register of deeds, and no new building, or part thereof, or addition to or enlargement of an existing building, that is part of a development project in conjunction with which severable development rights are exercised shall be occupied, until documents have been recorded in the office of the register of deeds transferring title from the owner of the severable development rights to the granting city or county and providing for their subsequent extinguishment. These documents shall also include any other information that the city or county ordinance may prescribe.

(e) In order to implement the purposes of this section a city or county may by ordinance adopt regulations consistent with the provisions of this section.

(f) A severable development right shall be treated as an interest in real property. Once a deed for severable development rights has been transferred by a city or county to the dedicator and recorded, the severable development rights shall vest and become freely alienable. (1987, c. 747, s. 7.)

Article 4.

Neighborhood Roads, Cartways, Church Roads, etc.

§ 136-67. Neighborhood public roads.

All those portions of the public road system of the State which have not been taken over and placed under maintenance or which have been abandoned by the Department of Transportation, but which remain open and in general use as a necessary means of ingress to and egress from the dwelling house of one or more families, and all those roads that have been laid out, constructed, or reconstructed with unemployment relief funds under the supervision of the Department of Health and Human Services, and all other roads or streets or portions of roads or streets whatsoever outside of the boundaries of any incorporated city or town in the State which serve a public use and as a means of ingress or egress for one or more families, regardless of whether the same have ever been a portion of any State or county road system, are hereby declared to be neighborhood public roads and they shall be subject to all of the provisions of G.S. 136-68, 136-69 and 136-70 with respect to the alteration, extension, or discontinuance thereof, and any interested party is authorized to institute such proceeding, and in lieu of personal service with respect to this class of roads, notice by publication once a week in any newspaper published in said county, or in the event there is no such newspaper, by posting at the courthouse door and three other public places, shall be deemed sufficient: Provided, that this definition of neighborhood public roads shall not be construed to embrace any street, road or driveway that serves an essentially private use, and all those portions and segments of old roads, formerly a part of the public road system, which have not been taken over and placed under maintenance and which have been abandoned by the Department of Transportation and which do not serve as a necessary means of ingress to and egress from an occupied dwelling house are hereby specifically excluded from the definition of neighborhood public roads, and the owner of the land, burdened with such portions and segments of such old roads, is hereby invested with the easement or right-of-way for such old roads heretofore existing.

Upon request of the board of county commissioners of any county, the Department of Transportation is permitted, but is not required, to place such neighborhood public roads as above defined in a passable condition without incorporating the same into the State or county system, and without becoming obligated in any manner for the permanent maintenance thereof.

This section shall not authorize the reopening on abandoned roads of any railroad grade crossing that has been closed by order of the Department of Transportation in connection with the building of an overhead bridge or underpass to take the place of such grade crossing. (1929, c. 257, s. 1; 1933, c. 302; 1941, c. 183; 1949, c. 1215; 1957, c. 65, s. 11; 1969, c. 982; 1973, c. 476, s. 138; c. 507, s. 5; 1977, c. 464, s. 7.1; 1997-443, s. 11A.122.)

§ 136-68. Special proceeding for establishment, alteration or discontinuance of cartways, etc.; petition; appeal.

The establishment, alteration, or discontinuance of any cartway, church road, mill road, or like easement, for the benefit of any person, firm, association, or corporation, over the lands of another, shall be determined by a special proceeding instituted before the clerk of the superior court in the county where the property affected is situated. Such special proceeding shall be commenced by a petition filed with said clerk and the service of a copy thereof on the person or persons whose property will be affected thereby. From any final order or judgment in said special proceeding, any interested party may appeal to the superior court for a jury trial de novo on all issues including the right to relief, the location of a cartway, tramway or railway, and the assessment of damages. The procedure established under Chapter 40A, entitled "Eminent Domain," shall be followed in the conduct of such special proceeding insofar as the same is applicable and in harmony with the provisions of this section. (1879, c. 82, s. 9; Code, s. 2023; Rev., s. 2683; C.S., s. 3835; 1931, c. 448; 1995, c. 513, s. 1.)

§ 136-69. Cartways, tramways, etc., laid out; procedure.

(a) If any person, firm, association, or corporation shall be engaged in the cultivation of any land or the cutting and removing of any standing timber, or the working of any quarries, mines, or minerals, or the operating of any industrial or manufacturing plants, or public or private cemetery, or taking action preparatory to the operation of any such enterprises, to which there is leading no public road or other adequate means of transportation, other than a navigable waterway, affording necessary and proper means of ingress thereto and egress therefrom, such person, firm, association, or corporation may institute a special proceeding as set out in the preceding section (G.S. 136-68), and if it shall be made to appear to the court necessary, reasonable and just that such person shall have a private way to a public road or watercourse or railroad over the lands of other persons, the court shall appoint a jury of view of three disinterested freeholders to view the premises and lay off a cartway, tramway, or railway of not less than 18 feet in width, or cableways, chutes, and flumes, and assess the damages the owner or owners of the land crossed may sustain thereby, and make report of their findings in writing to the clerk of the superior court. Exceptions to said report may be filed by any interested party and such exceptions shall be heard and determined by the clerk of the superior court. The clerk of the superior court may affirm or modify said report, or set the same aside and order a new jury of view. All damages assessed by a judgment of the clerk, together with the cost of the proceeding, shall be paid into the clerk's office before the petitioners shall acquire any rights under said proceeding.

(b) (See editor's note) Compensation to the landowner for the establishment of a cartway over the property of another shall be as provided in Chapter 40A Article 4 of the North Carolina General Statutes.

(c) Where a tract of land lies partly in one county and partly in an adjoining county, or where a tract of land lies wholly within one county and the public road nearest or from which the most practical roadway to said land would run, lies in an adjoining county and the practical way for a cartway to said land would lead over lands in an adjoining county, then and in that event the proceeding for the laying out and establishing of a cartway may be commenced in either the county in which the land is located or the adjoining county through which said cartway would extend to the public road, and upon the filing of such petition in either county the clerk of the court shall have jurisdiction to proceed for the appointment of a jury from the county in which the petition is filed and proceed for the laying out and establishing of a cartway as if the tract of land to be reached by the cartway and the entire length of the cartway are all located within the bounds of said county in which the petition may be filed. (1798, c. 508, s. 1, P.R.; 1822, c. 1139, s. 1, P.R.; R.C., c. 101, s. 37; 1879, c. 258; Code, s. 2056; 1887, c. 46; 1903, c. 102; Rev., s. 2686; 1909, c. 364, s. 1; 1917, c. 187, s. 1; c. 282, s. 1; C.S., s. 3836; 1921, c. 135; Ex. Sess., 1921, c. 73; 1929, c. 197, s. 1; 1931, c. 448; 1951, c. 1125, s. 1; 1961, c. 71; 1965, c. 414, s. 1; 1981, c. 826, s. 1; 1995, c. 513, ss. 2, 3a)

§ 136-70. Alteration or abandonment of cartways, etc., in same manner.

Cartways or other ways established under this Article or heretofore established, may be altered, changed, or abandoned in like manner as herein provided for their establishment upon petition instituted by any interested party: Provided, that all cartways, tramways, or railways established for the removal of timber shall automatically terminate at the end of a period of five years, unless a greater time is set forth in the petition and the judgment establishing the same. (1798, c. 508, ss. 1, 2, 3, P.R.; 1834, c. 16, s. 1; R.C., c. 101, s. 38; Code, s. 2057; 1887, c. 46, s. 2; c. 266; Rev., s. 2694; C.S., s. 3837; 1931, c. 448; 1995, c. 513, s. 3.)

§ 136-71. Church roads and easements of public utility lines laid out on petition; procedure.

Necessary roads or easements and right-of-ways for electric light lines, power lines, water lines, sewage lines, and telephone lines leading to any church or other place of public worship may be established in the same manner as set forth in the preceding sections of this Article upon petition of the duly constituted officials of such church. (1872-3, c. 189, ss. 1-3, 5; Code, ss. 2062, 2064; Rev., ss. 2687, 2689; C.S., s. 3838; 1931, c. 448; 1949, c. 382.)

§§ 136-71.1 through 136-71.5. Reserved for future codification purposes.

Article 4A.

Bicycle and Bikeway Act of 1974.

§ 136-71.6. How Article cited.

This Article may be cited as the North Carolina Bicycle and Bikeway Act of 1974. (1973, c. 1447, s. 1.)

§ 136-71.7. Definitions.

As used in this Article, except where the context clearly requires otherwise, the words and expressions defined in this section shall be held to have the meanings here given to them:

(1) Bicycle: A nonmotorized vehicle with two or three wheels tandem, a steering handle, one or two saddle seats, and pedals by which the vehicle is propelled.

(2) Bikeway: A thoroughfare suitable for bicycles, and which may either exist within the right-of-way of other modes of transportation, such as highways, or along a separate and independent corridor.

(3) Department: North Carolina Department of Transportation.

(4) Program: North Carolina Bicycle and Bikeway Program.

(5) Secretary: The Secretary of the North Carolina Department of Transportation. (1973, c. 1447, s. 2; 1975, c. 716, s. 7; 1977, c. 1021, s. 1.)

§ 136-71.8. Findings.

The General Assembly hereby finds that it is in the public interest, health, safety, and welfare for the State to encourage and provide for the efficient and safe use of the bicycle; and that to coordinate plans for bikeways most effectively with those of the State and local governments as they affect roads, streets, schools, parks and other publicly owned lands, abandoned roadbeds and conservation areas, while maximizing the benefits from the use of tax dollars, a single State agency, eligible to receive federal matching funds, should be designated to establish and maintain a statewide bikeways program. The General Assembly also finds that bikeways are a bona fide highway purpose, subject to the same rights and responsibilities, and eligible for the same considerations as other highway purposes and functions. (1973, c. 1447, s. 3; 1977, c. 1021, s. 1.)

§ 136-71.9. Program development.

The Department is designated as such State agency, responsible for developing and coordinating the program. (1973, c. 1447, s. 4.)

§ 136-71.10. Duties.

The Department will:

(1) Assist and cooperate with local governments and other agencies in the development and construction of local and regional bikeway projects;

(2) Develop and publish policies, procedures, and standards for planning, designing, constructing, maintaining, marking, and operating bikeways in the

State; for the registration and security of bicycles; and for the safety of bicyclists, motorists and the public;

(3)   Develop bikeway demonstration projects and safety training programs;

(4)   Develop and construct a State bikeway system. (1973, c. 1447, s. 5.)

§ 136-71.11. Designation of bikeways.

Bikeways may be designated along and upon the public roads. (1973, c. 1447, s. 5.)

§ 136-71.12. Funds.

The General Assembly hereby authorizes the Department to include needed funds for the program in its annual budgets for fiscal years after June 30, 1975, subject to the approval of the General Assembly.

The Department is authorized to spend any federal, State, local or private funds available to the Department and designated for the accomplishment of this Article. Cities, towns, and counties may use any funds available. (1973, c. 1447, s. 6; 2003-256, s. 1.)

§ 136-71.13: Repealed by Session Laws 2011-145, s. 28.17(b), effective July 1, 2011, and Session Laws 2011-266, s. 1.27, effective July 1, 2011.

Article 5.

Bridges.

§ 136-72. Load limits for bridges; penalty for violations.

The Department of Transportation shall have authority to determine the safe load-carrying capacity for any and all bridges on highways on the State highway system. It shall be unlawful for any person, firm, or corporation to drive, operate or tow on any bridge on the State highway system, any vehicle or combination of vehicles with a gross weight exceeding the safe load-carrying capacity established by the Department of Transportation and posted at each end of the said bridge. Any person, firm, or corporation violating the provisions of this section shall be guilty of a Class 1 misdemeanor. (1931, c. 145, s. 16; 1933, c. 172, s. 17; 1957, c. 65, s. 11; 1973, c. 507, s. 5; 1975, c. 373, s. 1; 1977, c. 306, c. 464, s. 7.1; 1993, c. 539, s. 985; 1994, Ex. Sess., c. 24, s. 14(c).)

§§ 136-73 through 136-75. Repealed by Session Laws 1979, c. 114, s. 1.

§ 136-76. Repealed by Session Laws 1965, c. 492.

§ 136-76.1. Bridge replacement program.

(a) The Department of Transportation is hereby directed to replace all bridges on the State highway system containing long through truss spans over 125 feet long with less than a 12 feet clear roadway width. The Department shall initiate a bridge replacement program as soon as possible and shall complete the replacement program of all such bridges by June 30, 1980. All such bridges now on the State highway system shall be replaced except those on roads where the traffic volume is low and the elimination of the bridge would be a minimum inconvenience to the public and the replacement cannot be justified. Such bridges not replaced shall be removed and taken off the State highway system. Provided, that the provisions of this subsection shall not apply to any bridge which has not been removed and replaced by June 30, 1980; these bridges shall continue to be included in the State Highway System, and shall be examined, repaired if necessary, updated and put into usable condition with weight limitations as safety may require.

(b) The Environment [Environmental] Policy Act contained in Article 1 of Chapter 113A shall not apply to the bridge replacement program provided for by this section. (1975, c. 889; 1977, c. 464, s. 7.1; 1981, c. 861.)

§ 136-77. Repealed by Session Laws 1979, c. 114, s. 1.

§ 136-78. Railroad companies to provide draws.

Railroad companies, erecting bridges across watercourses, shall attach and keep up good and sufficient draws, by which vessels may be allowed conveniently to pass. (1846, c. 51, ss. 1, 2; R.C., c. 101, s. 32; Code, s. 2051; Rev., s. 2701; C.S., s. 3800.)

§ 136-79. Repealed by Session Laws 1965, c. 491.

§ 136-80. Fastening vessels to bridges misdemeanor.

If any person shall fasten any decked vessel or steamer to any bridge that crosses a navigable stream, he shall be guilty of a Class 1 misdemeanor, and in the case of a bridge that crosses a county line, may be prosecuted in either county. (R.S., c. 104; R.C., c. 101, s. 31; 1858-9, c. 58, s. 1; Code, s. 2050; 1887, c. 93, s. 3; Rev., s. 3774; C.S., s. 3804; 1993, c. 539, s. 986; 1994, Ex. Sess., c. 24, s. 14(c).)

§ 136-81. Department of Transportation may maintain footways.

The Department of Transportation shall have the power to erect and maintain adequate footways over swamps, waters, chasms, gorges, gaps, or in any other places whatsoever, whenever said Department of Transportation shall find that such footways are necessary, in connection with the use of the highways, for the safety and convenience of the public. (1817, c. 940, ss. 1, 2, P.R.; R.C., c. 101, s. 17; Code, s. 2029; Rev., s. 2695; C.S., s. 3785; 1921, c. 2; 1931, c. 145; 1933, c. 172, s. 17; 1957, c. 65, s. 11; 1973, c. 507, s. 5; 1977, c. 464, s. 7.1.)

Article 6.

Ferries, etc., and Toll Bridges.

§ 136-82. Department of Transportation to establish and maintain ferries.

(a) Powers of Department. - The Department of Transportation is vested with authority to provide for the establishment and maintenance of ferries connecting the parts of the State highway system, whenever in its discretion the public good may require, and shall prescribe and collect tolls on the ferry routes as established by the Board of Transportation following the procedures set forth in this section.

(b) Establishment of Tolling. - The Board of Transportation may establish tolls on any untolled ferry route as set forth in this subsection. Prior to establishing tolls on an untolled ferry route, the Board of Transportation must receive a resolution approved by the Transportation Advisory Committee of each affected local transportation planning organization requesting tolls on that route. No later than March 1, 2014, the Department shall hold a separate public hearing in the geographic area of each untolled ferry route and invite each affected local transportation planning organization. At the public hearing, the Department shall present an explanation of the toll setting methodology, the impact of tolling on the availability of funding for other local transportation priorities, and the minimum and maximum toll rates. After the public hearing, an affected local transportation planning organization may consider and adopt a ferry tolling resolution. The Board of Transportation shall adopt the toll at its next regularly scheduled meeting after receipt of the ferry tolling resolutions required by this subsection. The Department shall collect the toll as soon as is feasible following its adoption, but in no case more than 180 days after adoption of the toll. The establishment of tolls by the Board of Transportation pursuant to the authority granted in this section shall be exempt from the provisions of Chapter 150B of the General Statutes. For purposes of this section, "affected local transportation planning organization" means any Metropolitan Planning Organization or Rural Transportation Planning Organization with geographic jurisdiction over any part of an untolled ferry route, and "untolled ferry route" means any ferry route for which no tolls were in effect as of June 30, 2013.

(c) Revisions of Tolls. - The Department of Transportation shall report to the Fiscal Research Division, the Joint Legislative Transportation Oversight Committee, and all affected local transportation planning organizations 30 days prior to any change in toll rates or change in the toll setting methodology by the Board of Transportation.

(d) Use of Toll Proceeds. - The Department of Transportation shall credit the proceeds from tolls collected on North Carolina Ferry System routes and receipts generated under subsection (e) of this section to reserve accounts within the Highway Fund for each of the Highway Divisions in which system terminals are located and fares are earned. For the purposes of this subsection, fares are earned based on the terminals from which a passenger trip originates and terminates. Commuter pass receipts shall be credited proportionately to each reserve account based on the distribution of trips originating and terminating in each Highway Division. The proceeds credited to each reserve account shall be used exclusively for prioritized North Carolina Ferry System ferry passenger vessel replacement projects in the Division in which the proceeds are earned. Proceeds may be used to fund ferry passenger vessel replacement projects or supplement funds allocated for ferry passenger vessel replacement projects approved in the Transportation Improvement Program.

(e) Powers of Department. - To accomplish the purpose of this section, the Department of Transportation is authorized to acquire, own, lease, charter or otherwise control all necessary vessels, boats, terminals or other facilities required for the proper operation of the ferries or to enter into contracts with persons, firms or corporations for the operation thereof and to pay the reasonable sums that in the opinion of the Department of Transportation represent the fair value of the public service rendered.

(f) Authority to Generate Certain Receipts. - The Department of Transportation, notwithstanding any other provision of law, may operate or contract for the following receipt-generating activities and use the proceeds for ferry passenger vessel replacement projects in the manner set forth in subsection (c) of this section:

(1) Operation of, concessions on the ferries and at ferry facilities to provide to passengers on the ferries food, drink, and other refreshments, personal comfort items, Internet access, and souvenirs publicizing the ferry system.

(2) The sale of naming rights to any ferry vessel, ferry route, or ferry facility.

(3) Advertising on or within any ferry vessel, including display advertising and advertising delivered to passengers through the use of video monitors, public address systems installed in passenger areas, and other electronic media.

(4) Any other receipt-generating activity not otherwise forbidden by applicable law pertaining to public health or safety.

(g) Confidentiality of Personal Information. - Identifying information obtained by the Department related to operation of the ferry system is not a public record under Chapter 132 of the General Statutes and is subject to the disclosure limitations in 18 U.S.C. § 2721 of the federal Driver's Privacy Protection Act. The Department shall maintain the confidentiality of all information required to be kept confidential under 18 U.S.C. § 2721(a), as well as any financial information, transaction history, and information related to the collection of a toll or user fee from a person, including, but not limited to, photographs or other recorded images or automatic vehicle identification or driver account information generated by radio-frequency identification or other electronic means. The Department may use identifying information only for purposes of collecting and enforcing tolls. Nothing in this section is intended to limit the right of any person to examine that person's own account information, or the right of any party, by authority of a proper court order, to inspect and examine identifying information. (1927, c. 223; 1933, c. 172, s. 17; 1957, c. 65, s. 11; 1973, c. 507, s. 5; 1977, c. 464, s. 7.1; 1989, c. 752, s. 101; 1995, c. 211, s. 1; 2011-145, s. 31.30(a); 2012-142, s. 24.18(a); 2013-360, s. 34.13(b).)

§ 136-82.1. Authority to insure vessels operated by Department of Transportation.

The Department of Transportation is vested with authority to purchase liability insurance, hull insurance, and protection insurance on all vessels and boats owned, leased, chartered or otherwise controlled and operated by the Department of Transportation. (1961, c. 486; 1973, c. 507, s. 5; 1977, c. 464, s. 27.)

§ 136-82.2: Repealed by Session Laws 2010-133, s. 1, effective December 1, 2010.

§ 136-83. Repealed by Session Laws 1977, c. 464, s. 22.

§§ 136-84 through 136-87: Repealed by Session Laws 1983, c. 684, s. 1.

§ 136-88. Authority of county commissioners with regard to ferries and toll bridges; rights and liabilities of owners of ferries or toll bridges not under supervision of Department of Transportation.

Subject to the provisions of G.S. 136-67, 136-99, and 153-198, the boards of commissioners of the several counties are vested, in regard to the establishment, operation, maintenance, and supervision of ferries and toll bridges on public roads not under the supervision and control of the Department of Transportation, with all the power and authority regarding ferries and toll bridges vested by law in county commissioners on the thirty-first day of March, 1931. And the owners or operators of ferries or toll bridges not under the supervision and control of the Department of Transportation shall be entitled to the same rights, powers, and privileges, and subject to the same duties, responsibilities and liabilities, to which owners or operators of ferries or toll bridges were entitled or were subject on the thirty-first day of March, 1931. (1957, c. 65, s. 11; 1973, c. 507, s. 5; 1977, c. 464, s. 7.1.)

§ 136-89. Safety measures; guard chains or gates.

Each and every person, firm or corporation, owning or operating a public ferry upon any sound, bay, river, creek or other stream, shall have securely affixed and attached thereto, at each end of the same, a detachable steel or iron chain, or in lieu thereof a steel or iron gate, and so affixed and arranged that the same shall be closed or fastened across the opposite end from the approach, whenever any motor vehicle, buggy, cart, wagon, or other conveyance shall be driven upon or shall enter upon the same; and shall be securely fastened or closed at each end of the ferry after such motor vehicle, buggy, cart, wagon, or other conveyance shall have been driven or shall have entered upon the same. And the said gates or chains shall remain closed or fastened, at each end, until the voyage across the stream upon which said ferry is operated shall have been completed. The Department of Transportation, as to ferries under its supervision, and the respective boards of county commissioners, as to other ferries, shall fix and determine a standard weight or size of chain, and a standard size, type, or character of gate, for use by said ferries, leaving optional with the said owner or operator the use of chains or gates.

Any person, firm or corporation violating any of the provisions of this section shall be guilty of a Class 1 misdemeanor. (1923, c. 133; C.S., ss. 3825(a), 3825(b), 3825(c); 1927, c. 223; 1931, c. 145, s. 38; 1933, c. 172, s. 17; 1957, c.

65, s. 11; 1973, c. 507, s. 5; 1977, c. 464, s. 7.1; 1993, c. 539, s. 987; 1994, Ex. Sess., c. 24, s. 14(c).)

Article 6A.

Carolina-Virginia Turnpike Authority.

§§ 136-89.1 through 136-89.11H: Repealed by Session Laws 1959, c. 25, s. 1.

Article 6B.

Turnpikes.

§§ 136-89.12 through 136-89.30: Repealed by Session Laws 1959, c. 25, s. 2.

Article 6C.

State Toll Bridges and Revenue Bonds.

§§ 136-89.31 through 136-89.47: Repealed by Session Laws 1977, c. 464, s. 22.

Article 6D.

Controlled-Access Facilities.

§ 136-89.48. Declaration of policy.

The General Assembly hereby finds, determines, and declares that this Article is necessary for the immediate preservation of the public peace, health and safety, the promotion of the general welfare, the improvement and development of transportation facilities in the State, the elimination of hazards at grade intersections, and other related purposes. (1957, c. 993, s. 1.)

§ 136-89.49. Definitions.

When used in this Article:

(1)   "Department" means the Department of Transportation.

(2)   "Controlled-access facility" means a State highway, or section of State highway, especially designed for through traffic, and over, from or to which highway owners or occupants of abutting property, or others, shall have only a controlled right or easement of access.

(3)   "Frontage road" means a way, road or street which is auxiliary to and located on the side of another highway, road or street for service to abutting property and adjacent areas and for the control of access to such other highway, road or street. (1957, c. 993, s. 2; 1973, c. 507, s. 5; 1977, c. 464, s. 7.1.)

§ 136-89.50. Authority to establish controlled-access facilities.

The Department of Transportation may designate, establish, abandon, improve, construct, maintain and regulate controlled-access facilities as a part of the State highway system, National System of Interstate Highways, and Federal Aid Primary System whenever the Department of Transportation determines that traffic conditions, present or future, justify such controlled-access facilities, or the abandonment thereof. (1957, c. 993, s. 3; 1973, c. 507, s. 5; 1977, c. 464, s. 7.1.)

§ 136-89.51. Design of controlled-access facility.

The Department of Transportation is authorized so to design any controlled-access facility and so to regulate, restrict, or prohibit access as best to serve the traffic for which such facility is intended. In this connection the Department of Transportation is authorized to divide and separate any controlled-access facility into separate roadways by the construction of raised curbings, central dividing sections, or other physical separations, or by designating such separate roadways by signs, markers, or stripes, and the proper lane for such traffic by appropriate signs, markers, stripes, and other devices. No person shall have any right of ingress or egress to, from or across controlled-access facilities to or from abutting lands, except at such designated points at which access may be permitted, upon such terms and conditions as may be specified from time to time by the Department of Transportation. (1957, c. 993, s. 4; 1973, c. 507, s. 5; 1977, c. 464, s. 7.1.)

§ 136-89.52. Acquisition of property and property rights.

For the purposes of this Article, the Department of Transportation may acquire private or public property and property rights for controlled-access facilities and service or frontage roads, including rights of access, air, view and light, by gift, devise, purchase, or condemnation in the same manner as now or hereafter authorized by law to acquire such property or property rights in connection with highways. The property rights acquired under the provisions of this Article may be in fee simple or an appropriate easement for right-of-way in perpetuity. In connection with the acquisition of property or property rights for any controlled-access facility or portion thereof, or frontage road in connection therewith, the Department of Transportation may, in its discretion, with the consent of the landowner, acquire an entire lot, parcel, or tract of land, if by so doing, the interests of the public will be best served, even though said entire lot, parcel, or tract is not immediately needed for the right-of-way proper.

Along new controlled-access highway locations, abutting property owners shall not be entitled to access to such new locations, and no abutter's easement of access to such new locations shall attach to said property. Where part of a tract of land is taken or acquired for the construction of a controlled-access facility on a new location, the nature of the facility constructed on the part taken, including the fact that there shall be no direct access thereto, shall be considered in determining the fair market value of the remaining property immediately after the taking. (1957, c. 993, s. 5; 1969, c. 946; 1973, c. 507, s. 5; 1977, c. 464, s. 7.1.)

§ 136-89.53. New and existing facilities; grade crossing eliminations.

The Department of Transportation may designate and establish controlled-access highways as new and additional facilities or may designate and establish an existing street or highway as included within a controlled-access facility. When an existing street or highway shall be designated as and included within a controlled-access facility the owners of land abutting such existing street or highway shall be entitled to compensation for the taking of or injury to their easements of access. The Department of Transportation shall have authority to provide for the elimination of intersections at grade of controlled-access facilities with existing State highways and county roads, and city and town streets, by grade separation or frontage road, or by closing off such roads and streets, or other public ways at the right-of-way boundary line of such controlled-access facility; and after the establishment of any controlled-access facility, no highway or street which is not part of said facility shall intersect the same at grade. No street or [of] any city or town and no State highway, county road, or other public way shall be opened into or connected with any such controlled-access facility without the consent and previous approval of the Department of Transportation. Such consent and approval shall be given only if the public interest shall be served thereby. (1957, c. 993, s. 6; 1973, c. 507, s. 5; 1977, c. 464, s. 7.1.)

§ 136-89.54. Authority of local units to consent.

The Department of Transportation, as the highway authority of the State, and the governing body of any county, city or town are authorized, after a public hearing to be held in the county affected, to enter into agreements with each other, and the Department of Transportation is authorized to enter into agreements with the federal government, respecting the financing, planning, establishment, improvement, maintenance, use, regulations, or vacation of controlled-access facilities or other public ways in their respective jurisdictions, to facilitate the purposes of this Article. (1957, c. 993, s. 7; 1973, c. 507, s. 5; 1977, c. 464, s. 7.1.)

§ 136-89.55. Local service roads.

In connection with the development of any controlled-access facility the Department of Transportation is authorized to plan, designate, establish, use, regulate, alter, improve, maintain, and vacate local service or frontage roads and streets or to designate as local service or frontage roads and streets any existing road or street, and to exercise jurisdiction over service or frontage roads in the same manner as is authorized over controlled-access facilities under the terms of this Article, if in its opinion such local service or frontage roads and streets are necessary or desirable; provided, however that after a local service or frontage road has been established, the same shall not be vacated or abandoned in such a manner as to reduce access to the facility without the consent of the abutting property owners or the payment of just compensation, so long as the controlled-access facility is maintained as such facility, and the Department of Transportation shall not have any authority to control or restrict the right of access of abutting property owners from their property to such local service or frontage roads or streets without the property owners' consent or the payment of just compensation, except such authority as the Department of Transportation has with respect to primary and secondary roads under the police power. Such local service or frontage roads or streets shall be of appropriate design, and shall be separated from the controlled-access facility proper by means of all devices designated as necessary or desirable. (1957, c. 993, s. 8; 1969, c. 795; 1973, c. 507, s. 5; 1977, c. 464, s. 7.1.)

§ 136-89.56. Commercial enterprises.

No commercial enterprises or activities shall be authorized or conducted by the Department of Transportation, or the governing body of any city or town, within or on the property acquired for or designated as a controlled-access facility, as defined in this Article, except for:

(1) Materials displayed at welcome centers which shall be directly related to travel, accommodations, tourist-related activities, tourist-related services, and attractions. The Department of Transportation shall issue rules regulating the display of these materials. These materials may contain advertisements for real estate; and

(2) Vending machines permitted by the Department of Transportation and placed by the Division of Services for the Blind, Department of Health and Human Services, as the State licensing agency designated pursuant to Section 2(a)(5) of the Randolph-Sheppard Act (20 USC 107a(a)(5)). The Department of Transportation shall regulate the placing of the vending machines in highway rest areas and shall regulate the articles to be dispensed. In order to permit the establishment of adequate fuel and other service facilities by private owners or their lessees for the users of a controlled-access facility, the Department of Transportation shall permit access to service or frontage roads within the publicly owned right-of-way of any controlled-access facility established or designated as provided in this Article, at points which, in the opinion of the Department of Transportation, will best serve the public interest. The location of

such fuel and other service facilities may be indicated to the users of the controlled-access facilities by appropriate signs, the size, style, and specifications of which shall be determined by the Department of Transportation.

The location of fuel, gas, food, lodging, camping, and attraction facilities may be indicated to the users of the controlled-access facilities by appropriate logos placed on signs owned, controlled, and erected by the Department of Transportation. The owners, operators or lessees of fuel, gas, food, lodging, camping, and attraction facilities who wish to place a logo identifying their business or service on a sign shall furnish a logo meeting the size, style and specifications determined by the Department of Transportation and shall pay the Department for the costs of initial installation and subsequent maintenance. The fees for logo sign installation and maintenance shall be set by the Board of Transportation based on cost. (1957, c. 993, s. 9; 1973, c. 507, s. 5; 1977, c. 464, s. 7.1; 1981, c. 481, s. 1; 1983, c. 604, s. 1; 1985, c. 456; c. 718, ss. 2, 3, 6; 1987, c. 417, s. 2; 1996, 2nd Ex. Sess., c. 18, s. 19.10(b); 1997-443, s. 11A.118(a); 2003-184, s. 2.)

§ 136-89.57. Repealed by Session Laws 1965, c. 474, s. 1.

§ 136-89.58. Unlawful use of National System of Interstate and Defense Highways and other controlled-access facilities.

On those sections of highways which are or become a part of the National System of Interstate and Defense Highways and other controlled-access facilities it shall be unlawful for any person:

(1)   To drive a vehicle over, upon or across any curb, central dividing section or other separation or dividing line on said highways.

(2)   To make a left turn or a semicircular or U-turn except through an opening provided for that purpose in the dividing curb section, separation, or line on said highways.

(3) To drive any vehicle except in the proper lane provided for that purpose and in the proper direction and to the right of the central dividing curb, separation section, or line on said highways.

(4) To drive any vehicle into the main travel lanes or lanes of connecting ramps or interchanges except through an opening or connection provided for that purpose by the Department of Transportation.

(5) To stop, park, or leave standing any vehicle, whether attended or unattended, on any part or portion of the right-of-way of said highways, except in the case of an emergency or as directed by a peace officer, or as designated parking areas.

(6) To willfully damage, remove, climb, cross or breach any fence erected within the rights-of-way of said highways.

(7) Repealed by Session Laws 1999-330, s. 6.

Any person who violates any of the provisions of this section shall be guilty of a Class 2 misdemeanor. (1959, c. 647; 1965, c. 474, s. 2; 1973, c. 507, s. 5; 1977, c. 464, s. 7.1; c. 731, s. 2; 1993, c. 539, s. 988; 1994, Ex. Sess., c. 24, s. 14(c); 1999-330, s. 6.)

§ 136-89.59. Highway rest area refreshments.

All civic, nonprofit, or charitable corporations and organizations are authorized to serve nonalcoholic refreshments to motorists at rest areas and welcome centers located on control-access facilities in accordance with the following conditions:

(1) Thirty-day permits shall be issued without cost by the Highway Division Engineer. Permits shall be subject to revocation by the Chief Engineer for violations of this section. The applicant must be a nonprofit organization showing a record of concern for automotive, highway, or driver safety.

(2) The activity must be carried on solely within the safety rest area free from any ramp or other service used for the movement of vehicles.

(3) The activity must be conducted for the express purpose of improving the safety of highway travel and the advertisement of any product by any organization shall not be permitted.

(4) The refreshment and any other service offered must be free of charge to the motorist.

(5) Signs shall be displayed by the corporation or organization, and the Department of Transportation is hereby authorized to promulgate rules and regulations governing the size, content and location of such signs. (1973, c. 1346; 1977, c. 464, s. 7.1; 1981, c. 545, ss. 1, 2; 2012-85, s. 7.)

§ 136-89.59A. Promotion of North Carolina farm products at rest areas and welcome centers.

Subject to the approval of the Department, the Department of Agriculture and Consumer Services may distribute promotional materials and free samples of North Carolina farm products at rest areas and welcome centers located on controlled-access facilities and operated by the State for the purpose of promoting North Carolina farm products. (2001-424, s. 17.1.)

Article 6E.

North Carolina Turnpike Authority.

§§136-89.60 to 136-89.76. Repealed by Session Laws 1971, c. 882, s. 4.

§ 136-89.77: Repealed by Session Laws 1965, c. 1077.

§§ 136-89.78 through 136-89.158. Reserved for future codification purposes.

Article 6F.

North Carolina Bridge Authority.

§§ 136-89.159 through 136-89.170: Repealed by Session Laws 2006-228, s. 1, effective August 10, 2006.

Article 6G.

Private Pilot Toll Project.

§§ 136-89.171 through 136-89.179: Repealed by Session Laws 2006-228, s. 2, effective August 10, 2006.

Article 6H.

Public Toll Roads and Bridges.

Part 1. Turnpike Authority and Bridges.

§ 136-89.180. Legislative findings.

The General Assembly finds that the existing State road system is becoming increasingly congested and overburdened with traffic in many areas of the State; that the sharp surge of vehicle miles traveled is overwhelming the State's ability to build and pay for adequate road improvements; and that an adequate answer to this challenge will require the State to be innovative and utilize several new approaches to transportation improvements in North Carolina.

Toll funding of highway and bridge construction is feasible in North Carolina and can contribute to addressing the critical transportation needs of the State. A toll program can speed the implementation of needed transportation improvements by funding some projects with tolls. (2002-133, s. 1.)

§ 136-89.181. Definitions.

The following definitions apply to this Article:

(1)   Department. - The North Carolina Department of Transportation.

(2) Turnpike Authority. - The public agency created by this Article.

(3) Authority Board. - The governing board of the Turnpike Authority.

(4) Turnpike project. - Either of the following:

a. A road, bridge, or tunnel project planned, or planned and constructed, in accordance with the provisions of this Article.

b. A segment of the State highway system the Authority Board converts to a tolled highway pursuant to the authorization in G.S. 136-89.187.

(5) Turnpike system. - All Turnpike projects. (2002-133, s. 1; 2008-225, s. 3.)

§ 136-89.182. North Carolina Turnpike Authority.

(a) Creation. - There is created a body politic and corporate to be known as the "North Carolina Turnpike Authority". The Authority is constituted as a public agency, and the exercise by the Authority of the powers conferred by this Article in the construction, operation, and maintenance of toll roads and bridges shall be deemed and held to be the performance of an essential governmental function.

(b) Administrative Placement. - The Authority shall be located within the Department of Transportation and shall be subject to and under the direct supervision of the Secretary of Transportation.

(c) Authority Board. - The North Carolina Turnpike Authority shall be governed by a nine-member Authority Board consisting of two members appointed by the General Assembly upon the recommendation of the President Pro Tempore of the Senate in accordance with G.S. 120-121, two members appointed by the General Assembly upon the recommendation of the Speaker of the House of Representatives in accordance with G.S. 120-121, four members appointed by the Governor, and the Secretary of Transportation. Each appointing authority shall appoint members who reside in diverse regions of the State. The Chair of the Authority shall be selected by the Authority Board.

(d) Board of Transportation Members. - Members of the North Carolina Board of Transportation may serve as members of the Authority Board.

(e) Staggered Terms. - One of the initial appointments to the Authority Board by the General Assembly upon the recommendation of the President Pro Tempore of the Senate, one of the initial appointments to the Authority Board by the General Assembly upon the recommendation of the Speaker of the House of Representatives, and three of the initial appointments of the Governor shall be appointed to terms ending January 14, 2007. One of the initial appointments to the Authority Board by the General Assembly upon the recommendation of the President Pro Tempore of the Senate, one of the initial appointments to the Authority Board by the General Assembly upon the recommendation of the Speaker of the House of Representatives, and one of the initial appointments of the Governor shall be appointed to terms ending January 14, 2005. The Secretary of Transportation shall serve as an ex officio voting member of the Board. Thereafter, at the expiration of each stipulated term of office, all appointments shall be to a term of four years from the date of the expiration of the term.

(f) Vacancies. - All members of the Authority Board shall remain in office until their successors are appointed and qualified. The original appointing authority may appoint a member to serve out the unexpired term of any member.

(g) Removal of Board Members. - Each member of the Authority Board, notwithstanding subsection (e) of this section, shall serve at the pleasure of the appointing authority. The Chair of the Authority serves at the pleasure of the Authority Board.

(h) Conflicts of Interest, Ethics. - Members of the Authority Board shall be subject to the provisions of G.S. 136-13, 136-13.1, and 136-14.

(i) Compensation. - The appointed members of the Authority Board shall receive no salary for their services but shall be entitled to receive per diem and travel allowances in accordance with the provisions of G.S. 138-5 and G.S. 138-6 as appropriate.

(j) Bylaws. - The Authority Board shall adopt, change, or amend bylaws with respect to the calling of meetings, quorums, voting procedures, the keeping of records, and other organizational, staffing, and administrative matters as the Authority Board may determine. Any bylaws, or subsequent changes or amendments to the bylaws, shall be included in the Annual Report as required by G.S. 136-89.193.

(k) Executive Director and Administrative Employees. - The Authority Board shall appoint an Executive Director, whose salary shall be fixed by the Authority, to serve at its pleasure. The Executive Director shall be the Authority's chief administrative officer and shall be responsible for the daily administration of the toll roads and bridges constructed, maintained, or operated pursuant to this Article. The Executive Director or his designee shall appoint, employ, dismiss, and, within the limits approved by the Authority Board, fix the compensation of administrative employees as the Executive Director deems necessary to carry out this Article.

(l) Office. - The offices of the Authority may be housed in one or more facilities of the Department of Transportation. (2002-133, s. 1; 2009-343, ss. 1, 2; 2011-145, s. 28.35(c).)

§ 136-89.183. Powers of the Authority.

(a) The Authority shall have all of the powers necessary to execute the provisions of this Article, including the following:

(1) The powers of a corporate body, including the power to sue and be sued, to make contracts, to adopt and use a common seal, and to alter the adopted seal as needed.

(2) To study, plan, develop, and undertake preliminary design work on up to nine Turnpike Projects. At the conclusion of these activities, the Turnpike Authority is authorized to design, establish, purchase, construct, operate, and maintain the following projects:

a. Triangle Expressway, including segments also known as N.C. 540, Triangle Parkway, and the Western Wake Freeway in Wake and Durham Counties. The described segments constitute three projects.

b. Repealed by Session Laws 2013-183, s. 5.1, effective July 1, 2013.

c. Monroe Connector/Bypass.

d., e. Repealed by Session Laws 2013-183, s. 5.1, effective July 1, 2013.

Any other project proposed by the Authority in addition to the projects listed in this subdivision requires prior consultation with the Joint Legislative Commission on Governmental Operations pursuant to G.S. 120-76.1 no less than 180 days prior to initiating the process required by Article 7 of Chapter 159 of the General Statutes.

With the exception of the four projects set forth in sub-subdivisions a. and c. of this subdivision, the Turnpike projects selected for construction by the Turnpike Authority, prior to the letting of a contract for the project, shall meet the following conditions: (i) two of the projects must be ranked in the top 35 based on total score on the Department-produced list entitled "Mobility Fund Project Scores" dated June 6, 2012, and, in addition, may be subject to G.S. 136-18(39a); (ii) of the projects not ranked as provided in (i), one may be subject to G.S. 136-18(39a); (iii) the projects shall be included in any applicable locally adopted comprehensive transportation plans; (iv) the projects shall be shown in the current State Transportation Improvement Program; and (v) toll projects must be approved by all affected Metropolitan Planning Organizations and Rural Transportation Planning Organizations for tolling.

f. Repealed by Session Laws 2008-225, s. 4, effective August 17, 2008.

Any other project proposed by the Authority in addition to the projects listed in this subdivision must be approved by the General Assembly prior to construction.

A Turnpike Project selected for construction by the Turnpike Authority shall be included in any applicable locally adopted comprehensive transportation plans and shall be shown in the current State Transportation Improvement Plan prior to the letting of a contract for the Turnpike Project.

(3) Repealed by Session Laws 2005-275, s. 2, effective August 12, 2005.

(4) To rent, lease, purchase, acquire, own, encumber, dispose of, or mortgage real or personal property, including the power to acquire property by eminent domain pursuant to G.S. 136-89.184.

(5) To fix, revise, charge, retain, enforce, and collect tolls and fees for the use of the Turnpike Projects. Prior to the effective date of any toll or fee for use of a Turnpike Facility, the Authority shall submit a description of the proposed

toll or fee to the Board of Transportation, the Joint Legislative Transportation Oversight Committee and the Joint Legislative Commission on Governmental Operations for review.

(6) To issue bonds or notes of the Authority as provided in this Article.

(6a) To invest the proceeds of bonds or notes of the Authority that are pending disbursement or other idle funds of the Authority in any investment authorized by G.S. 159-30.

(7) To establish, construct, purchase, maintain, equip, and operate any structure or facilities associated with the Turnpike System.

(8) To pay all necessary costs and expenses in the formation, organization, administration, and operation of the Authority.

(9) To apply for, accept, and administer loans and grants of money or real or personal property from any federal agency, the State or its political subdivisions, local governments, or any other public or private sources available.

(10) To adopt, alter, or repeal its own bylaws or rules implementing the provisions of this Article, in accordance with the review and comment requirements of G.S. 136-89.182(j).

(11) To utilize employees of the Department; to contract for the services of consulting engineers, architects, attorneys, real estate counselors, appraisers, and other consultants; to employ administrative staff as may be required in the judgment of the Authority; and to fix and pay fees or compensation to the Department, contractors, and administrative employees from funds available to the Authority.

(12) To receive and use appropriations from the State and federal government.

(13) To adopt procedures to govern its procurement of services and delivery of Turnpike Projects.

(14) To perform or procure any portion of services required by the Authority.

(15) To use officers, employees, agents, and facilities of the Department for the purposes and upon the terms as may be mutually agreeable.

(16) To contract for the construction, maintenance, and operation of a Turnpike Project.

(17) To enter into partnership agreements with the Department of Transportation, agreements with political subdivisions of the State, and agreements with private entities, and to expend such funds as it deems necessary, pursuant to such agreements, for the purpose of financing the cost of acquiring, constructing, equipping, operating, or maintaining any Turnpike Project. An agreement entered under this subdivision requires the concurrence of the Board of Transportation if the Department of Transportation is a party to the agreement.

(18) To utilize incentives in any contract for development or construction of a Turnpike Project, in order to promote expedited delivery of the project.

(19) To enter into reciprocal toll enforcement agreements with other toll agencies, as provided in G.S. 136-89.220.

(b) To execute the powers provided in subsection (a) of this section, the Authority shall determine its policies by majority vote of the members of the Authority Board present and voting, a quorum having been established. Once a policy is established, the Authority Board shall communicate it to the Executive Director or the Executive Director's designee, who shall have the sole and exclusive authority to execute the policy of the Authority. No member of the Authority Board shall have the responsibility or authority to give operational directives to any employee of the Authority other than the Executive Director or the Director's designee. (2002-133, s. 1; 2005-275, s. 2; 2006-228, s. 5; 2006-230, s. 1(b); 2008-225, s. 4; 2011-7, s. 1; 2011-145, s. 28.32(e); 2011-391, s. 56; 2012-85, s. 9; 2013-94, s. 1; 2013-183, ss. 5.1, 5.3.)

§ 136-89.183A. Accelerated Pilot Toll Bridge Project.

(a) Findings. - The General Assembly finds that there is a need for a bridge connecting the Currituck County mainland to the Currituck County Outer Banks; that the bridge should be implemented as a toll bridge; that the bridge should be implemented in a manner that protects the natural environment and quality of life on the Outer Banks; and that the character of the existing road system in Currituck County and Dare County Outer Banks should be preserved.

(b) Contract to Construct Accelerated Pilot Toll Bridge Project. - The Authority shall contract with a single private firm to design, obtain all necessary permits for, and construct the toll bridge described in G.S. 136-89.183(a)(2), known as the Mid-Currituck Bridge, in order to provide accelerated, efficient, and cost-effective completion of the project.

(c) Preconstruction Participation. - In addition to the authority granted by G.S. 136-89.191, the Department shall participate in the cost of preconstruction activities related to the project described in this section, if requested by the Authority.

(d) Environmental Protection. - The Authority shall ensure that the Mid-Currituck Bridge is implemented in a manner that accomplishes all of the following:

(1) Ensures the preservation of water quality in Currituck Sound.

(2) Mitigates the environmental impact of the bridge on the Currituck County mainland and the Outer Banks.

(3) Reduces traffic congestion and vehicle miles traveled, and preserves the character of the existing road system, in Dare County and Currituck County on the Outer Banks.

(e) Report on Project. - The Authority shall report to the Joint Legislative Transportation Oversight Committee on December 1, 2005, and each December 1 thereafter until completion, on the progress of the accelerated pilot toll bridge project described in this section. (2005-275, s. 3; 2008-225, s. 11.)

§ 136-89.183B. Accelerated Herbert C. Bonner Bridge Replacement Project.

(a) Contract for Accelerated Construction of the Herbert C. Bonner Replacement Bridge Project. - The Department of Transportation shall implement all reasonable measures to expedite completion of environmental reviews required by the National Environmental Policy Act. Within 90 days of receiving an approved Record of Decision from the Federal Highway

Administration, the Department shall contract with a single private firm to design and build a replacement bridge for the Herbert C. Bonner Bridge at Oregon Inlet, in accordance with G.S. 136-28.11, in order to expedite and accelerate the efficient, cost effective completion of the project.

(b) Replacement Bridge; Termini. - The General Assembly recommends that the replacement bridge constructed pursuant to this section shall be located with north and south termini located in general proximity to the termini of the existing Herbert C. Bonner Bridge. It is recognized, however, that the preferred alternative for the bridge location cannot be determined prior to compliance with all federal and State laws and regulations.

(c) Department to Report on Project. - The Department shall report to the Joint Legislative Transportation Oversight Committee on December 1, 2005, and each December 1 thereafter until completion, on the progress of the accelerated bridge project described in this section. (2005-275, s. 6(b); 2005-382, s. 3.)

§ 136-89.183C. Accelerated Yadkin River Veterans Memorial Bridge Replacement Project.

(a) Contract for Accelerated Construction of the Yadkin River Veterans Memorial Bridge Replacement Bridge Project. - The Authority shall study, plan, develop, undertake preliminary design work, and analyze and list all necessary permits, in preparation for construction of a replacement bridge and approaches for the Yadkin River Veterans Memorial Bridge over the Yadkin River and between Rowan and Davidson Counties, in order to provide accelerated, efficient, and cost-effective completion of the project.

(b) Replacement Bridge; Termini. - The bridge constructed pursuant to this section shall be a replacement bridge, with north and south termini located in general proximity to the termini of the existing Yadkin River Veterans Memorial Bridge. (2007-299, s. 1; 2012-42, s. 3.)

§ 136-89.184. Acquisition of real property.

(a) General. - The Authority may acquire public or private real property by purchase, negotiation, gift, or devise, or condemnation that it determines to be necessary and convenient for the construction, expansion, enlargement, extension, improvement, or operation of a Turnpike Project. When the Authority acquires real property owned by the State, the Secretary of the Department of Administration shall execute and deliver to the Authority a deed transferring fee simple title to the property to the Authority.

(b) Condemnation. - To exercise the power of eminent domain, the Authority shall commence a proceeding in its name and shall follow the procedure set forth in Article 9 of Chapter 136 of the General Statutes. (2002-133, s. 1.)

§ 136-89.185. Taxation of property of Authority.

Property owned by the Authority is exempt from taxation in accordance with Section 2 of Article V of the North Carolina Constitution. (2002-133, s. 1.)

§ 136-89.186. Audit.

The operations of the Authority shall be subject to the oversight of the State Auditor pursuant to Article 5A of Chapter 147 of the General Statutes. (2002-133, s. 1.)

§ 136-89.187. Conversion of free highways prohibited.

The Authority Board is prohibited from converting any segment of the nontolled State Highway System to a toll facility, except for a segment of N.C. 540 under construction as of July 1, 2006, located in Wake County and extending from the N.C. 54 exit on N.C. 540 to the N.C. 55 exit on N.C. 540. No segment may be converted to a toll route pursuant to this section unless first approved by the Metropolitan Planning Organization (MPO) or Rural Planning Organization (RPO) of the area in which that segment is located. (2002-133, s. 1; 2006-228, s. 3; 2008-225, s. 5.)

§ 136-89.188. Use of revenues.

(a) Revenues derived from Turnpike Projects authorized under this Article shall be used only for the following:

(1) Authority administration costs.

(2) Turnpike Project development, right-of-way acquisition, design, construction, operation, maintenance, reconstruction, rehabilitation, and replacement.

(3) Debt service on the Authority's revenue bonds or related purposes such as the establishment of debt service reserve funds.

(4) Debt service, debt service reserve funds, and other financing costs related to any of the following:

a. A financing undertaken by a private entity under a partnership agreement with the entity for a Turnpike Project.

b. Private activity bonds issued under law related to a Turnpike Project.

c. Any federal or State loan, line of credit, or loan guarantee relating to a Turnpike Project.

(5) A return on investment of any private entity under a partnership agreement with the entity for a Turnpike Project.

(6) Any other uses granted to a private entity under a partnership agreement with the entity for a Turnpike Project.

(b) The Authority may use up to one hundred percent (100%) of the revenue derived from a Turnpike Project for debt service on the Authority's revenue bonds or for a combination of debt service and operation and maintenance expenses of the Turnpike Projects.

(c) The Authority shall use not more than five percent (5%) of total revenue derived from all Turnpike Projects for Authority administration costs.

(d) Notwithstanding the provisions of subsections (a) and (b) of this section, toll revenues generated from a converted segment of the State highway system previously planned for operation as a nontoll facility shall only be used for the funding or financing of the right of way acquisition, construction, expansion, operations, maintenance, and Authority administration costs associated with the converted segment or a contiguous toll facility. (2002-133, s. 1; 2006-228, s. 4; 2013-183, s. 5.4.)

§ 136-89.189. Turnpike Authority revenue bonds.

The Authority shall be a municipality for purposes of Article 5 of Chapter 159 of the General Statutes, the State and Local Government Revenue Bond Act, and may issue revenue bonds pursuant to that Act to pay all or a portion of the cost of a Turnpike Project or to refund any previously issued bonds. In connection with the issuance of revenue bonds, the Authority shall have all powers of a municipality under the State and Local Government Revenue Bond Act, and revenue bonds issued by the Authority shall be entitled to the protection of all provisions of the State and Local Government Revenue Bond Act.

Except as provided in this section, the provisions of Chapter 159 of the General Statutes, the Local Government Finance Act, apply to revenue bonds issued by the Turnpike Authority.

(1) The term of a lease between the Turnpike Authority and the Department executed prior to July 27, 2009, for all or any part of a Turnpike Project may exceed 40 years, as agreed by the Authority and the Department.

(2) The maturity date of a refunding bond may extend to the earlier of the following:

a. Forty years from the date of issuance of the refunding bond.

b. The date the Turnpike Authority determines is the maturity date required for the Turnpike Project funded with the refunding bonds to generate sufficient revenues to retire the refunding bonds and any other outstanding indebtedness issued for that Project. The Authority's determination of the appropriate maturity date is conclusive and binding. In making its determination, the Authority may take into account appropriate financing terms and conventions. (2002-133, s. 1; 2009-56, s. 2; 2010-165, s. 10.)

§ 136-89.190. Sale of Turnpike Authority revenue bonds.

Revenue bonds of the Authority issued pursuant to G.S. 136-89.189 and the State and Local Government Revenue Bond Act shall be sold in accordance with and pursuant to Article 7 of Chapter 159 of the General Statutes. (2002-133, s. 1.)

§ 136-89.191. Cost participation by Department of Transportation.

The Department of Transportation may participate in the cost of preconstruction activities, construction, maintenance, or operation of a Turnpike Project. (2002-133, s. 1.)

§ 136-89.192. Applicability of formula.

Only those funds applied to a Turnpike Project from the State Highway Fund, State Highway Trust Fund, or federal-aid funds that might otherwise be used for other roadway projects within the State, and are otherwise already subject to the formula under G.S. 136-189.11 shall be included in the formula.

Other revenue from the sale of the Authority's bonds or notes, project loans, or toll collections shall not be included in the formula. (2002-133, s. 1; 2013-183, s. 4.6.)

§ 136-89.193. Annual plan of work; annual and quarterly reports.

(a) Annual Plan of Work. - The Authority shall annually develop a plan of work for the fiscal year, describing the activities and projects to be undertaken, accompanied by a budget. This annual plan of work shall be subject to the concurrence of the Board of Transportation.

(b) Annual Reports. - The Authority shall, promptly following the close of each fiscal year, submit an annual report of its activities for the preceding year to the Governor, the General Assembly, and the Department of Transportation. Each report shall be accompanied by an audit of its books and accounts.

(c) Semiannual Reports. - The Authority shall submit semiannual reports to the Joint Legislative Transportation Oversight Committee, and more frequent reports if requested. The reports shall summarize the Authority's activities during the preceding six months, and shall contain any information about the Authority's activities that is requested by the Committee.

(d) Report Prior to Let of Contracts. - The Authority shall consult with and report to the Joint Legislative Transportation Oversight Committee and the Joint Legislative Commission on Governmental Operations prior to the letting of any contract for Turnpike Project construction authorized under G.S. 136-183(a)(2).

(e) Repealed by Session Laws 2011-145, s. 28.35(a), effective July 1, 2011. (2002-133, s. 1; 2011-145, s. 28.35(a).)

§ 136-89.194. Laws applicable to the Authority; exceptions.

(a) Motor Vehicle Laws. - The Turnpike System shall be considered a "highway" as defined in G.S. 20-4.01(13) and a "public vehicular area" as defined in G.S. 20-4.01(32). All law enforcement and emergency personnel, including the State Highway Patrol and the Division of Motor Vehicles, shall have the same powers and duties on the Turnpike System as on any other highway or public vehicular area.

(b) Applicable Contracting. - For the purposes of implementing this Article, the Authority shall solicit competitive proposals for the construction of Turnpike Projects in accordance with the provisions of Article 2 of this Chapter. Contracts for professional engineering services and other kinds of professional or specialized services necessary in connection with construction of Turnpike Projects shall be solicited in accordance with procedures utilized by the Department of Transportation. Cost estimates prepared for the purpose of comparing bids for a Turnpike project are confidential and may not be disclosed until after the opening of bids for the project.

(c) Alternative Contracting Methods. - Notwithstanding the provisions of subsection (b) of this section, the Authority may authorize the use of alternative contracting methods if:

(1) The authorization applies to an individual project;

(2) The Authority has concluded, and documented in writing, that the alternative contracting method is necessary because the project cannot be completed utilizing the procedures of Article 2 of this Chapter within the necessary time frame or available funding or for other reasons the Authority deems in the public interest;

(3) The Authority has provided, to the extent possible, for the solicitation of competitive proposals prior to awarding a contract; and

(4) The approved alternative contracting method provides for reasonable compliance with the disadvantaged business participation goals of G.S. 136-28.4.

(d) Entry for Surveys. - The Turnpike Authority and its employees and contractors shall have the same right of entry for surveys, borings, soundings, or examinations as granted the Department of Transportation in G.S. 136-120.

(e) Plans and Contract Documents. - The requirements for registering right-of-way plans set in G.S. 136-19.4 apply to right-of-way plans of the Turnpike Authority. In applying G.S. 136-19.4 to the Authority, references to the "Department" are considered references to the "Turnpike Authority" and references to the "Board" are considered references to the "Authority Board."

Diaries and analyses for contracts of the Turnpike Authority are subject to the same restrictions on disclosure that apply to diaries and analyses for contracts of the Department under G.S. 136-28.5.

(f) Construction Claims. - G.S. 136-29 applies to the adjustment and resolution of Turnpike project construction claims. In applying G.S. 136-29 to the Turnpike Authority, references to the "Department of Transportation," the "Chief Engineer," and a "State highway" are considered references to the "Turnpike Authority," the "chief engineer of the Turnpike Authority," and a "Turnpike project."

(g) Contract Exemptions. - The following provisions concerning the purchase of goods and services by a State agency do not apply to the Turnpike Authority:

(1) Article 3 of Chapter 143 of the General Statutes. The Authority may use the services of the Department of Administration in procuring goods and services that are not specific to establishing and operating a toll revenue

system. However, the Authority shall: (i) submit all proposed contracts for supplies, materials, printing, equipment, and contractual services that exceed one million dollars ($1,000,000) authorized by this subdivision to the Attorney General or the Attorney General's designee for review as provided in G.S. 114-8.3; and, (ii) include in all proposed contracts to be awarded by the Authority under this subdivision a standard clause which provides that the State Auditor and internal auditors of the Authority may audit the records of the contractor during and after the term of the contract to verify accounts and data affecting fees and performance. The Authority shall not award a cost plus percentage of cost agreement or contract for any purpose.

(2) Article 3D of Chapter 147 of the General Statutes. The Authority may use the services of the Office of Information Technology Services in procuring goods and services that are not specific to establishing and operating a toll revenue system. All contract information for contracts for information technology are subject to disclosure in accordance with G.S. 147-33.95.

(h) APA. - Chapter 150B of the General Statutes does not apply to the Turnpike Authority, except as provided in this section and G.S. 136-89.218. (2002-133, s. 1; 2006-228, s. 6; 2008-225, s. 6; 2010-194, s. 20.1; 2011-326, s. 15(u); 2012-85, s. 8.)

§ 136-89.195. Internet report of funds expended.

The Department shall publish and update annually on its Internet web site a record of all expenditures of the Authority for highway construction, maintenance, and administration. The record shall include a total expenditure amount by county. For each Turnpike Project, the record shall include a readily identifiable project name or location, the nature of the project, the amount of the project, the contractor for the project, the date of project letting, and the actual or expected project completion date. (2002-133, s. 1.)

§ 136-89.196. Removal of tolls.

The Authority shall, upon fulfillment of and subject to any restrictions included in the agreements entered into by the Authority in connection with the issuance of the Authority's revenue bonds, remove tolls from a Turnpike Project. (2002-133, s. 1.)

§ 136-89.197. Maintenance of nontoll routes.

The Department shall maintain an existing, alternate, comparable nontoll route corresponding to each Turnpike Project constructed pursuant to this Article. (2002-133, s. 1.)

§ 136-89.198. Authority to toll existing interstate highways.

(a) General. - Notwithstanding any other provision of this Article, the Authority may collect tolls on any existing interstate highway for which the United States Department of Transportation has granted permission by permit, or any other lawful means, to do so. The revenue generated from the collected tolls shall be used by the Authority to repair and maintain the interstate on which the tolls were collected. These revenues shall not be used to repair, maintain, or upgrade any State primary or secondary road adjacent to or connected with the interstate highways.

(b) Method. - The Authority shall establish toll locations on the permitted interstate highway in accordance with federal guidelines. Toll locations shall be erected at or near the borders of the State and at such other locations that are not impracticable, unfeasible, or that would result in an unsafe or hazardous condition.

(c) Severability. - If any provision of this section or its application is held invalid, the invalidity does not affect other provisions or applications of this section that can be given effect without the invalid provisions or application, and to this end the provisions of this section are severable. (2005-276, s. 28.21(b).)

§ 136-89.199. Designation of high-occupancy toll and managed lanes.

Notwithstanding any other provision of this Article, the Authority may designate one or more lanes of any highway, or portion thereof, within the State, including lanes that may previously have been designated as HOV lanes under G.S. 20-146.2, as high-occupancy toll (HOT) or other type of managed lanes; provided, however, that such designation shall not reduce the number of existing non-toll general purpose lanes. In making such designations, the Authority shall specify the high-occupancy requirement or other conditions for use of such lanes, which may include restricting vehicle types, access controls, or the payment of tolls for vehicles that do not meet the high-occupancy requirements or conditions for use. (2013-183, s. 5.5; 2013-410, s. 38(e).)

§ 136-89.200: Reserved for future codification purposes.

§ 136-89.201: Reserved for future codification purposes.

§ 136-89.202: Reserved for future codification purposes.

§ 136-89.203: Reserved for future codification purposes.

§ 136-89.204: Reserved for future codification purposes.

§ 136-89.205: Reserved for future codification purposes.

§ 136-89.206: Reserved for future codification purposes.

§ 136-89.207: Reserved for future codification purposes.

§ 136-89.208: Reserved for future codification purposes.

§ 136-89.209: Reserved for future codification purposes.

Part 2. Collection of Tolls on Turnpike Projects.

§ 136-89.210. Definitions.

The definitions in G.S. 136-89.181 and the following definitions apply in this Article:

(1) Reserved.

(2) Open road toll. - A toll payable under an open road tolling system.

(3)   Open road tolling system. - A system of collecting a toll for the use of a highway that does not provide a way to pay the toll in cash while traveling on the highway. (2008-225, s. 2; 2013-410, s. 12.)

§ 136-89.211. Tolls for use of Turnpike project.

In exercising its authority under G.S. 136-89.183 to set tolls for the use of a Turnpike project, the Authority may not do any of the following:

(1)   Set open road tolls that vary for the same class of motor vehicle depending on the method by which the Authority identifies a motor vehicle that drives on the Turnpike project. This does not preclude the Authority from allowing a discount for a motor vehicle equipped with an electronic toll collection transponder or a motor vehicle that has prepaid its toll.

(2)   Exempt a motor vehicle that is not a law enforcement vehicle, an emergency fire or rescue vehicle, or an emergency medical services vehicle from the requirement of paying a toll for the use of a Turnpike project. (2008-225, s. 2; 2010-133, s. 2.)

§ 136-89.212. Payment of toll required for use of Turnpike project.

(a)   A motor vehicle that is driven on a Turnpike project is subject to a toll imposed by the Authority for the use of the project. If the toll is an open road toll, the person who is the registered owner of the motor vehicle is liable for payment of the toll unless the registered owner establishes that the motor vehicle was in the care, custody, and control of another person when it was driven on the Turnpike project.

(b)   A person establishes that a motor vehicle was in the care, custody, and control of another person when it was driven on a Turnpike project by submitting to the Authority a sworn affidavit stating one of the following:

(1)   The name and address of the person who had the care, custody, and control of the motor vehicle when it was driven. If the motor vehicle was leased or rented under a long-term lease or rental, as defined in G.S. 105-187.1, the

affidavit must be supported by a copy of the lease or rental agreement or other written evidence of the agreement.

(2)   The motor vehicle was stolen. The affidavit must be supported by an insurance or police report concerning the theft or other written evidence of the theft.

(3)   The person transferred the motor vehicle to another person by sale or otherwise before it was driven on the Turnpike project. The affidavit must be supported by insurance information, a copy of the certificate of title, or other evidence of the transfer.

(c)   If a person establishes that a motor vehicle was in the care, custody, and control of another person under subsection (b) of this section, the other person shall be liable for the payment of the toll, and the Authority may send a bill to collect and enforce the toll in accordance with this Article; provided, however, that such other person may contest such toll in accordance with this Article. (2008-225, s. 2; 2013-183, s. 5.6.)

§ 136-89.213. Administration of tolls and requirements for open road tolls.

(a)   Administration. - The Authority is responsible for collecting tolls on Turnpike projects. In exercising its authority under G.S. 136-89.183 to perform or procure services required by the Authority, the Authority may contract with one or more providers to perform part or all of the collection functions and may enter into agreements to exchange information, including confidential information under subsection (a1) of this section, that identifies motor vehicles and their owners with one or more of the following entities: the Division of Motor Vehicles of the Department of Transportation, another state, another toll operator, a toll collection-related organization, or a private entity that has entered into a partnership agreement with the Authority pursuant to G.S. 136-89.183(a)(17). Further, the Authority may assign its authority to fix, revise, charge, retain, enforce, and collect tolls and fees under this Article to a private entity that has entered into a partnership agreement with the Authority pursuant to G.S. 136-89.183(a)(17).

(a1)   Identifying information obtained by the Authority through an agreement is not a public record and is subject to the disclosure limitations in 18 U.S.C. § 2721, the federal Driver's Privacy Protection Act. The Authority shall maintain the confidentiality of all information required to be kept confidential under 18 U.S.C. § 2721(a), as well as any financial information, transaction history, and information related to the collection of a toll or user fee from a person, including, but not limited to, photographs or other recorded images or automatic vehicle identification or driver account information generated by radio-frequency identification or other electronic means. Notwithstanding the provisions of this section:

(1) The account holder may examine his own account information, and the Authority may use the account information only for purposes of collecting and enforcing tolls.

(2) A party, by authority of a proper court order, may inspect and examine confidential account information.

(b) Open Road Tolls. - If a Turnpike project uses an open road tolling system, the Authority must operate a facility that is in the immediate vicinity of the Turnpike project or provide an alternate means to accept cash payment of the toll and must place signs on the Turnpike project that give drivers the following information:

(1) Notice that the driver is approaching a highway for which a toll is required. Signs providing this information must be placed before the toll is incurred.

(2) The methods by which the toll may be paid.

(3) If applicable, directions to the nearby facility that accepts cash payment of the toll. (2008-225, s. 2; 2012-78, s. 12; 2013-183, s. 5.6.)

§ 136-89.214. Bill for unpaid open road toll.

(a) Bill. - If a motor vehicle travels on a Turnpike project that uses an open road tolling system and a toll for traveling on the project is not paid prior to travel or at the time of travel, the Authority must send a bill by first-class mail to the registered owner of the motor vehicle or the person who had care, custody, and control of the vehicle as established under G.S. 136-89.212(b) for the amount of the unpaid toll. The Authority must send the bill within 90 days after the travel occurs, or within 90 days of receipt of a sworn affidavit submitted under G.S.

136-89.212(b) identifying the person who had care, custody, and control of the motor vehicle. If a bill is not sent within the required time, the Authority waives collection of the toll. The Authority must establish a billing period for unpaid open road tolls that is no shorter than 15 days. A bill for a billing period must include all unpaid tolls incurred by the same person during the billing period.

(b) Information on Bill. - A bill sent under this section must include all of the following information:

(1) The name and address of the registered owner of the motor vehicle that traveled on the Turnpike project or of the person identified under G.S. 136-89.212(b).

(2) The date the travel occurred, the approximate time the travel occurred, and each segment of the Turnpike project on which the travel occurred.

(3) An image of the registration plate of the motor vehicle, if the Authority captured an electronic image of the motor vehicle when it traveled on the Turnpike project.

(4) The amount of the toll due and an explanation of how payment may be made.

(5) The date by which the toll must be paid to avoid the imposition of a processing fee under G.S. 136-89.215 and the amount of the processing fee.

(6) A statement that a vehicle owner who has unpaid tolls is subject to a civil penalty and may not renew the vehicle's registration until the tolls and civil penalties are paid.

(7) A clear and concise explanation of how to contest liability for the toll.

(8) If applicable, a copy of the affidavit submitted under G.S. 136-89.212(b) identifying the person with care, custody, and control of the motor vehicle. (2008-225, s. 2; 2010-133, s. 3; 2013-183, s. 5.6.)

§ 136-89.215. Required action upon receiving bill for open road toll and processing fee for unpaid toll.

(a) Action Required. - A person who receives a bill from the Authority for an unpaid open road toll must take one of the following actions within 30 days of the date of the bill:

(1) Pay the bill.

(2) Send a written request to the Authority for a review of the toll.

(b) Fee. - If a person does not take one of the actions required under subsection (a) of this section within the required time, the Authority may add a processing fee to the amount the person owes. The processing fee may not exceed six dollars ($6.00). A person may not be charged more than forty-eight dollars ($48.00) in processing fees in a 12-month period.

The Authority must set the processing fee at an amount that does not exceed the costs of collecting the unpaid toll. (2008-225, s. 2; 2010-133, s. 4; 2013-183, s. 5.6.)

§ 136-89.216. Civil penalty for failure to pay open road toll.

(a) Penalty. - A person who receives two or more bills for unpaid open road tolls and who has not paid the amount due on those bills within 30 days is subject to a civil penalty of twenty-five dollars ($25.00). Only one penalty may be assessed in a six-month period.

(b) Payment. - The Authority must send a notice by first-class mail to a person who is assessed a civil penalty under this section. A person who is assessed a civil penalty must pay the unpaid toll for which the civil penalty was imposed, the amount of any processing fee due, and the civil penalty within 30 days of the date of the notice.

(c) Penalty Proceeds. - A civil penalty imposed under this section is payable to the Authority. The clear proceeds of a civil penalty imposed under this section must be credited to the Civil Penalty and Forfeiture Fund established in G.S. 115C-457.1. The guidelines used by the Office of State Budget and Management to determine an agency's actual costs of collecting a civil penalty and the clear proceeds of the civil penalty apply to the determination of the clear proceeds of a civil penalty imposed under this section. (2008-225, s. 2; 2010-133, s. 5.)

§ 136-89.217. Vehicle registration renewal blocked for unpaid open road toll.

(a) Registration Block. - Failure of a person to pay an open road toll billed to the person under G.S. 136-89.214, any processing fee added under G.S. 136-89.215, and any civil penalty imposed under G.S. 136-89.216, as well as any toll, processing fee, or civil penalty owed to another tolling jurisdiction with which the Authority has a valid reciprocal toll enforcement agreement under G.S. 136-89.220, is grounds under G.S. 20-54 to withhold the registration renewal of a motor vehicle registered in that person's name. The Authority must notify the Commissioner of Motor Vehicles of a person who owes a toll, a processing fee, or a civil penalty. When notified, the Commissioner of Motor Vehicles must withhold the registration renewal of any motor vehicle registered in that person's name.

(b) Repealed by S.L. 2010-133, s. 6, effective December 1, 2010. (2008-225, s. 2; 2010-133, s. 6; 2012-85, s. 10.)

§ 136-89.218. Procedures for contesting liability for unpaid open road toll.

(a) Informal Review. - A person who receives a bill for an unpaid open road toll and who disputes liability for the toll may contest the toll by sending to the Authority a request for review of the toll. The person may include a sworn affidavit described in G.S. 136-89.212 that establishes that someone else had the care, custody, and control of the motor vehicle subject to the toll when the toll was incurred. The person must send the request for review to the Authority within 30 days of the date of the bill sent by the Authority. A person who does not send a request for review to the Authority within this time limit waives the right to a review. If a person sends a timely request for review to the Authority, the Authority may not collect the disputed toll and any processing fee added to the bill for the toll until the conclusion of the review process in this section.

(b) Administrative Hearing. - If the Authority conducts an informal review under subsection (a) of this section and determines that the person who requested the review is liable for the toll, the Authority must send the person a notice informing the person of the Authority's determination. The person may contest this determination by filing a petition for a contested case hearing at the Office of Administrative Hearings in accordance with Article 3 of Chapter 150B of the General Statutes.

(c) Judicial Review. - Article 4 of Chapter 150B of the General Statutes governs judicial review of a final decision made in a contested case authorized under subsection (b) of this section. (2008-225, s. 2; 2010-133, s. 7.)

§ 136-89.219: Reserved for future codification purposes.

§ 136-89.220. Reciprocal toll enforcement agreements.

The Authority may enter into reciprocal agreement with other tolling jurisdictions to enforce toll violations. Such an agreement shall provide that, when another toll agency certifies that the registered owner of a vehicle registered in this State has failed to pay a toll, processing fee, or civil penalty due to that toll agency, the unpaid toll, processing fee, or civil penalty may be enforced by the Authority placing a renewal block as if it were an unpaid toll, processing fee, or civil penalty owed to this State under G.S. 136-89.217. Such agreement shall only be enforceable, however, if all of the following are true:

(1) The other toll agency has its own effective reciprocal procedure for toll violation enforcement and does, in fact, reciprocate in enforcing toll violations within this State by withholding the registration renewal of registered owners of motor vehicles from the state of the other toll agency.

(2) The other toll agency provides due process and appeal protections to avoid the likelihood that a false, mistaken, or unjustified claim will be pursued against the owner of a vehicle registered in this State.

(3) The owner of a vehicle registered in this State may present evidence to the other toll agency by mail or other means to invoke rights of due process without having to appear personally in the jurisdiction where the violation allegedly occurred.

(4) The reciprocal violation enforcement arrangement between the Authority and the other toll agency provides that each party shall charge the other for costs associated with registration holds in their respective jurisdictions. (2012-85, s. 11.)

Article 7.

Miscellaneous Provisions.

§ 136-90. Obstructing highways and roads misdemeanor.

If any person shall willfully alter, change or obstruct any highway, cartway, mill road or road leading to and from any church or other place of public worship, whether the right-of-way thereto be secured in the manner provided for by law or by purchase, donation or otherwise, such person shall be guilty of a Class 1 misdemeanor. If any person shall hinder or in any manner interfere with the making of any road or cartway laid off according to law, he shall be guilty of a Class 1 misdemeanor. (1872-3, c. 189, s. 6; 1883, c. 383; Code, s. 2065; Rev., s. 3784; C.S., s. 3789; 1993, c. 539, s. 989; 1994, Ex. Sess., c. 24, s. 14(c).)

§ 136-91. Placing glass, etc., or injurious obstructions in road.

(a) No person shall throw, place, or deposit any glass or other sharp or cutting substance or any injurious obstruction in or upon any highway or public vehicular area.

(b) As used in this section:

(1) "Highway" shall be defined as it is in G.S. 20-4.01; and

(2) "Public vehicular area" shall be defined as it is in G.S. 20-4.01.

(c) Any person violating the provisions of this section shall be guilty of a Class 3 misdemeanor. (1917, c. 140, ss. 18, 21; C.S., ss. 2599, 2619; 1971, c. 200; 1993, c. 539, s. 990; 1994, Ex. Sess., c. 24, s. 14(c); 2001-441, s. 3.)

§ 136-92. Obstructing highway drains prohibited.

It is unlawful to obstruct a drain along or leading from any public road in the State. A person who violates this section is responsible for an infraction. (1917, c. 253; C.S., s. 3791; 1993, c. 539, s. 991; 1994, Ex. Sess., c. 24, s. 14(c); 1995, c. 163, s. 15.)

§ 136-92.1. Exemption from temporary driveway permitting for forestry operations.

Forestry operations and silviculture operations, including the harvesting of timber, and other related management activities that require temporary ingress from a property to State roads shall be exempt from the temporary driveway permit process of the Department for State roads, except for controlled access facilities, if the operator of the temporary driveway has attended an educational course on timbering access and obtained a safety certification. Driveway access points covered by this section shall be temporary and shall be removed upon the earlier of six months or the end of forestry or silviculture operations on the property. (2013-265, s. 17.)

§ 136-93. Openings, structures, pipes, trees, and issuance of permits.

(a) No opening or other interference whatsoever shall be made in any State road or highway other than streets not maintained by the Department of Transportation in cities and towns, nor shall any structure be placed thereon, nor shall any structure which has been placed thereon be changed or removed except in accordance with a written permit from the Department of Transportation or its duly authorized officers, who shall exercise complete and permanent control over such roads and highways. No State road or State highway, other than streets not maintained by the Department of Transportation in cities and towns, shall be dug up for laying or placing pipes, conduits, sewers, wires, railways, or other objects, and no obstruction placed thereon, without a written permit as hereinbefore provided for, and then only in accordance with the regulations of said Department of Transportation or its duly authorized officers or employees; and the work shall be under the supervision and to the satisfaction of the Department of Transportation or its officers or employees, and the entire expense of replacing the highway in as good condition as before shall be paid by the persons, firms, or corporations to whom the permit is given, or by whom the work is done. The Department of Transportation, or its duly authorized officers, may, in its discretion, before granting a permit under the provisions of this section, require the applicant to file a satisfactory bond, payable to the State of North Carolina, in such an amount as may be deemed sufficient by the Department of Transportation or its duly authorized officers, conditioned upon the proper compliance with the requirements of this section by the person, firm, or corporation granted such permit. Any person making any opening in a State road or State highway, or placing any structure thereon, or changing or removing any structure thereon without obtaining a written permit as herein provided, or not in compliance with the terms of such permit, or otherwise violating the provisions of this section, shall be guilty of a Class 1 misdemeanor: Provided, this section shall not apply to railroad crossings. The railroads shall keep up said crossings as now provided by law.

(b) Except as provided in G.S. 136-133.1(g), no vegetation, including any tree, shrub, or underbrush, in or on any right-of-way of a State road or State highway shall be planted, cut, trimmed, pruned, or removed without a written selective vegetation removal permit issued pursuant to G.S. 136-133.2 and in accordance with the rules of the Department. Requests for a permit for selective vegetation cutting, thinning, pruning, or removal shall be made by the owner of an outdoor advertising sign or the owner of a business facility to the appropriate person in the Division of Highways office on a form prescribed by the Department. For purposes of this section, G.S. 136-133.1, 136-133.2, and 136-133.4, the phrase "outdoor advertising" shall mean the outdoor advertising expressly permitted under G.S. 136-129(a)(4) [G.S. 136-129(4)] or G.S. 136-129(a)(5) [G.S. 136-129(5)]. These provisions shall not be used to provide visibility to on-premises signs.

(c) For outdoor advertising, vegetation cut or removal limits shall be restricted to a maximum selective vegetation cut or removal zone for each sign face pursuant to the provisions of G.S. 136-133.1.

(d) If the application for vegetation cutting, thinning, pruning, or removal is for a site located within the corporate limits of a municipality, the municipality shall be given 30 days to review and provide comments on the application if the municipality has previously advised the Department in writing of the desire to review such applications and the name of the local official to whom notice of such application should be directed. (1921, c. 2, s. 13; 1923, c. 160, s. 2; C.S., s. 3846(u); 1933, c. 172, s. 17; 1943, c. 410; 1957, c. 65, s. 11; 1973, c. 507, s. 5; 1977, c. 464, s. 7.1; 1993, c. 539, s. 992; 1994, Ex. Sess., c. 24, s. 14(c); 2011-397, s. 1.)

§ 136-93.1. Express permit review program.

(a) Program Created. - The Department shall develop a fee-supported express permit review program in each highway division. The program is voluntary for permit applicants and applies to permits, approvals, or certifications that allow for a connection to the State highway system through the use of a driveway, street, signal, drainage, or any other encroachment.

(b) Implementation. - An individual highway division may opt out of the express permit review program created under this section if the highway division routinely reviews and issues special commercial permits within an average of 45 days. Any express permit review program created under this section shall be supported by the fees established pursuant to subsection (e) of this section.

(c) Procedure. - In reviewing a permit application under the express permit review program, the Department shall undergo the following steps:

(1) The Department shall, within three business days of receipt, determine whether an express permit review application is complete. If the Department determines the express permit review application is not complete, the Department shall return the express permit review application and all fees to the permit applicant to allow for a complete express permit review application to be resubmitted to the Department.

(2) If the Department determines the express permit review application is complete, the Department shall, within 45 days, issue or deny the permit based upon its review of the application. Failure of the Department to issue or deny the permit within 45 days is a denial of the express permit review application.

(d) Staffing. - In order to implement the express permit review program, the Department may utilize either of the following or a combination thereof:

(1) Existing Department staff and resources.

(2) Contracted engineering firms supporting each highway division to provide express permit reviews, comments, and recommendations for issuing express permits. If the Department utilizes contracted engineering firms to provide work under this section, any fees received by the Department pursuant to subsection (e) of this section shall be credited towards the cost of the Department utilizing these contracted engineering firms. Any additional costs associated with engaging the contracted engineering firm shall be agreed to by the permit applicant prior to incurring the costs and shall be paid by the permit applicant.

(e) Fees. - The Department may determine the fees for an express application review under the express review program conducted by highway division staff. Unless a contracted engineering firm is utilized, the maximum permit application fee to be charged under this section for an express review of a project application requiring all of the permits listed under subsection (a) of this section shall not exceed four thousand dollars ($4,000). Notwithstanding Chapter 150B of the General Statutes, the Department shall establish the procedure by which the amount of the fees under this subsection are established and applied for an express review program permitted by this section. The fee schedule established by the Department shall be applicable to all divisions participating in an express permit review program.

(f) Use of Fees. - All fees collected under this section shall be used to fund the cost of administering and implementing express permit review programs created under this section. These costs include the salaries of the program's staff and costs of contracted engineering firms.

(g) Repealed by Session Laws 2011-145, s. 28.35(a), effective July 1, 2011. (2008-176, s. 1; 2011-145, s. 28.35(a).)

§ 136-93.2. Monetary value of trees.

The monetary value for existing trees removed and eligible for reimbursement to the Department as provided in G.S. 136-93 or G.S. 136-133.1 from State rights-of-way shall be determined on an annual basis by the Department. In determining the value of existing trees removed, the average cost per caliper inch shall be based on the lower value of either the average wholesale commercial nursery prices for hardwood and conifer plants, times a 2.5 multiplier for installation and warranty or the average cost per caliper inch for tree planting contracts let by the Department in the previous calendar year. The values shall be determined and published by the Department no later than December 15 of each year. The values established pursuant to this section shall be used in calculating the monetary value of trees removed from State rights-of-way beginning January 1 of each year. If the Department fails to publish changes in values by December 15, then the values existing on December 15 shall be applicable to existing trees removed and eligible for reimbursement for the following year. (2011-397, s. 2.)

§ 136-93.3. Selective pruning within highway rights-of-way to enable view of agritourism activities.

The Department of Transportation shall adopt rules to authorize selective pruning within highway rights-of-way for vegetation that obstructs motorists' views of properties on which agritourism activities, as that term is defined in G.S. 99E-30, occur. The Department of Transportation is exempt from the provisions of G.S. 150B that require the preparation of fiscal notes for any rule proposed pursuant to this section. (2013-413, s. 45.)

§ 136-94. Gates projecting over rights-of-way forbidden.

It shall be unlawful for any person, firm or corporation to erect, maintain or operate upon his own land, or the land of another, any farm gate or other gate which, when opened, will project over the right-of-way of any State highway.

Any person violating the provisions of this section shall be guilty of a Class 3 misdemeanor. (1927, c. 130; 1993, c. 539, s. 993; 1994, Ex. Sess., c. 24, s. 14(c).)

§ 136-95. Water must be diverted from public road by ditch or drain.

When any ditch or drain is cut in such a way as to turn water into any public road, the person cutting the ditch or drain shall be compelled to cut another ditch or drain as may be necessary to take the water from said road. (Code, s. 2036; Rev., s. 2697; C.S., s. 3790.)

§ 136-96. Road or street not used within 15 years after dedication deemed abandoned; declaration of withdrawal recorded; joint tenants or tenants in common; defunct corporations.

Every strip, piece, or parcel of land which shall have been at any time dedicated to public use as a road, highway, street, avenue, or for any other purpose whatsoever, by a deed, grant, map, plat, or other means, which shall not have been actually opened and used by the public within 15 years from and after the dedication thereof, shall be thereby conclusively presumed to have been abandoned by the public for the purposes for which same shall have been dedicated; and no person shall have any right, or cause of action thereafter, to enforce any public or private easement therein, except where such dedication was made less than 20 years prior to April 28, 1953, such right may be asserted within one year from and after April 28, 1953; provided, that no abandonment of any such public or private right or easement shall be presumed until the dedicator or some one or more of those claiming under him shall file and cause to be recorded in the register's office of the county where such land lies a declaration withdrawing such strip, piece or parcel of land from the public or private use to which it shall have theretofore been dedicated in the manner aforesaid; provided further, that where the fee simple title is vested in tenants in common or joint tenants of any land embraced within the boundaries of any such road, highway, street, avenue or other land dedicated for public purpose whatsoever, as described in this section, any one or more of such tenants, on his own or their behalf and on the behalf of the others of such tenants, may execute and cause to be registered in the office of the register of deeds of the county where such land is situated the declaration of withdrawal provided for in this section, and, under Chapter 46 of the General Statutes of North Carolina, entitled "Partition," and Chapter 1, Article 29A of the General Statutes of North Carolina, known as the "Judicial Sales Act," and on petition of any one or more of such tenants such land thereafter may be partitioned by sale only as between or among such tenants, and irrespective of who may be in actual possession of such land, provided further, that in such partition proceedings any such tenants in common or joint tenants may object to such withdrawal certificate and the court shall thereupon order the same cancelled of record; that where any corporation has dedicated any strip, piece or parcel of land in the manner herein set out, and said dedicating corporation is not now in existence, it shall be conclusively presumed that the said corporation has no further right, title or interest in said strip, piece, or parcel of land, regardless of the provisions of conveyances from said corporation, or those holding under said corporation, retaining title and interest in said strip, piece, or parcel of land so dedicated; the right, title and interest in said strip, piece, or parcel of land shall be conclusively presumed to be vested in those persons, firms or corporations owning lots or parcels of land adjacent thereto, subject to the provisions set out herein before in this section.

The provisions of this section shall have no application in any case where the continued use of any strip of land dedicated for street or highway purposes shall be necessary to afford convenient ingress or egress to any lot or parcel of land sold and conveyed by the dedicator of such street or highway. This section shall apply to dedications made after as well as before April 28, 1953.

The provisions of this section shall not apply when the public dedication is part of a future street shown on the street plan adopted pursuant to G.S. 136-66.2. Upon request, a city shall adopt a resolution indicating that the dedication described in the proposed declaration of withdrawal is or is not part of the street plan adopted under G.S. 136-66.2. This resolution shall be attached to the declaration of withdrawal and shall be registered in the office of the register of deeds of the county where the land is situated. (1921, c. 174; C.S., ss. 3846(rr), 3846(ss), 3846(tt); 1939, c. 406; 1953, c. 1091; 1957, c. 517; 1987, c. 428.)

§ 136-96.1. Special proceeding to declare a right-of-way dedicated to public use.

(a) A special proceeding under Article 3, Chapter 1 of the General Statutes may be brought to declare a right-of-way dedicated to public use if:

(1) The landowners of tracts constituting two-thirds of the road frontage of the land abutting the right-of-way in question join in the action;

(2) The right-of-way is depicted on an unrecorded map, plat, or survey;

(3) The right-of-way has been actually open and used by the public; and

(4) Recorded deeds for at least three separate parcels abutting the right-of-way recite the existence of the right-of-way as a named street or road.

(b) In a special proceeding brought pursuant to this section, the clerk of court shall issue an order declaring the right-of-way to be dedicated to public use upon finding that the provisions of subsection (a) of this section have been proven.

(c) Any right-of-way found to be dedicated to public use pursuant to this section that is proposed for addition to the State highway system shall meet the requirements of G.S. 136-102.6.

(d) This section shall not apply to any right-of-way established by adverse possession or by cartway proceeding. (2001-501, s. 1.)

§ 136-96.2. Withdrawal of public use dedication by property owners associations.

(a) Qualification for Withdrawal of Dedication. - A property owners association that owns subdivision streets or segments of streets may file in the office of the register of deeds, in the county where the streets are located, a declaration withdrawing any purported dedication to public use or withdrawing an offer of dedication to public use of such streets and declaring such streets to be private when all of the following conditions are met:

(1) The subdivision within which the streets exist is located entirely outside the corporate limits of any municipality and bounded on the east by the Atlantic Ocean.

(2) The subdivision was created by a plat recorded at least 30 years prior to the recording of the declaration of withdrawal.

(3) The recorded plat of the subdivision bears a certificate signed by a county representative purporting to accept on behalf of the county the dedication of the streets shown on the plat.

(4) At least two-thirds of the total length of all the streets shown on the plat have been paved, opened, and used for vehicular traffic for a period of at least 25 years prior to the recording of the declaration of withdrawal.

(5) The subdivision streets have only one means of ingress and egress intersecting with a State highway.

(6) The streets have never been maintained by the county, and the county claims no interest in the streets.

(7) The Department of Transportation has never maintained the streets or accepted them for maintenance and claims no ownership interest in the streets.

(8) The developer of the subdivision or the successor to the developer has deeded the streets to an incorporated property owners association and, therefore, such property owners association is the record owner of the streets.

(9) The streets within the subdivision are being maintained and insured by the property owners association that represents all property owners.

(10) The declaration of withdrawal has been approved by a two-thirds vote of all members of the property owners association present in person or by proxy at a special meeting of all such members duly called for that purpose.

(b) Approval by Board of County Commissioners; Signature of Clerk. - A declaration described under subsection (a) of this section may not be recorded unless it bears the signature of the clerk to the board of commissioners of the county where the streets covered in the declaration are located attesting to the adoption by the board of commissioners of a resolution approving such declaration. The board of commissioners may adopt such a resolution only upon a finding that each of the circumstances listed in subsection (a) of this section exists. In approving such a resolution, the board of commissioners may provide that:

(1) The withdrawal of dedication shall not apply to (i) streets or segments of streets where withdrawal of dedication would terminate all reasonable legal means of access to any property or (ii) streets or segments of streets that are necessary to connect a public street located outside the subject subdivision with another public street located outside the subject subdivision.

(2) No gate or other obstruction may be placed across any street or segments of streets unless such gate or obstruction is approved by the board of commissioners upon a finding by the board that other methods of preventing unauthorized parking or preserving public safety on such streets or segments of streets have proved inadequate.

(3) The clerk to the board of commissioners shall sign the declaration of withdrawal only upon completion of the improvements to the covered streets in accordance with a plan for such improvements submitted by the property owners association that complies with any published street standards required by the county on the date that the subdivision plat was recorded as certified by the county engineer.

(c) Effect of Withdrawal of Dedication. - The recording of a declaration authorized by and in accordance with this section shall declare and make the streets described in the declaration the private property of the property owners association that owns such streets, and any offer of dedication of such streets that may have been created by the recording of the plat creating the subdivision shall be conclusively presumed to be withdrawn. However, the right, title, or interest vested in the property owners association remains subject to (i) public pedestrian access on, over, and upon the road or easement as existed immediately before its closing and (ii) any public utility use or facility located on, over, or under the road easement immediately before its closing, until the landowner or any successor thereto pays to the utility involved, and the utility accepts, the reasonable cost of removing and relocating the facility. (2011-289, s. 1.)

§ 136-97. Responsibility of counties for upkeep, etc., terminated.

(a) The board of county commissioners or other road-governing bodies of the various counties in the State are hereby relieved of all responsibility or liability for the upkeep or maintenance of any of the roads or bridges thereon constituting the State highway system, after the same shall have been taken over, and the control thereof assumed by the Department of Transportation.

(b) The Department of Transportation, as part of maintaining the highways, bridges, and watercourses of this State, may haul all debris removed from on, under, or around a bridge to an appropriate disposal site for solid waste, where the debris shall be disposed of in accordance with law. (1921, c. 2, s. 50; C.S., s. 3846(dd); 1933, c. 172, s. 17; 1957, c. 65, s. 11; 1973, c. 507, ss. 5, 20; 1977, c. 464, s. 7.1; 1989, c. 752, s. 102; 1989 (Reg. Sess., 1990), c. 1066, s. 139; 1991, c. 689, s. 209.)

§ 136-98. Counties authorized to participate in costs of road construction and maintenance, participation is voluntary.

(a) Repealed by Session Laws 2007-428, s. 4, effective August 23, 2007.

(b) Nothing in this Article prohibits counties from establishing service districts for road maintenance under Part 1, Article 16 of Chapter 153A of the General Statutes.

(c) A county is authorized to participate in the cost of rights-of-way, construction, reconstruction, improvement, or maintenance of a road on the State highway system under agreement with the Department of Transportation. County participation in improvements to the State highway system is voluntary. The Department shall not transfer any of its responsibilities to counties without specific statutory authority. (1931, c. 145, s. 35; 1957, c. 65, s. 11; 1973, c. 507, s. 5; 1977, c. 464, s. 7.1; 1995, c. 434, s. 2; 2007-428, s. 4; 2008-180, s. 7.)

§§ 136-99 through 136-101. Repealed by Session Laws 1971, c. 1106.

§ 136-102. Billboard obstructing view at entrance to school, church or public institution on public highway.

(a) It shall be unlawful for any person, firm, or corporation to construct or maintain outside the limits of any city or town in this State any billboard larger than six square feet at or nearer than 200 feet to the point where any walk or drive from any school, church, or public institution located along any highway enters such highway except under the following conditions:

(1) Such billboard is attached to the side of a building or buildings which are or may be erected within 200 feet of any such walk or drive and the attachment thereto causes no additional obstruction of view.

(2) A building or other structure is located so as to obstruct the view between such walk or drive and such billboard.

(3) Such billboard is located on the opposite side of the highway from the entrance to said walk or drive.

(b) Any person, firm, or corporation convicted of violating the provisions of this section shall be guilty of a Class 3 misdemeanor and punished only by a fine of ten dollars ($10.00), and each day that such violation continues shall be considered a separate offense. (1947, c. 304, ss. 1, 2; 1993, c. 539, s. 994; 1994, Ex. Sess., c. 24, s. 14 (c).)

§ 136-102.1. Blue Star Memorial and American Ex-Prisoners of War Highway.

All of the United States Highway #70, wherever located in North Carolina shall be known and designated as the "Blue Star Memorial and American Ex-Prisoners of War Highway." The designation shall pay tribute to the many North Carolinians killed during World War II and to all North Carolina's ex-prisoners of war. (1963, c. 140; 2001-196, s. 1.)

§ 136-102.2. Authorization required for test drilling or boring upon right-of-way; filing record of results with Department of Transportation.

No person, firm or corporation shall make any test drilling or boring upon the right-of-way of any transportation system, under the jurisdiction of the Department of Transportation, until written authorization has been obtained from the owner or the person in charge of the land on which the highway easement is located. A complete record showing the results of the test drilling or boring shall be filed forthwith with the chairman [Secretary] of the Department of Transportation and shall be a public record. This section shall not apply to the Department of Transportation making test drilling or boring for highway purposes only. (1967, c. 923, s. 1; 1973, c. 507, s. 5; 1977, c. 464, s. 7.1; 2009-266, s. 25.)

§ 136-102.3. Filing record of results of test drilling or boring with Secretary of Administration and Secretary of Environment and Natural Resources.

Any person, firm or corporation making any test drilling or boring upon any public land, owned or controlled by the State of North Carolina[,] shall, forthwith after completion, file a complete record of the results of the test drilling or boring with the Secretary of Administration and with the Secretary of Environment and Natural Resources, of each test hole bored or drilled. Such records filed shall become a matter of public record. Provided, that after exploratory drilling and boring has been completed, and a lease or contract has been executed for operation, production or development of the area, the results of test drillings or borings made incidental to the operation, production or development of the area under lease or contract shall not be subject to the provisions of G.S. 136-102.2 to 136-102.4 unless otherwise provided in such lease or contract. (1967, c. 923, s. 2; 1973, c. 1262, s. 86; 1975, c. 879, s. 46; 1977, c. 771, s. 4; 1989, c. 727, s. 218(90); 1997-443, s. 11A.119(a).)

§ 136-102.4. Penalty for violation of §§ 136-102.2 and 136-102.3.

Violation of G.S. 136-102.2 and 136-102.3 shall be a Class 1 misdemeanor. (1967, c. 923, s. 3; 1993, c. 539, s. 995; 1994, Ex. Sess., c. 24, s. 14 (c).)

§ 136-102.5. Signs on fishing bridges.

When requested to do so by any county or municipality that has enacted an ordinance under G.S. 153-9(66) and 160-200(47) regulating or prohibiting fishing on any bridge of the North Carolina State highway system, the Department of Transportation shall erect signs on such bridges indicating the prohibition or regulation of the ordinance enacted under G.S. 153-9(66) and 160-200(47). (1971, c. 690, s. 5; 1973, c. 507, s. 5; 1977, c. 464, s. 7.1.)

§ 136-102.6. Compliance of subdivision streets with minimum standards of the Board of Transportation required of developers.

(a)   The owner of a tract or parcel of land which is subdivided from and after October 1, 1975, into two or more lots, building sites, or other divisions for sale or building development for residential purposes, where such subdivision includes a new street or the changing of an existing street, shall record a map or plat of the subdivision with the register of deeds of the county in which the land is located. The map or plat shall be recorded prior to any conveyance of a portion of said land, by reference to said map or plat.

(b)   The right-of-way of any new street or change in an existing street shall be delineated upon the map or plat with particularity and such streets shall be designated to be either public or private. Any street designated on the plat or map as public shall be conclusively presumed to be an offer of dedication to the public of such street.

(c)   The right-of-way and design of streets designated as public shall be in accordance with the minimum right-of-way and construction standards established by the Board of Transportation for acceptance on the State highway system. If a municipal or county subdivision control ordinance is in effect in the area proposed for subdivision, the map or plat required by this section shall not be recorded by the register of deeds until after it has received final plat approval by the municipality or county, and until after it has received a certificate of approval by the Division of Highways as herein provided as to those streets regulated in subsection (g). The certificate of approval may be issued by a district engineer of the Division of Highways of the Department of Transportation.

(d) The right-of-way and construction plans for such public streets in residential subdivisions, including plans for street drainage, shall be submitted to the Division of Highways for review and approval, prior to the recording of the subdivision plat in the office of the register of deeds. The plat or map required by this section shall not be recorded by the register of deeds without a certification pursuant to G.S. 47-30.2 and, if determined to be necessary by the Review Officer, a certificate of approval by the Division of Highways of the plans for the public street as being in accordance with the minimum standards of the Board of Transportation for acceptance of the subdivision street on the State highway system for maintenance. The Review Officer shall not certify a map or plat subject to this section unless the new streets or changes in existing streets are designated either public or private. The certificate of approval shall not be deemed an acceptance of the dedication of the streets on the subdivision plat or map. Final acceptance by the Division of Highways of the public streets and placing them on the State highway system for maintenance shall be conclusive proof that the streets have been constructed according to the minimum standards of the Board of Transportation.

(e) No person or firm shall place or erect any utility in, over, or upon the existing or proposed right-of-way of any street in a subdivision to which this section applies, except in accordance with the Division of Highway's policies and procedures for accommodating utilities on highway rights-of-way, until the Division of Highways has given written approval of the location of such utilities. Written approval may be in the form of exchange of correspondence until such times as it is requested to add the street or streets to the State system, at which time an encroachment agreement furnished by the Division of Highways must be executed between the owner of the utility and the Division of Highways. The right of any utility placed or located on a proposed or existing subdivision public street right-of-way shall be subordinate to the street right-of-way, and the utility shall be subject to regulation by the Department of Transportation. Utilities are defined as electric power, telephone, television, telegraph, water, sewage, gas, oil, petroleum products, steam, chemicals, drainage, irrigation, and similar lines. Any utility installed in a subdivision street not in accordance with the Division of Highways accommodation policy, and without prior approval by the Division of Highways, shall be removed or relocated at no expense to the Division of Highways.

(f) Prior to entering any agreement or any conveyance with any prospective buyer, the developer and seller shall prepare and sign, and the buyer of the subject real estate shall receive and sign an acknowledgment of receipt of a separate instrument known as the subdivision streets disclosure statement (hereinafter referred to as disclosure statement). Said disclosure statement shall fully and completely disclose the status (whether public or private) of the street upon which the house or lot fronts. If the street is designated by the developer and seller as a public street, the developer and seller shall certify that the right-of-way and design of the street has been approved by the Division of Highways, and that the street has been or will be constructed by the developer and seller in accordance with the standards for subdivision streets adopted by the Board of Transportation for acceptance on the highway system. If the street is designated by the developer and seller as a private street, the developer and seller shall include in the disclosure statement an explanation of the consequences and responsibility as to maintenance of a private street, and shall fully and accurately disclose the party or parties upon whom responsibility for construction and maintenance of such street or streets shall rest, and shall further disclose that the street or streets will not be constructed to minimum standards, sufficient to allow their inclusion on the State highway system for maintenance. The disclosure statement shall contain a duplicate original which shall be given to the buyer. Written acknowledgment of receipt of the disclosure statement by the buyer shall be conclusive proof of the delivery thereof.

(g) The provisions of this section shall apply to all subdivisions located outside municipal corporate limits. As to subdivisions inside municipalities, this section shall apply to all proposed streets or changes in existing streets on the State highway system as shown on the comprehensive plan for the future development of the street system made pursuant to G.S. 136-66.2, and in effect at the date of approval of the map or plat.

(h) The provisions of this section shall not apply to any subdivision that consists only of lots located on Lakes Hickory, Norman, Mountain Island and Wylie which are lakes formed by the Catawba River which lots are leased upon October 1, 1975. No roads in any such subdivision shall be added to the State maintained road system without first having been brought up to standards established by the Board of Transportation for inclusion of roads in the system, without expense to the State. Prior to entering any agreement or any conveyance with any prospective buyer of a lot in any such subdivision, the seller shall prepare and sign, and the buyer shall receive and sign an acknowledgment of receipt of a statement fully and completely disclosing the status of and the responsibility for construction and maintenance of the road upon which such lot is located.

(i) The purpose of this section is to insure that new subdivision streets described herein to be dedicated to the public will comply with the State standards for placing subdivision streets on the State highway system for maintenance, or that full and accurate disclosure of the responsibility for construction and maintenance of private streets be made. This section shall be construed and applied in a manner which shall not inhibit the ability of public utilities to satisfy service requirements of subdivisions to which this section applies.

(j) The Division of Highways and district engineers of the Division of Highways of the Department of Transportation shall issue a certificate of approval for any subdivision affected by a transportation corridor official map established by the Board of Transportation only if the subdivision conforms to Article 2E of this Chapter or conforms to any variance issued in accordance with that Article.

(k) A willful violation of any of the provisions of this section shall be a Class 1 misdemeanor. (1975, c. 488, s. 1; 1977, c. 464, ss. 7.1, 8; 1987, c. 747, s. 21; 1993, c. 539, s. 996; 1994, Ex. Sess., c. 24, s. 14(c); 1997-309, s. 4; 1998-184, s. 3.)

§ 136-102.7. Hurricane evacuation standard.

Evacuation Standard. - The hurricane evacuation standard to be used for any bridge or highway construction project pursuant to this Chapter shall be no more than 18 hours, as recommended by the State Emergency Management officials. (2005-275, s. 5.)

§ 136-102.8. Subdivision streets; traffic calming devices.

The Department shall establish policies and procedures for the installation or utilization of traffic tables or traffic calming devices erected on State-maintained subdivision streets adopted by the Department, pursuant to G.S. 136-102.6, if all of the following requirements are met:

(1) A traffic engineering study has been approved by the Department detailing types and locations of traffic calming devices.

(2) Installation and utilization of traffic tables or traffic calming devices is within one of the following areas:

a. A subdivision with a homeowners association.

b. A neighborhood in which the property owners have established a contractual agreement outlining responsibility for traffic calming devices installed in the neighborhood.

(3) The traffic tables or traffic calming devices are paid for and maintained by the subdivision homeowners association, or its successor, or pursuant to a neighborhood agreement.

(4) The homeowners association has the written support, for the installation of each traffic table or traffic calming device approved by the Department pursuant to this section, of at least seventy percent (70%) of the member property owners, or the neighborhood agreement is signed by at least seventy percent (70%) of the neighborhood property owners.

(5) The homeowners association, or neighborhood pursuant to its agreement, posts a performance bond with the Department sufficient to fund maintenance or removal of the traffic tables or calming devices, if the homeowners association, or neighborhood pursuant to its agreement, fails to maintain them, or is dissolved. The bond shall remain in place for a period of three years from the date of installation. (2009-310, s. 1.)

§ 136-102.9. Use of aircraft managed by the Department of Transportation.

Of the aircraft managed by the Department of Transportation, the use of aircraft for economic development purposes shall take precedence over all other uses except in cases of emergency or disaster response. The Department of Transportation shall annually review the rates charged for the use of aircraft and shall adjust the rates, as necessary, to account for upgraded aircraft and inflationary increases in operating costs, including jet fuel prices. If an aircraft is used to attend athletic events or for any other purpose related to collegiate athletics, the rate charged shall be equal to the direct cost of operating the aircraft as established by the aircraft's manufacturer, adjusted for inflation. (2010-31, s. 14.6(c).)

Article 8.

Citation to Highway Bond Acts.

§ 136-102.50: Repealed by Session Laws 1998-98, s. 40.

Article 9.

Condemnation.

§ 136-103. Institution of action and deposit.

(a) In case condemnation shall become necessary the Department of Transportation shall institute a civil action by filing in the superior court of any county in which the land is located a complaint and a declaration of taking declaring that such land, easement, or interest therein is thereby taken for the use of the Department of Transportation.

(b) Said declaration shall contain or have attached thereto the following:

(1) A statement of the authority under which and the public use for which said land is taken.

(2) A description of the entire tract or tracts affected by said taking sufficient for the identification thereof.

(3) A statement of the estate or interest in said land taken for public use and a description of the area taken sufficient for the identification thereof.

(4) The names and addresses of those persons who the Department of Transportation is informed and believes may have or claim to have an interest in said lands, so far as the same can by reasonable diligence be ascertained and if any such persons are infants, non compos mentis, under any other disability, or their whereabouts or names unknown, it must be so stated.

(5) A statement of the sum of money estimated by said Department of Transportation to be just compensation for said taking.

(c) Said complaint shall contain or have attached thereto the following:

(1) A statement of the authority under which and the public use for which said land is taken.

(2) A description of the entire tract or tracts affected by said taking sufficient for the identification thereof.

(3) A statement of the estate or interest in said land taken for public use and a description of the area taken sufficient for the identification thereof.

(4) The names and addresses of those persons who the Department of Transportation is informed and believes may have or claim to have an interest in said lands, so far as the same can by reasonable diligence be ascertained and if any such persons are infants, non compos mentis, under any other disability, or their whereabouts or names unknown, it must be so stated.

(5) A statement as to such liens or other encumbrances as the Department of Transportation is informed and believes are encumbrances upon said real estate and can by reasonable diligence be ascertained.

(6) A prayer that there be a determination of just compensation in accordance with the provisions of this Article.

(d) The filing of said complaint and said declaration of taking shall be accompanied by the deposit of the sum of money estimated by said Department of Transportation to be just compensation for said taking and upon the filing of said complaint and said declaration of taking and deposit of said sum, summons shall be issued and together with a copy of said complaint and said declaration of taking and notice of the deposit be served upon the person named therein in the manner now provided for the service of process in civil actions. The Department of Transportation may amend the complaint and declaration of taking and may increase the amount of its deposit with the court at any time while the proceeding is pending, and the owner shall have the same rights of withdrawal of this additional amount as set forth in G.S. 136-105 of this Chapter. (1959, c. 1025, s. 2; 1961, c. 1084, s. 1; 1963, c. 1156, s. 1; 1973, c. 507, s. 5; 1977, c. 464, s. 7.1; 1997-456, s. 27.)

§ 136-103.1. Outside counsel.

The Attorney General is authorized to employ outside counsel as he deems necessary for the purpose of obtaining title abstracts and title certificates for transportation system rights-of-way and for assistance in the trial of condemnation cases involving the acquisition of rights-of-way and other interests in land for the purpose of transportation construction. Compensation, as approved by the Attorney General, shall be paid out of the appropriations from the Highway Fund. (1973, c. 507, s. 4; 2009-266, s. 26.)

§ 136-104. Vesting of title and right of possession; recording memorandum or supplemental memorandum of action.

Upon the filing of the complaint and the declaration of taking and deposit in court, to the use of the person entitled thereto, of the amount of the estimated compensation stated in the declaration, title to said land or such other interest therein specified in the complaint and the declaration of taking, together with the right to immediate possession hereof shall vest in the Department of Transportation and the judge shall enter such orders in the cause as may be required to place the Department of Transportation in possession, and said land shall be deemed to be condemned and taken for the use of the Department of Transportation and the right to just compensation therefor shall vest in the person owning said property or any compensable interest therein at the time of the filing of the complaint and the declaration of taking and deposit of the money in court, and compensation shall be determined and awarded in said action and established by judgment therein.

Where there is a life estate and a remainder either vested or contingent, in lieu of the investment of the proceeds of the amount determined and awarded as just compensation to which the life tenant would be entitled to the use during the life estate, the court may in its discretion order the value of said life tenant's share during the probable life of such life tenant be ascertained as now provided by law and paid directly to the life tenant out of the final award as just compensation established by the judgment in the cause and the life tenant may have the relief provided for in G.S. 136-105.

On and after July 1, 1961, the Department of Transportation, at the time of the filing of the complaint and declaration of taking and deposit of estimated compensation, shall record a memorandum of action with the register of deeds in all counties in which the land involved therein is located and said memorandum shall be recorded among the land records of said county. Upon the amending of any complaint and declaration of taking affecting the property taken, the Department of Transportation shall record a supplemental memorandum of action. The memorandum of action shall contain

(1) The names of those persons who the Department of Transportation is informed and believes may have or claim to have an interest in said lands and who are parties to said action;

(2) A description of the entire tract or tracts affected by said taking sufficient for the identification thereof;

(3) A statement of the estate or interest in said land taken for public use;

(4) The date of institution of said action, the county in which said action is pending, and such other reference thereto as may be necessary for the identification of said action.

As to those actions instituted by the Department of Transportation under the provisions of this Article prior to July 1, 1961, the Department of Transportation shall, on or before October 1, 1961, record a memorandum of action with the register of deeds in all counties in which said land is located as hereinabove set forth; however, the failure of the Department of Transportation to record said memorandum shall not invalidate those actions instituted prior to July 1, 1961. (1959, c. 1025, s. 2; 1961, c. 1084, s. 2; 1963, c. 1156, s. 2; 1973, c. 507, s. 5; 1975, c. 522, s. 1; 1977, c. 464, s. 7.1.)

§ 136-105. Disbursement of deposit; serving copy of disbursing order on Department of Transportation.

The person named in the complaint and declaration of taking may apply to the court for disbursement of the money deposited in the court, or any part thereof, as full compensation, or as a credit against just compensation without prejudice to further proceedings in the cause to determine just compensation. Upon such application, the judge shall, unless there is a dispute as to title, order that the money deposited be paid forthwith to the person entitled thereto in accordance with the application. The judge shall have power to make such orders with respect to encumbrances, liens, rents, taxes, assessments, insurance, and other charges, if any, as shall be just and equitable.

No notice to the Department of Transportation of the hearing upon the application for disbursement of deposit shall be necessary, but a copy of the order disbursing the deposit shall be served upon the Secretary of Transportation, or such other process agents as may be designated by the Department of Transportation. (1959, c. 1025, s. 2; 1961, c. 1084, s. 3; 1965, c. 55, s. 14; 1969, c. 649; 1973, c. 507, s. 5; 1977, c. 464, ss. 7.1, 26.)

§ 136-106. Answer, reply and plat.

(a)   Any person whose property has been taken by the Department of Transportation by the filing of a complaint and a declaration of taking, may within the time hereinafter set forth file an answer to the complaint only praying for a determination of just compensation. No answer shall be filed to the declaration of taking and notice of deposit. Said answer shall, in addition, contain the following:

(1)   Such admissions or denials of the allegations of the complaint as are appropriate.

(2)   The names and addresses of the persons filing said answer, together with a statement as to their interest in the property taken.

(3)   Such affirmative defenses or matters as are pertinent to the action.

(b)   A copy of the answer shall be served on the Department of Transportation, or such other process agents as may be designated by the Department of Transportation, in Raleigh, provided that failure to serve the answer shall not deprive the answer of its validity. The affirmative allegations of said answer shall be deemed denied. The Department of Transportation may, however, file a reply within 30 days from receipt of a copy of the answer.

(c)   The Department of Transportation, within 90 days from the receipt of the answer shall file in the cause a plat of the land taken and such additional area as may be necessary to properly determine the damages, and a copy thereof shall be mailed to the parties or their attorney; provided, however, the Department of Transportation shall not be required to file a map or plat in less than six months from the date of the filing of the complaint. (1959, c. 1025, s. 2; 1961, c. 1084, s. 4; 1963, c. 1156, ss. 3, 4; 1965, c. 55, s. 15; 1973, c. 507, s. 5; 1977, c. 464, ss. 7.1, 28.)

§ 136-107. Time for filing answer.

Any person named in and served with a complaint and declaration of taking shall have 12 months from the date of service thereof to file answer. Failure to answer within said time shall constitute an admission that the amount deposited is just compensation and shall be a waiver of any further proceeding to determine just compensation; in such event the judge shall enter final judgment in the amount deposited and order disbursement of the money deposited to the owner. Provided, however, at any time prior to the entry of the final judgment the judge may, for good cause shown and after notice to the plaintiff, extend the time for filing answer for 30 days. Provided that when the procedures of Article 9 of Chapter 136 are employed by the Department of Administration, any person named in or served with a complaint and declaration of taking shall have 120 days from the date of service thereof within which to file an answer. (1959, c. 1025, s. 2; 1973, c. 507, s. 5; 1975, c. 625; 1981, c. 245, s. 2.)

§ 136-108. Determination of issues other than damages.

After the filing of the plat, the judge, upon motion and 10 days' notice by either the Department of Transportation or the owner, shall, either in or out of term, hear and determine any and all issues raised by the pleadings other than the issue of damages, including, but not limited to, if controverted, questions of necessary and proper parties, title to the land, interest taken, and area taken. (1959, c. 1025, s. 2; 1963, c. 1156, s. 5; 1973, c. 507, s. 5; 1977, c. 464, s. 7.1.)

§ 136-109. Appointment of commissioners.

(a)   Upon request of the owner in the answer, or upon motion filed by either the Department of Transportation or the owner within 60 days after the filing of answer, the clerk shall appoint, after the determination of other issues as provided by G.S. 136-108 of this Chapter, three competent, disinterested freeholders residing in the county to go upon the property and under oath appraise the damage to the land sustained by reason of the taking and report same to the court within a time certain. If no request or motion is made for the appointment of commissioners within the time permitted, the cause shall be transferred to the civil issue docket for trial as to the issue of just compensation.

(b) Such commissioners, if appointed, shall have the power to make such inspection of the property, hold such hearings, swear such witnesses, and take such evidence as they may, in their discretion, deem necessary, and shall file into court a report of their determination of the damages sustained.

(c) Said report of commissioners shall in substance be in written form as follows:

TO THE SUPERIOR COURT OF _____ COUNTY

We, _____, _____ and _____ Commissioners appointed by the Court to assess the damages that have been and will be sustained by _____, the owner of certain land lying in _____ County, North Carolina, which has been taken by the Department of Transportation for highway purposes, do hereby certify that we convened, and, having first been duly sworn, visited the premises, and took such evidence as was presented to us, and after taking into full consideration the quality and quantity of the land and all other facts which reasonably affect its fair market value at the time of the taking, we have determined the fair market value of the part of the land taken to be the sum of $_____ and the damage to the remainder of the land of the owner by reason of the taking to be the sum of $_____ (if applicable).

We have determined the general and special benefits resulting to said owner from the construction of the highway to be the sum of $_____ (if applicable).

GIVEN under our hands, this the _____ day of _____, _____

_____ (SEAL)

_____ (SEAL)

_____

(SEAL)

(d) A copy of the report shall at the time of filing be mailed to each of the parties. Within 30 days after the filing of the report, either the Department of Transportation or the owner, may except thereto and demand a trial de novo by a jury as to the issue of damages. Whereupon the action shall be placed on the civil issue docket of the superior court for trial de novo by a jury as to the issue of damages, provided, that upon agreement of both parties trial by jury may be waived and the issue determined by the judge. The report of commissioners shall not be competent as evidence upon the trial of the issue of damages in the superior court, nor shall evidence of the deposit by the Department of Transportation into the court be competent upon the trial of the issue of damages. If no exception to the report of commissioners is filed within the time prescribed final judgment shall be entered by the judge upon a determination and finding by him that the report of commissioners, plus interest computed in accordance with G.S. 136-113 of this Chapter, awards to the property owners just compensation. In the event that the judge is of the opinion and, in his discretion, determines that such award does not provide just compensation he shall set aside said award and order the case placed on the civil issue docket for determination of the issue of damages by a jury. (1959, c. 1025, s. 2; 1961, c. 1084, s. 5; 1963, c. 1156, s. 6; 1973, c. 108, s. 85; c. 507, s. 5; 1977, c. 464, s. 7.1; 1999-456, s. 59.)

§ 136-110. Parties; orders; continuances.

The judge may appoint some competent attorney to appear for and protect the rights of any party or parties in interest who are unknown, or whose residence is unknown and who has not appeared in the proceeding by an attorney or agent. The judge shall appoint guardians ad litem for such parties as are minors, incompetents, or other parties who may be under a disability and without general guardian, and the judge shall have the authority to make such additional parties as are necessary to the complete determination of the proceeding and enter such other orders either in law or equity as may be necessary to carry out the provisions of this Article.

Upon the coming on of the cause for hearing pursuant to G.S. 136-108 or upon the coming on of the cause for trial, the judge, in order that the material ends of justice may be served, upon his own motion, or upon motion of any of the parties thereto and upon proper showing that the effect of condemnation upon the subject property cannot presently be determined, may, in his discretion, continue the cause until the highway project under which the appropriation occurred is open to traffic, or until such earlier time as, in the opinion of the judge, the effect of condemnation upon said property may be determined. (1959, c. 1025, s. 2; 1963, c. 1156, s. 7.)

§ 136-111. Remedy where no declaration of taking filed; recording memorandum of action.

Any person whose land or compensable interest therein has been taken by an intentional or unintentional act or omission of the Department of Transportation and no complaint and declaration of taking has been filed by said Department of Transportation may, within 24 months of the date of the taking of the affected property or interest therein or the completion of the project involving the taking, whichever shall occur later, file a complaint in the superior court setting forth the names and places of residence of the parties, so far as the same can by reasonable diligence be ascertained, who own or have, or claim to own or have estates or interests in the said real estate and if any such persons are under a legal disability, it must be so stated, together with a statement as to any encumbrances on said real estate; said complaint shall further allege with particularity the facts which constitute said taking together with the dates that they allegedly occurred; said complaint shall describe the property allegedly owned by said parties and shall describe the area and interests allegedly taken. Upon the filing of said complaint summons shall issue and together with a copy of said complaint be served on the Department of Transportation as provided by G.S. 1A-1, Rule 4(j)(4). The allegations of said complaint shall be deemed denied; however, the Department of Transportation within 60 days of service of summons and complaint may file answer thereto, and if said taking is admitted by the Department of Transportation, it shall, at the time of filing answer, deposit with the court the estimated amount of compensation for said taking and notice of said deposit shall be given to said owner. Said owner may apply for disbursement of said deposit and disbursement shall be made in accordance with the applicable provisions of G.S. 136-105 of this Chapter. If a taking is admitted, the Department of Transportation shall, within 90 days of the filing of the answer to the complaint, file a map or plat of the land taken. The procedure hereinbefore set out shall be followed for the purpose of determining all matters raised by the pleadings and the determination of just compensation.

The plaintiff at the time of filing of the complaint shall record a memorandum of action with the register of deeds in all counties in which the land involved therein is located, said memorandum to be recorded among the land records of said county. The memorandum of action shall contain

(1) The names of those persons who the plaintiff is informed and believes may have or claim to have an interest in said lands and who are parties to said action;

(2) A description of the entire tract or tracts affected by the alleged taking sufficient for the identification thereof;

(3) A statement of the estate or interest in said land allegedly taken for public use; and

(4) The date on which plaintiff alleges the taking occurred, the date on which said action was instituted, the county in which it was instituted, and such other reference thereto as may be necessary for the identification of said action. (1959, c. 1025, s. 2; 1961, c. 1084, s. 6; 1963, c. 1156, s. 8; 1965, c. 514, ss. 1, 1 1/2; 1971, c. 1195; 1973, c. 507, s. 5; 1977, c. 464, ss. 7.1, 29; 1985, c. 182.)

§ 136-112. Measure of damages.

The following shall be the measure of damages to be followed by the commissioners, jury or judge who determines the issue of damages:

(1) Where only a part of a tract is taken, the measure of damages for said taking shall be the difference between the fair market value of the entire tract immediately prior to said taking and the fair market value of the remainder immediately after said taking, with consideration being given to any special or general benefits resulting from the utilization of the part taken for highway purposes.

(2) Where the entire tract is taken the measure of damages for said taking shall be the fair market value of the property at the time of taking. (1959, c. 1025, s. 2.)

§ 136-113. Interest as a part of just compensation.

To said amount awarded as damages by the commissioners or a jury or judge, the judge shall, as a part of just compensation, add interest at the legal rate as provided in G.S. 24-1 on said amount from the date of taking to the date of judgment; but interest shall not be allowed from the date of deposit on so much thereof as shall have been paid into court as provided in this Article. (1959, c. 1025, s. 2; 1983, c. 812.)

§ 136-114. Additional rules.

In all cases of procedure under this Article where the mode or manner of conducting the action is not expressly provided for in this Article or by the statute governing civil procedure or where said civil procedure statutes are inapplicable the judge before whom such proceeding may be pending shall have the power to make all the necessary orders and rules of procedure necessary to carry into effect the object and intent of this Chapter and the practice in such cases shall conform as near as may be to the practice in other civil actions in said courts. (1959, c. 1025, s. 2.)

§ 136-115. Definitions.

For the purpose of this Article

(1)   The word "judge" shall mean the resident judge of the superior court in the district where the cause is pending, or special judge residing in said district, or the judge of the superior court assigned to hold the courts of said district or the emergency or special judge holding court in the county where the cause is pending.

(2)   The words "person," "owner," and "party" shall include the plural; the word "person" shall include a firm or public or private corporation, and the word "Department" shall mean the Department of tation. (1959, c. 1025, s. 2; 1961, c. 1084, s. 7; 1965, c. 422; 1973, c. 507, s. 5; 1975, c. 19, s. 47; 1977, c. 464, s. 30.)

§ 136-116. Final judgments.

Final judgments entered in actions instituted under the provisions of this Article shall contain a description of the property affected, together with a description of the property and estate of interest acquired by the Department of Transportation and a copy of said judgment shall be certified to the register of deeds in the county in which the land or any part thereof lies and be recorded among the land records of said county. (1959, c. 1025, s. 2; 1973, c. 507, s. 5; 1977, c. 464, s. 7.1.)

§ 136-117. Payment of compensation.

If there are adverse and conflicting claimants to the deposit made into the court by the Department of Transportation or the additional amount determined as just compensation, on which final judgment is entered in said action, the judge may direct the full amount determined to be paid into said court by the Department of Transportation and may retain said cause for determination of who is entitled to said moneys and may by further order in the cause direct to whom the same shall be paid and may in its discretion order a reference to ascertain the facts on which such determination and order are to be made. (1959, c. 1025, s. 2; 1973, c. 507, s. 5; 1977, c. 464, s. 7.1.)

§ 136-118. Agreements for entry.

The provisions of this Article shall not prevent the Department of Transportation and the owner from entering into a written agreement whereby the owner agrees and consents that the Department of Transportation may enter upon his property without filing the complaint and declaration of taking and depositing estimated compensation as herein provided and the Department of Transportation shall have the same rights under such agreement with the owner in carrying on work on such project as it would have by having filed a complaint and a declaration of taking and having deposited estimated compensation as provided in this Article. (1959, c. 1025, s. 2; 1961, c. 1084, s. 8; 1973, c. 507, s. 5; 1977, c. 464, s. 7.1.)

§ 136-119. Costs and appeal.

The Department of Transportation shall pay all court costs taxed by the court. Either party shall have a right of appeal to the Supreme Court for errors of law committed in any proceedings provided for in this Article in the same manner as in any other civil actions and it shall not be necessary that an appeal bond be posted.

The court having jurisdiction of the condemnation action instituted by the Department of Transportation to acquire real property by condemnation shall award the owner of any right, or title to, or interest in, such real property such sum as will in the opinion of the court reimburse such owner for his reasonable cost, disbursements, and expenses, including reasonable attorney fees, appraisal, and engineering fees, actually incurred because of the condemnation proceedings, if (i) the final judgment is that the Department of Transportation cannot acquire real property by condemnation; or (ii) the proceeding is abandoned by the Department of Transportation.

The judge rendering a judgment for the plaintiff in a proceeding brought under G.S. 136-111 awarding compensation for the taking of property, shall determine and award or allow to such plaintiff, as a part of such judgment, such sum as will in the opinion of the judge reimburse such plaintiff for his reasonable cost, disbursements and expenses, including reasonable attorney, appraisal, and engineering fees, actually incurred because of such proceeding. (1959, c. 1025, s. 2; 1971, c. 1102, s. 1; 1973, c. 507, s. 5; 1977, c. 464, s. 7.1.)

§ 136-120. Entry for surveys.

The Department of Transportation without having filed a complaint and a declaration of taking as provided in this Article is authorized to enter upon any lands and structures upon lands to make surveys, borings, soundings or examinations as may be necessary in carrying out and performing its duties under this Chapter, and such entry shall not be deemed a trespass, or taking within the meaning of this Article; provided, however, that the Department of Transportation shall make reimbursement for any damage resulting to such land as a result of such activities and the owner, if necessary, shall be entitled to proceed under the provisions of G.S. 136-111 of this Chapter to recover for such damage. (1959, c. 1025, s. 2; 1973, c. 507, s. 5; 1977, c. 464, s. 7.1.)

§ 136-121. Refund of deposit.

In the event the amount of the final judgment is less than the amount deposited by the Department of Transportation pursuant to the provisions of this Article, the Department of Transportation shall be entitled to recover the excess of the amount of the deposit over the amount of the final judgment and court costs incident thereto: Provided, however, in the event there are not sufficient funds on deposit to cover said excess the Department of Transportation shall be entitled to a judgment for said sum against the person or persons having received said deposit. (1959, c. 1025, s. 2; 1973, c. 507, s. 5; 1977, c. 464, s. 7.1.)

§ 136-121.1. Reimbursement of owner for taxes paid on condemned property.

(a)   A property owner whose property is totally taken in fee simple by any condemning agency (as defined in G.S. 133-7(1)) exercising the power of eminent domain, under this Chapter or any other statute or charter provision, shall be entitled to reimbursement from the condemning agency of the pro rata portion of real property taxes paid that are allocable to a period subsequent to vesting of title in the agency, or the effective date of possession of the real property, whichever is earlier.

(b)   An owner who meets the following conditions is entitled to reimbursement from the condemning agency for all deferred taxes paid by the owner pursuant to G.S. 105-277.4(c) as a result of the condemnation:

(1)   The owner is a natural person whose property is taken in fee simple by a condemning agency exercising the power of eminent domain under this Chapter or any other statute.

(2)   The owner also owns agricultural land, horticultural land, or forestland that is contiguous to the condemned property and that is in active production.

A potential condemning agency that seeks to acquire property by gift or purchase shall give the owner written notice of the provisions of this section. The definitions in G.S. 105-277.2 apply in this subsection. (1975, c. 439, s. 1; 1997-270, s. 2.)

ARTICLE 10.

Preservation, etc., of Scenic Beauty of Areas along Highways.

§ 136-122. Legislative findings and declaration of policy.

The General Assembly finds that the rapid growth and the spread of urban development along and near the State highways is encroaching upon or eliminating many areas having significant scenic or aesthetic values, which if restored, preserved and enhanced would promote the enjoyment of travel and the protection of the public investment in highways within the State and would constitute important physical, aesthetic or economic assets to the State. It is the intent of the General Assembly in enacting this statute to provide a means whereby the Department of Transportation may acquire the fee or any lesser interest or right in real property in order to restore, preserve and enhance natural or scenic beauty of areas traversed by the highways of the State highway system.

The General Assembly hereby declares that it is a public purpose and in the public interest of the people of North Carolina, to expend public funds, in connection with the construction, reconstruction or improvement of State highways, for the acquisition of the fee or any lesser interest in real property in the vicinity of public highways forming a part of the State highway system, in order to restore, preserve and enhance natural or scenic beauty. The General Assembly hereby finds, determines and declares that this Article is necessary for the immediate preservation and promotion of public convenience, safety and welfare. (1967, c. 1247, s. 1; 1973, c. 507, s. 5; 1977, c. 464, s. 7.1.)

§ 136-123. Restoration, preservation and enhancement of natural or scenic beauty.

(a) The Department of Transportation is hereby authorized and empowered to acquire by purchase, exchanges or gift, the fee-simple title or any lesser interest therein in real property in the vicinity of public highways forming a part of the State highway system, for the restoration, preservation and enhancement of natural or scenic beauty; provided that no lands, rights-of-way or facilities of a public utility as defined by G.S. 62-3(23), or of an electric membership corporation or telephone membership corporation, may be acquired, except that the Department of Transportation upon payment of the full cost thereof may require the relocation of electric distribution or telephone lines or poles; provided further, that such lands may be acquired by the Department of Transportation with the consent of the public utility or membership corporation.

(b) No landscaping or highway beautification project undertaken by the Department or any other unit of government may use oyster shells as a ground cover. The Department or any other unit of government that possesses oyster shells shall make them available to the Department of Environment and Natural Resources, Division of Marine Fisheries, without remuneration, for use in any oyster bed revitalization programs or any other program that may use the shells. (1967, c. 1247, s. 2; 1973, c. 507, s. 5; 1977, c. 464, s. 7.1; 2007-84, s. 1; 2008-198, s. 4.)

§ 136-124. Availability of federal aid funds.

The Department of Transportation shall not be required to expend any funds for the acquisition of property under the provisions of this Article unless federal aid funds are made available for this purpose. (1967, c. 1247, s. 3; 1973, c. 507, s. 5; 1977, c. 464, s. 7.1.)

§ 136-125. Regulation of scenic easements.

The Department of Transportation shall have the authority to promulgate rules and regulations governing the use, maintenance and protection of the areas or interests acquired under this Article. Any violation of such rules and regulations shall be a Class 1 misdemeanor. (1967, c. 1247, s. 4; 1973, c. 507, s. 5; 1977, c. 464, s. 7.1; 1993, c. 539, s. 997; 1994, Ex. Sess., c. 24, s. 14(c).)

Article 10A.

Litter Prevention Account.

§ 136-125.1. Litter Prevention Account.

There is established under the control and direction of the Department of Transportation the Litter Prevention Account. The Account shall be a nonreverting special revenue account within the Highway Fund and shall consist of moneys credited to the Account under G.S. 20-81.12(b15) from the sale of litter prevention special registration plates. The Department of Transportation shall allocate the funds in the Account to reduce litter in the State. (2000-159, s. 9(a).)

§ 136-125.2: Repealed by Session Laws 2011-145, s. 28.35(a), effective July 1, 2011.

Article 11.

Outdoor Advertising Control Act.

§ 136-126. Title of Article.

This Article may be cited as the Outdoor Advertising Control Act. (1967, c. 1248, s. 1.)

§ 136-127. Declaration of policy.

The General Assembly hereby finds and declares that outdoor advertising is a legitimate commercial use of private property adjacent to roads and highways but that the erection and maintenance of outdoor advertising signs and devices in areas in the vicinity of the right-of-way of the interstate and primary highway systems within the State should be controlled and regulated in order to promote the safety, health, welfare and convenience and enjoyment of travel on and protection of the public investment in highways within the State, to prevent unreasonable distraction of operators of motor vehicles and to prevent interference with the effectiveness of traffic regulations and to promote safety on the highways, to attract tourists and promote the prosperity, economic well-being and general welfare of the State, and to preserve and enhance the natural scenic beauty of the highways and areas in the vicinity of the State highways and to promote the reasonable, orderly and effective display of such signs, displays and devices, and to secure the right of validly permitted outdoor advertising to be clearly viewed by the traveling public. It is the intention of the General Assembly to provide and declare herein a public policy and statutory basis for the regulation and control of outdoor advertising. (1967, c. 1248, s. 2; 1999-404, s. 6; 2011-397, s. 9.)

§ 136-128. Definitions.

As used in this Article:

(1) "Erect" means to construct, build, raise, assemble, place, affix, attach, create, paint, draw, or in any other way bring into being or establish.

(1a) "Illegal sign" means one which was erected and/or maintained in violation of State law.

(1b) "Information center" means an area or site established and maintained at safety rest areas for the purpose of informing the public of places of interest within the State and providing such other information as the Department of Transportation may consider desirable.

(2) "Interstate system" means that portion of the National System of Interstate and Defense Highways located within the State, as officially designated, or as may hereafter be so designated, by the Department of Transportation, or other appropriate authorities and are also so designated by interstate numbers. As to highways under construction so designated as interstate highways pursuant to the above procedures, the highway shall be a part of the interstate system for the purposes of this Article on the date the location of the highway has been approved finally by the appropriate federal authorities.

(2a) "Nonconforming sign" shall mean a sign which was lawfully erected but which does not comply with the provisions of State law or State rules and regulations passed at a later date or which later fails to comply with State law or State rules or regulations due to changed conditions. Illegally erected or maintained signs are not nonconforming signs.

(3) "Outdoor advertising" means any outdoor sign, display, light, device, figure, painting, drawing, message, plaque, poster, billboard, or any other thing which is designed, intended or used to advertise or inform, any part of the advertising or information contents of which is visible from any place on the main-traveled way of the interstate or primary system, whether the same be permanent or portable installation.

(4) "Primary systems" means the federal-aid primary system in existence on June 1, 1991, and any highway which is not on that system but which is on the National Highway System. As to highways under construction so designated as

primary highways pursuant to the above procedures, the highway shall be a part of the primary system for purposes of this Article on the date the location of the highway has been approved finally by the appropriate federal or State authorities.

(5) "Safety rest area" means an area or site established and maintained within or adjacent to the highway right-of-way by or under public supervision or control, for the convenience of the traveling public.

(6) "State law" means a State constitutional provision or statute, or an ordinance, rule or regulation enacted or adopted by a State agency or political subdivision of a State pursuant to a State Constitution or statute.

(7) "Unzoned area" shall mean an area where there is no zoning in effect.

(8) "Urban area" shall mean an area within the boundaries or limits of any incorporated municipality having a population of five thousand or more as determined by the latest available federal census.

(9) "Visible" means capable of being seen (whether or not legible) without visual aid by a person of normal visual acuity. (1967, c. 1248, s. 3; 1973, c. 507, s. 5; 1975, c. 568, ss. 1-4; 1977, c. 464, s. 7.1; 1997-456, s. 27; 1999-404, s. 7; 2000-101, s. 1.)

§ 136-129. Limitations of outdoor advertising devices.

No outdoor advertising shall be erected or maintained within 660 feet of the nearest edge of the right-of-way of the interstate or primary highway systems in this State so as to be visible from the main-traveled way thereof after the effective date of this Article as determined by G.S. 136-140, except the following:

(1) Directional and other official signs and notices, which signs and notices shall include those authorized and permitted by Chapter 136 of the General Statutes, which include but are not limited to official signs and notices pertaining to natural wonders, scenic and historic attractions and signs erected and maintained by a public utility, electric or telephone membership corporation, or municipality for the purpose of giving warning of or information as to the location of an underground cable, pipeline or other installation.

(2) Outdoor advertising which advertises the sale or lease of property upon which it is located.

(2a) Outdoor advertising which advertises the sale of any fruit or vegetable crop by the grower at a roadside stand or by having the purchaser pick the crop on the property on which the crop is grown provided: (i) the sign is no more than two feet long on any side; (ii) the sign is located on property owned or leased by the grower where the crop is grown; (iii) the grower is also the seller; and (iv) the sign is kept in place by the grower for no more than 30 days.

(3) Outdoor advertising which advertises activities conducted on the property upon which it is located.

(4) Outdoor advertising, in conformity with the rules and regulations promulgated by the Department of Transportation, located in areas which are zoned industrial or commercial under authority of State law.

(5) Outdoor advertising, in conformity with the rules and regulations promulgated by the Department of Transportation, located in unzoned commercial or industrial areas. (1967, c. 1248, s. 4; 1972, c. 507, s. 5; 1975, c. 568, s. 5; 1977, c. 464, s. 7.1; 1991 (Reg. Sess., 1992), c. 946, s. 1; 1999-404, s. 8.)

§ 136-129.1. Limitations of outdoor advertising devices beyond 660 feet.

No outdoor advertising shall be erected or maintained beyond 660 feet of the nearest edge of the right-of-way of the interstate or primary highway systems in this State outside of the urban areas so as to be visible and intended to be read from the main-traveled way except the following:

(1) Directional and other official signs and notices, which signs and notices shall include those authorized and permitted by Chapter 136 of the General Statutes, which include but are not limited to official signs and notices pertaining to natural wonders, scenic and historic attractions and signs erected and maintained by a public utility, electric or telephone membership corporation, or municipality for the purpose of giving warning of or information as to the location of an underground cable, pipeline or other installation.

(2) Outdoor advertising which advertises the sale or lease of property upon which it is located.

(3) Outdoor advertising which advertises activities conducted on the property upon which it is located. (1975, c. 568, s. 6; 1999-404, s. 9.)

§ 136-129.2. Limitation of outdoor advertising devices adjacent to scenic highways, State and National Parks, historic areas and other places.

(a) In addition to the limitations contained in G.S. 136-129 and G.S. 136-129.1, in order to further the purposes set forth in Article 10 of this Chapter and to promote the reasonable, orderly, and effective display of outdoor advertising devices along highways adjacent to scenic and historical areas, while protecting the public investment in these highways and promoting the safety and recreational value of public travel, and to preserve natural beauty, no outdoor advertising sign shall be erected adjacent to any highway which is either:

(1) a. A scenic highway or scenic byway designated by the Board of Transportation;

b. Within 1,200 feet, on the same side of the highway, of the boundary line of a North Carolina State Park, a National Park, a State or national wildlife refuge, or a designated wild and scenic river; or

c. Within 500 feet, on the same side of the highway, of the boundary lines of any historic districts and other properties listed in the National Register of Historic Places or State rest areas, or within the boundary lines of any historic district;

except as permitted under G.S. 136-129(1), (2), (2a), or (3); or

(2) Within one-third of the applicable distances under sub-subdivision (a)(1)b. and (a)(1)c. of this section, along the opposite side of the highway from any of the properties designated in sub-subdivision (a)(1)b. and (a)(1)c. of this section, except as permitted under G.S. 136-129(1), (2), (2a), (3), (4), or (5).

(b) The distances set forth in this section shall be measured horizontally in linear feet extending in each direction along the edge of the pavement of the highway from any point on the boundary of the subject property, or any point on the opposite side of the highway perpendicular to any point on the boundary line of the subject property.

(c) As used in sub-subdivision (a)(1)b. and (a)(1)c. of this section, the term "highway" means a highway that is designated as a part of the interstate or federal-aid primary highway system as of June 1, 1991, or any highway which is or becomes a part of the National Highway System. (1993, c. 524, s. 1.)

§ 136-130. Regulation of advertising.

The Department of Transportation is authorized to promulgate rules and regulations in the form of ordinances governing:

(1) The erection and maintenance of outdoor advertising permitted in G.S. 136-129,

(2) The erection and maintenance of outdoor advertising permitted in G.S. 136-129.1,

(2a) The erection and maintenance of outdoor advertising permitted in G.S. 136-129.2,

(3) The specific requirements and procedures for obtaining a permit for outdoor advertising as required in G.S. 136-133 and for the administrative procedures for appealing a decision at the agency level to refuse to grant or in revoking a permit previously issued, and

(4) The administrative procedures for appealing a decision at the agency level to declare any outdoor advertising illegal and a nuisance as pursuant to G.S. 136-134, as may be necessary to carry out the policy of the State declared in this Article. (1967, c. 1248, s. 5; 1973, c. 507, s. 5; 1975, c. 568, s. 7; 1977, c. 464, ss. 7.1, 31; 1993, c. 524, s. 2.)

§ 136-131. Removal of existing nonconforming advertising.

The Department of Transportation is authorized to acquire by purchase, gift, or condemnation all outdoor advertising and all property rights pertaining thereto which are prohibited under the provisions of G.S. 136-129, 136-129.1 or 136-129.2, provided such outdoor advertising is in lawful existence on the effective date of this Article as determined by G.S. 136-140, or provided that it is lawfully erected after the effective date of this Article as determined by G.S. 136-140.

In any acquisition, purchase or condemnation, just compensation to the owner of the outdoor advertising, where the owner of the outdoor advertising does not own the fee, shall be limited to the fair market value at the time of the taking of the outdoor advertising owner's interest in the real property on which the outdoor advertising is located and such value shall include the value of the outdoor advertising.

In any acquisition, purchase or condemnation, just compensation to the owner of the fee or other interest in the real property upon which the outdoor advertising is located where said owner does not own the outdoor advertising located thereon shall be limited to the difference in the fair market value of the entire tract immediately before and immediately after the taking by the Department of Transportation of the right to maintain such outdoor advertising thereon and in arriving at the fair market value after the taking, any special or general benefits accruing to the property by reason of the acquisition shall be taken into consideration.

In any acquisition, purchase or condemnation, just compensation to the owner of the fee in the real property upon which the outdoor advertising is located, where said owner also owns the outdoor advertising located thereon, shall be limited to the fair market value of the outdoor advertising plus the difference in the fair market value of the entire tract immediately before and immediately after the taking by the Department of Transportation of the right to maintain such outdoor advertising thereon and in arriving at the fair market value after the taking, any special or general benefits accruing to the property by reason of the acquisition shall be taken into consideration. (1967, c. 1248, s. 6; 1973, c. 507, s. 5; 1975, c. 568, ss. 8-10; 1977, c. 464, s. 7.1; 1993, c. 524, s. 3.)

§ 136-131.1. (See editor's note for expiration of section) Just compensation required for the removal of billboards on federal-aid primary highways by local authorities.

No municipality, county, local or regional zoning authority, or other political subdivision, shall, without the payment of just compensation in accordance with the provisions that are applicable to the Department of Transportation as provided in paragraphs 2, 3, and 4 of G.S. 136-131, remove or cause to be removed any outdoor advertising adjacent to a highway on the National System of Interstate and Defense Highways or a highway on the Federal-aid Primary Highway System for which there is in effect a valid permit issued by the Department of Transportation pursuant to the provisions of Article 11 of Chapter 136 of the General Statutes and regulations promulgated pursuant thereto. (1981 (Reg. Sess., 1982), c. 1147, ss. 1, 2; 1983, c. 318, s. 1; 1987 (Reg. Sess., 1988), c. 1024, s. 1; 1989, c. 166, s. 1; 1993 (Reg. Sess., 1994), c. 725, s. 1; 1998-23, s. 7; 1998-212, s. 27.5(a); 2002-11, s. 1.)

§ 136-131.2. Modernization of outdoor advertising devices.

No municipality, county, local or regional zoning authority, or other political subdivision shall, without the payment of just compensation as provided for in G.S. 136-131.1, regulate or prohibit the repair or reconstruction of any outdoor advertising for which there is in effect a valid permit issued by the Department of Transportation so long as the square footage of its advertising surface area is not increased. As used in this section, reconstruction includes the changing of an existing multipole outdoor advertising structure to a new monopole structure. (2013-413, s. 8(b).)

§ 136-132. Condemnation procedure.

For the purpose of this Article, the Department of Transportation shall use the procedure for condemnation of real property as provided by Article 9 of Chapter 136 of the General Statutes. (1967, c. 1248, s. 7; 1973, c. 507, s. 5; 1977, c. 464, s. 7.1.)

§ 136-133. Permits required.

(a) No person shall erect or maintain any outdoor advertising within 660 feet of the nearest edge of the right-of-way of the interstate or primary highway system, except those allowed under G.S. 136-129, subdivisions (2) and (3) in this Article, or beyond 660 feet of the nearest edge of the right-of-way of the interstate or primary highway system, except those allowed under G.S. 136-129.1, subdivisions (2) and (3), without first obtaining a permit from the Department of Transportation or its agents pursuant to the procedures set out by rules adopted by the Department of Transportation. The permit shall be valid until revoked for nonconformance with this Article or rules adopted by the Department of Transportation. Any person aggrieved by the decision of the Department of Transportation or its agents in refusing to grant or in revoking a permit may appeal the decision in accordance with the rules adopted by the Department of Transportation pursuant to this Article to the Secretary of Transportation who shall make the final decision on the agency appeal. The Department of Transportation shall have the authority to charge permit fees to defray the costs of administering the permit procedures under this Article. The fees for directional signs as set forth in G.S. 136-129(1) and G.S. 136-129.1(1) shall not exceed a forty dollar ($40.00) initial fee and a thirty dollar ($30.00) annual renewal fee. The fees for outdoor advertising structures, as set forth in G.S. 136-129(4) and (5) shall not exceed a one hundred twenty dollar ($120.00) initial fee and a sixty dollar ($60.00) annual renewal fee.

(b) If outdoor advertising is under construction and the Department of Transportation determines that a permit has not been issued for the outdoor advertising, the Department may require that all work on the outdoor advertising cease until the owner of the outdoor advertising shows that the outdoor advertising does not violate this section. The stopwork order shall be prominently posted on the outdoor advertising structure, and no further notice of the stopwork order is required. The failure of an owner of outdoor advertising to comply immediately with the stopwork order shall subject the outdoor advertising to removal by the Department of Transportation or its agents. Outdoor advertising is under construction when it is in any phase of construction prior to the attachment and display of the advertising message in final position for viewing by the traveling public. The cost of removing outdoor advertising by the Department of Transportation or its agents pursuant to this section shall be assessed against the owner of the unpermitted outdoor advertising by the Department of Transportation. No stopwork order may be issued when the Department of Transportation process agent has been served with a court order allowing the sign to be constructed.

(c) No electrical permit shall be denied to an outdoor advertising sign described in G.S. 136-129(4) and G.S. 136-129(5) for which the Department has issued a permit which has not been revoked, and the electrical permit is otherwise compliant with technical utility standards. (1967, c. 1248, s. 8; 1973,

c. 507, s. 5; 1975, c. 568, s. 11; 1977, c. 464, ss. 7.1, 32; 1983, c. 604, s. 2; 1989, c. 677; 1999-404, s. 1; 2011-397, s. 3.)

§ 136-133.1. Outdoor advertising vegetation cutting or removal.

(a) The owner of an outdoor advertising sign permitted under G.S. 136-129(a)(4) [G.S. 136-129(4)] or G.S. 136-129(a)(5) [G.S. 136-129(5)] who obtains a selective vegetation removal permit, and the owner's designees, may cut, thin, prune, or remove vegetation in accordance with this section, G.S. 136-93(b), 136-133.2, and 136-133.4. The maximum cut or removal zone for vegetation for each sign face shall be determined as follows:

(1) The point located on the edge of the right-of-way that is the closest point to the centerline of the sign face shall be point A.

(2) The point located 200 feet down the right-of-way line in the direction of the sign viewing zone shall be point B.

(3) The point on the edge of the pavement of the travel way, including acceleration and deceleration ramps, that is the closest to the centerline of the sign shall be point C.

(4) The point 50 feet down the edge of the pavement in the direction of the sign viewing zone from point C shall be point D.

(5) The point 380 feet down the edge of the pavement in the direction of the sign viewing zone from point C shall be point E; provided, however, the following shall apply within the corporal limits and territorial jurisdiction of any city, as defined in Chapter 160A of the General Statutes:

a. On interstates or other routes with fully controlled access, the point 340 feet down the edge of the pavement in the direction of the sign viewing zone from point C shall be point E.

b. On highways other than interstates and other routes with fully controlled access, the point 250 feet down the edge of the pavement in the direction of the sign viewing zone from point C shall be point E.

(6) Lines drawn from point A to point D and from point B to point E shall define the limits of the vegetation cut or removal area.

(a1) Notwithstanding any law to the contrary, in order to promote the outdoor advertiser's right to be clearly viewed as set forth in G.S. 136-127, the Department of Transportation, at the request of a selective vegetation removal permittee, may approve plans for the cutting, thinning, pruning, or removal of vegetation outside of the cut or removal zone defined in subsection (a) of this section along acceleration or deceleration ramps so long as the view to the outdoor advertising sign will be improved and the total aggregate area of cutting or removal does not exceed the maximum allowed in subsection (a) of this section.

(b) Vegetation permitted to be cut, thinned, pruned, or removed shall be defined as any tree, shrub, or underbrush within the zone created by points A, B, D, and E. Any existing tree that was in existence at the time that an outdoor advertising structure was erected shall only be eligible for removal in accordance with subsections (c), (d), and (e) of this section. Native dogwoods and native redbuds shall be preserved. For the purposes of this section, an existing tree is defined as a tree that had a diameter of four inches or greater as measured six inches from the ground at the time that the outdoor advertising structure was erected. An outdoor advertising sign is considered erected when the sign is completely constructed with a sign face.

(c) The applicant for a selective vegetation removal permit shall submit to the Department a site plan locating thereon any trees existing at the time that the outdoor advertising sign was erected, as defined in subsection (b) of this section, that are requested to be cut, thinned, pruned, or removed, and noting their species and total caliper inches. The applicant shall also tag, with highly visible material or flagging, any tree that is, at the time of the application for a selective vegetation removal permit, greater than four inches in diameter as measured six inches from the ground and requested to be cut, thinned, pruned, or removed. The selective vegetation removal request may be investigated on-site by Department personnel and a representative of the applicant. In the event that the Department disputes the accuracy of the existing tree information on the site plan noted above, the Department shall notify the applicant in writing and may request the following:

(1) A tree survey.

(2) That the applicant amends the site plan.

(3) That the applicant deletes the trees in dispute from the desired cutting.

If a notice of disputed tree information is received from the Department, the applicant can either employ the services of a North Carolina licensed landscape architect or certified arborist to perform a tree survey, amend the site plan, or notify the Department in writing that any or all of the disputed trees are deleted from the application. If the applicant selects a tree survey, the landscape architect or certified arborist will submit a report under seal that contains a tree inventory of existing trees in the removal zone for the outdoor advertising structure and include the age of any tree that existed at the time that the sign was erected. The report will categorize tree species and include a site map of sufficient detail and dimensions. A tree survey will not be required for subsequent applications to cut, thin, prune, or remove trees at the same site for trees that have been previously permitted. Any dispute relating to whether or not the tree existed at the time the outdoor advertising sign was erected shall be conclusively resolved by information in the report from the licensed landscape architect or certified arborist.

(d) Except as provided in subsection (e) of this section, trees existing at the time the outdoor advertising sign was erected may only be removed within the zone created in subsection (a) of this section if the applicant satisfies one of the following two options selected by the applicant: (i) reimbursement to the Department pursuant to G.S. 136-93.2 or (ii) trees that existed at the time of the erection of the sign may be removed if the applicant agrees to remove two nonconforming outdoor advertising signs for each sign at which removal of existing trees is requested. The surrendered nonconforming signs must be fully disassembled before any removal of existing trees is permitted and shall not be eligible for future outdoor advertising permits in perpetuity.

(e) Removal of trees and vegetation of any age, including complete removal, except for native dogwoods and native redbuds, shall be permitted within the cut or removal zone established in subsection (a) of this section if the applicant for the selective vegetation removal permit, in lieu of compliance with subsection (d) of this section, agrees to submit to the Department a plan for beautification and replanting related to the site for which the vegetation permit request is made. The Department shall develop rules for compensatory replanting, including the criteria for determining which sites qualify for replanting, and shall, in consultation with the applicant and local government representatives, determine which sites must be replanted, and the types of plants and trees to be replanted. The replanting and maintenance shall be conducted by the applicant or his or her agents in accordance with the rules adopted by the Department. If the conditions detailed in this subsection are agreed to by the applicant and approved by the Department, there shall be no reimbursement to the Department under G.S. 136-93.2 for removal of trees that existed at the time the outdoor sign was erected, nor shall the applicant be required to remove two nonconforming outdoor advertising signs for removal of existing trees at the site.

(f) Tree branches within a highway right-of-way that encroach into the zone created by points A, B, D, and E may be cut or pruned. Except as provided in subsection (g) of this section, no person, firm, or entity shall cut, trim, prune, or remove or otherwise cause to be cut, trimmed, pruned, or removed vegetation that is in front of, or adjacent to, outdoor advertising and within the limits of the highway right-of-way for the purpose of enhancing the visibility of outdoor advertising unless permitted to do so by the Department in accordance with this section, G.S. 136-93(b), 136-133.2, and 136-133.4.

(g) Notwithstanding any law to the contrary, the owner of an outdoor advertising sign defined by subsection (a) of this section or the owner's designees may, working only from the private property side of the fence, without charge and without obtaining a selective vegetation removal permit, cut, trim, prune, or remove any tree or other vegetation except for native dogwoods or native redbuds that is (i) less than four inches in diameter at the height of the controlled access fence, (ii) located within 200 feet on either side of the existing sign location as defined by point A and point B in G.S. 136-133.1(a)(1) and (2), and (iii) a distance of three feet from a controlled access fence within the limits of the highway right-of-way. The activities permitted by this subsection must be performed from the private property owner side of the controlled access fence and with the consent of the owner of the land that is used to access said fence.

(h) No additional funds from the Highway Trust Fund shall be used for the purpose of vegetation replacement under the provisions of this section.

(i) The Department may revoke an outdoor advertising permit for the unlawful destruction or illegal cutting of vegetation within the right-of-way of any State-owned or State-maintained highway only if both of the following conditions are met:

(1) The unlawful destruction or illegal cutting occurred within 500 feet of either side of the corresponding sign location measured along the edge of pavement of the main travel way of the nearest controlled route and was willfully caused by one or more of the following:

a. The sign owner.

b. The permit holder.

c. The lessee or advertiser employing the sign.

d. Any employees, agents, or assigns of persons listed in sub-subdivisions a. through c. of this subdivision, including, but not limited to, independent contractors hired by any of the above persons, or the owner of the property upon which the sign is located, if expressly authorized by the above persons to use or maintain the sign.

(2) There is substantial, material evidence that the unlawful destruction or illegal cutting of vegetation would create, increase, or improve a view to the outdoor advertising sign for passing motorists from the main travel way of the nearest controlled route. (2011-397, s. 4; 2013-413, s. 8(a).)

§ 136-133.2. Issuance or denial of a selective vegetation removal permit.

Except as provided in G.S. 136-133.1(g), permits to remove vegetation may be granted for outdoor advertising locations that have been permitted for at least two years prior to the date of application. The Department shall approve or deny an application submitted pursuant to this section, including the fee required by G.S. 136-18.7 and all required documentation, within 30 days of the receipt of an application for a selective vegetation removal permit. If written notice of approval or denial is not given to the applicant within the 30-day period, then the application shall be deemed approved. If the application is denied, the Department shall advise the applicant, in writing, by registered or certified mail, return receipt requested, addressed to the party to be noticed, and delivering to the addressee, the reasons for the denial. (2011-397, s. 5.)

§ 136-133.3. Appeals of selective vegetation removal permit decisions.

(a) An applicant for a selective vegetation removal permit issued pursuant to G.S. 136-133.2 may appeal a decision of the Department pertaining to the denial or conditioning of a permit for selective vegetation removal pursuant to the provisions of this section.

(b) Within 30 days of service of the Department's decision to deny or condition a selective vegetation removal permit issued pursuant to G.S. 136-133.4, the applicant shall submit a written appeal to the Secretary of Transportation setting forth with particularity the facts and arguments upon which the appeal is based. The appeal shall be sent to the Secretary by registered or certified mail, return receipt requested, addressed to the Secretary, and delivering to the addressee, with a copy to the Department official who issued the decision.

(c) Upon receipt of the written appeal, the Secretary of Transportation shall review the written appeal and the Department's decision, as well as any available documents, exhibits, or other evidence bearing on the appeal, and shall render the agency's final decision, supported by findings of fact and conclusions of law. The final agency decision shall be served upon the appealing party by registered or certified mail, return receipt requested, addressed to the applicant, and delivering to the addressee, within 90 days after the Secretary receives the written appeal. A copy of the agency's final decision shall also be delivered to the Department official who issued the initial decision.

(d) A person aggrieved by a decision made pursuant to this section may seek judicial review of the final agency decision pursuant to G.S. 136-134.1. (2011-397, s. 6.)

§ 136-133.4. Selective vegetation removal permits.

(a) Selected vegetation within the approved limits shall be cut, thinned, pruned, or removed by the permittee or the permittee's agent in accordance with accepted International Society of Arboriculture (ISA) standards.

(b) Permits are valid for a period of one year. The permittee may cut, thin, prune, or remove vegetation more than one time per year. A 48-hour notification shall be provided to the Department by the permittee before entering the right-of-way.

(c) The permittee, or the permittee's agent, shall not impede the flow of traffic on any highway while performing vegetation removal authorized by a permit. Access to the work site on controlled access highways must be gained without using the main travel way of the highway. The Department shall determine the traffic control signage that may be required. The permittee shall furnish, erect, and maintain the required signs as directed by the Department. The permittee, or the permittee's agent, shall wear safety vests that conform to OSHA standards while performing the work.

(d) Any damage to vegetation designated to remain at the site, to highway fences, signs, paved areas, or other facilities shall be repaired or replaced by the permittee to the condition prior to the occurrence of the damage caused by the permittee or the permittee's agent. All trimmings, laps, and debris shall be removed from the right-of-way and disposed of in areas provided by the permittee. No burning or burying of trimmings, laps, or debris shall be permitted on the highway right-of-way. When chipping is used to dispose of trimmings, chips may be neatly spread on a right-of-way at locations which the Department determines will not be harmful to the environment or affect traffic safety.

(e) Willful failure to substantially comply with all the requirements specified in the selective vegetation removal permit, unless otherwise mutually resolved by the Department and the permittee, shall result in a five-year moratorium for vegetation removal at the site, a summary revocation of the outdoor advertising permit if such willful failure meets the standards in G.S. 136-133.1(i), payment of Department investigative costs, and forfeiture of any applicable performance bond as determined by the Secretary. The moratorium shall begin upon execution of a settlement agreement or entry of a final disposition in the case. (2011-397, s. 7.)

§ 136-133.5. Denial of a permit for proposed outdoor advertising.

(a) When a district engineer determines that a proposed outdoor advertising structure would not conform to the standards of outdoor advertising as set out in the Outdoor Advertising Control Act, the district engineer shall refuse to issue a permit for that proposed outdoor advertising structure.

(b) When a violation of the Outdoor Advertising Control Act has been discovered, the district engineer shall notify the permit applicant by registered or certified mail, return receipt requested, addressed to the party to be noticed, and delivering to the addressee, in writing, the reason for the denial and the statutes or rules forming the basis for the denial and include a copy of the Act.

(c) The Department shall not issue permits for new outdoor advertising signs at a sign location for a period of five years where the unlawful destruction or illegal cutting of vegetation has occurred within 500 feet on either side of the proposed sign location and as measured along the edge of the pavement of the main travel way of the nearest controlled route. For the purposes of this section, unlawful destruction or illegal cutting is defined as the destruction or cutting of trees, shrubs, or other vegetation on the State-owned or State-maintained rights-of-way by anyone other than the Department or its authorized agents, or without written permission of the Department. Before a permit is denied pursuant to this subsection, the Department shall reveal some evidence that the unlawful destruction or illegal cutting would create, increase, or improve a view to a proposed outdoor advertising sign from the main travel way of the nearest controlled route. The five-year period shall begin on the date the Department executes a settlement agreement or final disposition of the case is entered. The five-year prohibition period for a new sign permit shall apply to all sign locations, including the following:

(1)   Sign locations where the unlawful destruction or illegal cutting of vegetation occurs prior to the time the location becomes a conforming location.

(2)   Sign locations where a revocation of an existing permit has been upheld and a sign has been removed.

(3)   Sign locations where the unlawful destruction or illegal cutting occurs prior to receipt of an outdoor advertising permit.

(4)   Sign locations where the unlawful destruction or illegal cutting occurs following receipt of an outdoor advertising permit application, but prior to the issuance of the permit by the Department.

(d)   The Department shall not issue permits for new outdoor advertising signs at a sign location where existing trees, if they were to reach the average mature size for that species, would make the proposed sign faces, when erected, not completely visible from the viewing zone. "Existing trees" are those trees that at the time of the permit application are four inches or greater in diameter as measured six inches from the ground. "Viewing zone" means the area which is 500 feet as measured along the edge of the main travel way of the controlled route on each side of the proposed sign structure which will have a sign face.

(e)   An outdoor advertising permit requested pursuant to G.S. 136-129(a)(4) [G.S. 136-129(4)] shall not be issued to a location if the zoning to commercial or industrial zones was adopted within one year prior to the filing of the permit application and is not part of comprehensive zoning or constitutes spot zoning, which, for purposes of this subsection, shall be defined as zoning designed primarily for the purpose of permitting outdoor advertising signs and in an area which would not normally permit outdoor advertising. Zoning shall not be considered "primarily for the purpose of permitting outdoor advertising signs" if the zoning would permit more than one principal commercial or industrial use, other than outdoor advertising, and the size of the land being zoned can practically support any one of the commercial or industrial uses.

(f) Outdoor advertising permits shall not be issued to a location for a period of 12 months prior to the proposed letting of a new construction contract that may affect the spacing or location requirements for an outdoor advertising structure until the project is completed. The prohibition authorized by this subsection shall not extend for a period longer than 18 months. Priority in spacing shall be given by the Department to the first submitted application for an outdoor advertising permit at the location.

(g) Outdoor advertising permits shall not be issued for a location on a North Carolina or United States route designated as a scenic byway. (2011-397, s. 8.)

§ 136-134. Illegal advertising.

Any outdoor advertising erected or maintained adjacent to the right-of-way of the interstate or primary highway system after the effective date of this Article as determined by G.S. 136-140, in violation of the provisions of this Article or rules adopted by the Department of Transportation, or any outdoor advertising maintained without a permit regardless of the date of erection shall be illegal and shall constitute a nuisance. The Department of Transportation or its agents shall give 30 days' notice to the owner of the illegal outdoor advertising with the exception of the owner of unlawful portable outdoor advertising for which the Department of Transportation shall give five days' notice, if such owner is known or can by reasonable diligence be ascertained, to remove the outdoor advertising or to make it conform to the provisions of this Article or rules adopted by the Department of Transportation hereunder. The Department of Transportation or its agents shall have the right to remove the illegal outdoor advertising at the expense of the owner if the owner fails to remove the outdoor advertising or to make it conform to the provisions of this Article or rules issued by the Department of Transportation within 30 days after receipt of such notice or five days for owners of portable outdoor advertising. The Department of Transportation or its agents may enter upon private property for the purpose of removing the outdoor advertising prohibited by this Article or rules adopted by the Department of Transportation hereunder without civil or criminal liability. The costs of removing the outdoor advertising, whether by the Department of Transportation or its agents, shall be assessed against the owner of the illegal outdoor advertising by the Department of Transportation. Any person aggrieved by the decision declaring the outdoor advertising structure illegal shall be granted the right to appeal the decision in accordance with the terms of the rules and regulations enacted by the Department of Transportation pursuant to this Article to the Secretary of Transportation who shall make the final decision on the agency appeal. (1967, c. 1248, s. 9; 1973, c. 507, s. 5; 1975, c. 568, s. 12; 1977, c. 464, ss. 7.1, 32; 1999-404, s. 2.)

§ 136-134.1. Judicial review.

Any person who is aggrieved by a final decision of the Secretary of Transportation after exhausting all administrative remedies made available to him by rules and regulations enacted pursuant to this Article is entitled to judicial review of such decision under this Article. In order to obtain judicial review of the Secretary of Transportation's decision under this Article, the person seeking review must file a petition in the Superior Court of Wake County within 30 days after written copy of the decision of the Secretary of Transportation is served upon the person seeking review. Failure to file such a petition within the time stated shall operate as a waiver of the right of such person to review under this Chapter.

The petition shall state explicitly what exceptions are taken to the decision of the Secretary of Transportation and what relief petitioner seeks. Within 10 days after the petition is filed with the court, the person seeking the review shall serve copies of the petition by registered mail, return receipt requested, upon the Department of Transportation. Within 30 days after receipt of the copy of the petition for review, or within such additional time as the court may allow, the Department of Transportation shall transmit to the reviewing court a certified copy of the written decision.

At any time before or during the review proceeding, the aggrieved party may apply to the reviewing court for an order staying the operation of the decision of the Secretary of Transportation pending the outcome of the review. The court may grant or deny the stay in its discretion upon such terms as it deems proper. The review of the decision of the Secretary of Transportation under this Article shall be conducted by the court without a jury and shall hear the matter de novo pursuant to the rules of evidence as applied in the General Court of Justice. The court, after hearing the matter may affirm, reverse or modify the decision if the decision is:

(1)   In violation of constitutional provisions; or

(2)   Not made in accordance with this Article or rules or regulations promulgated by the Department of Transportation; or

(3)   Affected by other error of law.

The party aggrieved shall have the burden of showing that the decision was violative of one of the above.

A party to the review proceedings, including the agency, may appeal to the appellate division from the final judgment of the Superior Court under the rules of procedure applicable in civil cases. The appealing party may apply to the Superior Court for a stay for its final determination or a stay of the administrative decision, whichever shall be appropriate, pending the outcome of the appeal to the appellate division. (1975, c. 568, s. 13; 1977, c. 464, ss. 32, 33.)

§ 136-134.2. Notification requirements.

When the Department of Transportation notifies a permit applicant, permit holder, or the owner of an outdoor advertising structure that the application is denied, the permit revoked, or the structure is in violation of this Article or rules issued pursuant to this Article, it shall do so in writing by certified mail, return receipt requested, and shall include a copy of this Article and all rules issued pursuant to this Article.

If the Department of Transportation fails to include a copy of this Article and the rules, the time period during which the permit applicant, permit holder, or owner of the outdoor advertising structure has to request a review hearing shall be tolled until the Department of Transportation provides the required materials. (1999-404, s. 3.)

§ 136-135. Enforcement provisions.

Any person, firm, corporation or association, placing, erecting or maintaining outdoor advertising along the interstate system or primary system in violation of this Article or rules adopted by the Department of Transportation shall be guilty of a Class 1 misdemeanor. In addition thereto, the Department of Transportation may seek injunctive relief in the Superior Court of Wake County or of the county where the outdoor advertising is located and require the outdoor advertising to conform to the provisions of this Article or rules adopted pursuant hereto, or require the removal of the said illegal outdoor advertising. (1967, c. 1248, s. 10; 1973, c. 507, s. 5; 1975, c. 568, s. 14; 1977, c. 464, s. 32; 1993, c. 539, s. 998; 1994, Ex. Sess., c. 24, s. 14(c); 1999-404, s. 4.)

§ 136-136. Zoning changes.

All zoning authorities shall give written notice to the Department of Transportation of the establishment or revision of any commercial and industrial zones within 660 feet of the right-of-way of interstate or primary highway systems. Notice shall be by registered mail sent to the offices of the Department of Transportation in Raleigh, North Carolina, within 15 days after the effective date of the zoning change or establishment. (1967, c. 1248, s. 11; 1973, c. 507, s. 5; 1977, c. 464, s. 7.1; 1999-404, s. 10.)

§ 136-137. Information directories.

The Department of Transportation is authorized to maintain maps and to permit informational directories and advertising pamphlets to be made available at safety rest areas and to establish information centers at safety rest areas and install signs on the right-of-way for the purpose of informing the public of facilities for food, lodging and vehicle services and of places of interest and for providing such other information as may be considered desirable. (1967, c. 1248, s. 12; 1973, c. 507, s. 5; 1977, c. 464, s. 7.1.)

§ 136-138. Agreements with United States authorized.

The Department of Transportation is authorized to enter into agreements with other governmental authorities relating to the control of outdoor advertising in areas adjacent to the interstate and primary highway systems, including the establishment of information centers and safety rest areas, and to take action in the name of the State to comply with the terms of the agreements. (1967, c. 1248, s. 13; 1973, c. 507, s. 5; 1977, c. 464, s. 7.1.)

§ 136-139. Alternate control.

In addition to any other control provided for in this Article, the Department of Transportation may regulate outdoor advertising in accordance with the standards provided by this Article and regulations promulgated pursuant thereto, by the acquisition by purchase, gift, or condemnation of easements or any other interests in real property prohibiting or controlling the erection and maintenance of advertising within 660 feet of the right-of-way line of the interstate and primary system of the State. (1967, c. 1248, s. 14; 1973, c. 507, s. 5; 1977, c. 464, s. 7.1.)

§ 136-140. Availability of federal aid funds.

The Department of Transportation shall not be required to expend any funds for the regulation of outdoor advertising under this Article, nor shall the provisions of this Article, with the exception of G.S. 136-138 hereof, have any force and effect until federal funds are made available to the State for the purpose of carrying out the provisions of this Article, and the Department of Transportation has entered into an agreement with the United States Secretary of Transportation as authorized by G.S. 136-138 hereof and as provided by the Highway Beautification Act of 1965 or subsequent amendment thereto. (1967, c. 1248, s. 15; 1973, c. 507, s. 5; 1975, c. 568, s. 15; 1977, c. 464, s. 7.1.)

§ 136-140.1. Adopt-A-Highway.

(a) Notwithstanding any other provision of this Article, the Department of Transportation may permit individuals or groups participating in its Adopt-A-Highway Program access to controlled access facilities for the purpose of removing litter from the right-of-way. Acknowledgment of participation in the program may be indicated by appropriate signs that shall be owned, controlled, and erected by the Department of Transportation. The size, style, specifications, and content of the signs shall be determined in the sole discretion of the Department of Transportation. The Department of Transportation may issue rules and policies necessary to administer the program.

(b)   Adopt-A-Highway participants may use contract services to clean the roadside of the sections of highway the participants have adopted only in accordance with the rules and policies issued by the Department of Transportation. (1995, c. 324, s. 18.1.)

§ 136-140.2. Reserved for future codification purposes.

§ 136-140.3. Reserved for future codification purposes.

§ 136-140.4. Reserved for future codification purposes.

§ 136-140.5. Reserved for future codification purposes.

ARTICLE 11A.

Exemption and Deferment from Removal of Certain Directional Signs, Displays, and Devices.

§ 136-140.6. Declaration of policy.

Notwithstanding any other provision of law, the State of North Carolina hereby finds and declares that the removal of certain directional signs, displays, and devices, lawfully erected under State law in force at the time of their erection, which do not conform to the requirements of subsection (C) of 23 U.S.C. 131, which provide directional information about goods and services in the interest of the traveling public, and which were in existence on May 6, 1976, may work a substantial economic hardship in certain defined areas, and shall be exempt according to Section 131 United States Code and the rules and regulations promulgated pursuant thereto. (1977, c. 639.)

§ 136-140.7. Definitions.

As used in this Article: "Motorist services directional signs" means signs, displays, and devices giving directional information about goods and services in the interest of the traveling public, including but not limited to:

(1) Places of public lodging;

(2) Places where food is served to the public on a regular basis;

(3) Places where automotive fuel or emergency automotive repair services, including truck stops, are regularly available to the public;

(4) Educational institutions;

(5) Places of religious worship;

(6) Public or private recreation areas, including campgrounds, resorts and attractions, natural wonders, wildlife and water fowl refuges, and nature trails;

(7) Plays, concerts and fairs;

(8) Antiques, gift and souvenir shops;

(9) Agricultural products in a natural state, including vegetables and fruit. (1977, c. 639.)

§ 136-140.8. Exemption procedures.

The North Carolina Department of Transportation shall upon receipt of a declaration, petition, resolution, certified copy of an ordinance, or other clear direction from a board of county commissioners, municipality, county, city, provided that such resolution is not in conflict with existing statute or ordinance, that removal of motorist services directional signs would cause an economic hardship in a defined area, shall forward such declaration, resolution, or finding to the Secretary of the North Carolina Department of Transportation for inclusion as a defined hardship area qualifying for exemption pursuant to 23 U.S.C. 131 (O). Any such declaration or resolution submitted to the North Carolina Department of Transportation shall further find that such motorist service signs provided directional information about goods and services in the interest of the traveling public and shall request the retention by the State of said directional motorist services signs as defined herein. The North Carolina Department of Transportation shall thereupon comply with all regulations issued both now and hereafter by the Federal Highway Administration necessary for application for the exemption provided in 23 U.S.C. 131 (O), provided such motorist services directional signs were lawfully erected under State law at the time of their erection and were in existence on May 5, 1976. The petitioner seeking exemption of those signs defined in G.S. 136-140.7 shall furnish the information required by the United States Department of Transportation to the North Carolina Department of Transportation and the North Carolina Department of Transportation shall request exemption from the United States Department of Transportation. (1977, c. 639.)

§ 136-140.9. Deferment.

The North Carolina Department of Transportation shall adopt programs to assure that removal of directional signs, displays or devices, providing directional information about goods and services in the interest of the traveling public, not otherwise exempted by economic hardship, be deferred until July 1, 1979. (1977, c. 639.)

§§ 136-140.10 through 136-140.14. Reserved for future codification purposes.

Article 11B.

Tourist-Oriented Directional Sign Program.

§ 136-140.15. Scope of operations.

(a) Program. - The Department of Transportation shall administer a tourist-oriented directional signs (TODS) program.

(b) Definitions. - The following definitions apply in this Article:

(1) TODS. - Tourist-oriented directional signs (TODS) are guide signs that display the business identification of and directional information for tourist-oriented businesses and tourist-oriented facilities or for classes of businesses or facilities that are tourist-oriented.

(2) Tourist-oriented business. - A business, the substantial portion of whose products or services is of significant interest to tourists. The term may include a business involved with seasonal agricultural products. When used in this Article, the term "business" means a tourist-oriented business.

(3) Tourist-oriented facility. - A business, service, or activity facility that derives a major portion of income or visitors during the normal business season from road users not residing in the immediate area of the facility. When used in this Article, the term "facility" means a tourist-oriented facility.

(c) Limitation. - The Department shall not install TODS for a business or facility if the signs would be required at intersections where, due to the number of conflicting locations of other highway signs or traffic control devices or other physical or topographical features of the roadside, their presence would be impractical or unfeasible or result in an unsafe or hazardous condition.

(d) Duplication. - If a business or facility is currently shown on another official highway guide sign, such as a logo sign or supplemental guide sign, on the same approach to an intersection where a TODS panel for that business or facility would be located, the business or facility may elect to keep the existing highway guide sign or have it removed and participate in the TODS program. If the business or facility elects to retain the existing highway guide sign, the business or facility is ineligible for the TODS program at that intersection. (2001-383, s. 1.)

§ 136-140.16. Eligibility criteria.

A business or facility is eligible to participate in the TODS program if it meets all of the following conditions:

(1) It is open to the general public and is not restricted to "members only".

(2) It does not restrict access to its facilities by the general public.

(3) It complies with all applicable laws, ordinances, rules, and regulations concerning the provision of public accommodations without regard to race, religion, color, age, sex, national origin, disability, and any other category protected by federal or State constitutional or statutory law concerning the granting of licenses and approvals for public facilities.

(4) It meets the following standards:

a. It is in continuous operation at least eight hours a day, five days a week during its normal season or the normal operating season for the type of business or facility.

b. It is licensed and approved by the appropriate State and local agencies regulating the particular type of business or activity. (2001-383, s. 1.)

§ 136-140.17. Terminating participation in program.

A business or facility may terminate its participation in the TODS program at any time. The business or facility is not entitled to a refund of any part of any fees paid because of voluntary termination of participation by the business or facility, for any reason, before the end of its current contract period. (2001-383, s. 1.)

§ 136-140.18. Temporary modification of TODS panels.

(a) The Department shall allow a participating business or facility to close for remodeling or to repair damage from fire or other natural disaster if its TODS panels are covered or removed while the business or facility is closed. No refund of fees or extension of the time remaining in the contract for participation will be provided for the period of closure.

(b) The Department may, at its discretion, remove or cover TODS panels for roadway construction or maintenance, for routine maintenance of the TODS assembly, for traffic research study, or for any other reason it considers appropriate. Businesses or facilities are not entitled to any refunds of fee amounts for the period that the TODS panels are covered or removed under this subsection unless the period exceeds seven days.

(c) The TODS panels for seasonal businesses or facilities shall have an appropriate message added during the period in which the businesses or facilities are open to the public as part of their normal seasonal operation. (2001-383, s. 1.)

§ 136-140.19. Department to adopt rules to implement the TODS program.

The Department shall adopt rules to implement the TODS program created by this Article. The rules shall include all of the following:

(1) The Department shall set fees to cover the initial costs of signs, sign maintenance, and administering the program.

(2) The Department shall establish a standard for the size, color, and letter height of the TODS as specified in the National Manual of Uniform Traffic Control Devices for Streets and Highways.

(3) TODS shall not be placed more than five miles from the business or facility.

(4) TODS shall not be placed where prohibited by local ordinance.

(5) The number of TODS panels shall not exceed six per intersection with only one business or facility on each panel.

(6) If a business or facility is not directly on a State highway, it is eligible for TODS panels only if both of the following requirements are met:

a. It is located on a street that directly connects with a State road.

b. It is located so that only one directional sign, placed on a State road, will lead the tourist to the business or facility.

(7) A TODS shall not be placed immediately in advance of the business or facility if the business or facility and its on-premise advertising signs are readily visible from the roadway.

(8) The Department shall limit the placement of TODS to highways other than fully controlled access highways and to rural areas in and around towns or cities with a population of less than 40,000. (2001-383, s. 1.)

Vision Books Order Form

Fax Orders: 1-980-299-5965

Phone Orders: 1-704-898-0770

E-mail Orders: www.visionbooks.org

Mail Orders: Vision Books, LLC
                     P.O. Box 42406
                     Charlotte, NC 28215

Shipp To:
Name_____
Address_____
City_____State_____Zip_____
Phone_____Fax_____
Email_____@_____

Bill To: We can bill a third party on your behalf.
Name_____
Address_____
City_____State_____Zip_____
Phone____(_____)_____Fax_____
Email_____@_____

Pamphlet Number ($15.00 Each)	Qty	Total Cost
_____	_____	_____
_____	_____	_____
_____	_____	_____
_____	_____	_____
_____	_____	_____
_____	_____	_____
_____	_____	_____
Full Volume Set 1-92	92 Pamphlets	1,380.00

Free Shipping & Handling on Full Volume Orders
Add $1.00 Shipping & Handling Per Pamphlet $_____

Total Cost $_____

Thank you for your support. Mmanagement!

DID YOU ENJOY THIS BOOK?

Vision Books, LLC would like to hear from you! If you or someone you know has been fasely imprisoned, we would like to hear your story. If the 'North Carolina Criminal Law and Procedure' has had an effect in your life or if you have suggestions, we would like to hear from you. Send your letters to:

Vision Books, LLC
Attn: Staff Writers
P.O. Box 42406
Charlotte, NC 28215
Email: staff@visionbooks.org

Order Additional Copies:

Fax Orders: 1-980-299-5965

Phone Orders: 1-704-898-0770

E-mail Orders: www.visionbooks.org

Mail Orders: Vision Books, LLC
                      P.O. Box 42406
                      Charlotte, NC 28215